WILDERNESS BROTHERS

MW00603976

Prospecting, Horse Packing, & Homesteading on the Western Frontier

Based On The Diaries

of

Luman G. Caswell 1895-1903

G. Wayne Minshall

Copyright © 2012
by Streamside Scribe Press

All rights reserved. No part of the material protected by this copyright notice may be reproduced or utilized in any form or by any means, electronic or mechanical, including photocopying, recording, or by any informational storage and retrieval system without written permission from the copyright owner, except for brief quotations in a review.

ISBN: 978-0-9849490-0-7
Library of Congress Control Number: 2011945330

1. Western US History. 2. Adventure. 3. Wilderness. 4. Gold Mining. 5. Homesteading. 6. Self-reliant Living (lifestyle). 7. Idaho. 8. Colorado. 9. Nevada. 10. Montana.

PRINTED IN THE UNITED STATES OF AMERICA

PREFACE

The latter half of the 19th century was marked by frustration and pent up energy among the middle and lower classes due to thwarted dreams and dismal prospects of many individuals in the eastern and mid-western United States and much of Europe. This energy was given release by the discovery of gold and other precious metals, vast open spaces, and seemingly limitless opportunities afforded by the opening of the American West. This was a simpler time when the difference between right and wrong seemed clear and the choices less complex. The necessities of life could still be wrung from the land and the land and its bounties were free for the taking, with seemingly endless natural resources.

Prospecting for gold wasn't simply a matter of luck. For most, success required large doses of hard work, perseverance, and skill. Even to the less serious individuals, gold could mean instant gratification of base pleasures or a supplemental income. The prospect of finding gold was like that of winning a major lottery today. For those who found and hung on to it, gold was a great equalizer in the disparity among classes. Discovering gold offered the promise of freedom from poverty and mindless toil. It was the means to a comfortable life and a chance to fulfill one's dreams. To the fortunate discoverer who made a substantial find and held on to the riches it brought, came the chance to marry and have a family, a fancy house, and respectability.

The Caswell brothers Benjamin and Luman came to Idaho when it was still a frontier—when the way of life was that of the pioneers before them and the homesteaders that followed. Like many others, they were looking for adventure and gold. But, unlike most, they were successful in their quest. At the heart of their story is the decade in which they scratched out a living in the rugged mountain fastness of the central part of the new state, in an area bounded by the Snake and Salmon Rivers. During this time they demonstrated a wide array of creativity, skills, and aptitudes that enabled them to be largely self-sufficient until their primary goal was attained. Equally interesting are the accounts of how they came to Idaho, of their brother Dan, who joined them later, and two other partners, and of what became of the five of them after they found their own El Dorado. What follows is their saga as best as I can reconstruct it through genealogical searches, newspaper and other published accounts, visits to actual sites, interviews with grandchildren, and assorted other research sources all woven into and around Luman's sparse account recorded in a series of unpublished diaries between 1895 and 1903.

The search for the details surrounding Luman's accounts has been like tracking a deer: an initial sighting and picking up of the trail, long stretches without tracks or clear direction, a sparsity of sign. There were other sporadic sightings of the quarry, tantalizing and discontinuous: losing the trail, backtracking, picking up new clues, making wrong assumptions, reaching apparent dead ends, finding the track again, and on it went. As I have sought to unearth the particulars of the lives of Ben and Lu, their brother Dan and their two mining partners A. O. Huntley and Wesley Ritchey, my quest has been obscured by the haze of a century of faded memories and poorly-recorded events. The beginnings and end of the tale are lodged in the cold statistics of births, marriages, deaths, and census records. However, the central portion covering the years 1889 through 1903, recorded in Lu's journals, in later recounting to his daughter Louisa, and in newspaper articles is much better documented. Though the details are clouded by the passage of time, the story of the Caswells and their discovery of gold in Idaho at Thunder Mountain in 1894 is a fascinating one. Like the emotional rush of a bronc buster following a good ride, these were heady times for the Caswells and their partners, but ones that could be savored only briefly and incompletely in the rapid passage of time and that ended all too abruptly and too soon.

ACKNOWLEDGMENTS

I would like to formally recognize and express my gratitude to the following individuals and organizations: Judy Minshall for abiding another of my passions, tolerating my stories, retracing routes with me, obtaining books and other materials, searching the web and endless spools of microfilm, reviewing the manuscript multiple times, and refining my efforts to capture the events recorded here in readable and grammatically correct prose; Jim Barnes, the "Big Kahuna of Family History" for sharing with me his passion for western history and solving its mysteries and for his skill with genealogical research and unearthing of critical facts and leads; and Stewart Taylor (Luman Caswell's grandson); Linda Kiesel (Daniel Caswell's granddaughter); Elsa Phelps, Freda Babbitt and husband Gene, and Wes Higgins (Melvina Caswell Higgins' grandchildren); and Dena Perrine (Cortland Caswell's granddaughter) for providing clues and course corrections. Stewart in particular fortified me with a wealth of facts and photographs regarding especially his grandfather and grandmother but also of other Caswell relatives. Genealogists in addition to Jim Barnes, who sustained me when the going got tough and the path unsure: Dale McCullough, Julie Miller, Elizabeth L. Cuff, and Ellen Sedell. Colbert E. Cushing, Tim Hall, and Dale McCullough reviewed and edited all or major parts of the entire manuscript at various stages of completion and provided many helpful comments and words of encouragement. I thank Jim and Holly Akenson for their invaluable insights into Big Creek history and locations, and especially to Jim for sharing his knowledge of Caswell and Cabin Creek history. Carolyn Bowler, Archivist, Idaho State Historical Society, was especially helpful in obtaining access to original copies of Luman Caswell's diaries and Caswell family and historic photographs. Larry Kingsbury (Payette National Forest, US Forest Service (USFS) archaeologist and custodian of the Cabin Creek National Historic site) and his assistant Gayle Dixon provided a variety and abundance of supportive information about the

Big Creek area and its residents. I also acknowledge in appreciation the many unnamed and otherwise unheralded county records clerks in Colorado, Idaho, and Oregon and the librarians at Idaho State University, the Idaho State Historical Society Library and Archives, Mesa State College, the US National Archives, Yellowstone National Park, and elsewhere for their skill and tireless efforts in locating and retrieving deeds, books, articles, maps, and other information sources used in my research. Idaho State Historical Society granted permission to publish photographs from their archives and access to the unpublished typescript and original diaries of Luman G. Caswell in file MS 2/437. David Burns (Payette National Forest USFS), my Big Creek research project coordinator, first called my attention to and provided my first copy of Luman Caswell's diaries. Keith Weber (Director GIS Training and Research Center, Idaho State University) made available the facilities and services of the Center and his patient and untiring assistant Kindra Serr, constructed the maps. James E Morris determined the distances used in locating travel points between Cabin Creek and Warren referred to in the diaries. Jennye Minshall, a bibliophile like her mother and grandmother, discovered a surprising number of valuable information sources and facts in places I would have never thought to look. Ross Engle (deceased) and Kate Harris helped locate hard to gather information. I am grateful to Idaho State University, and especially the Department of Biological Sciences, for the freedom, support, and facilities to pursue my own journeys into the wilderness, both virtual and real.

Contents

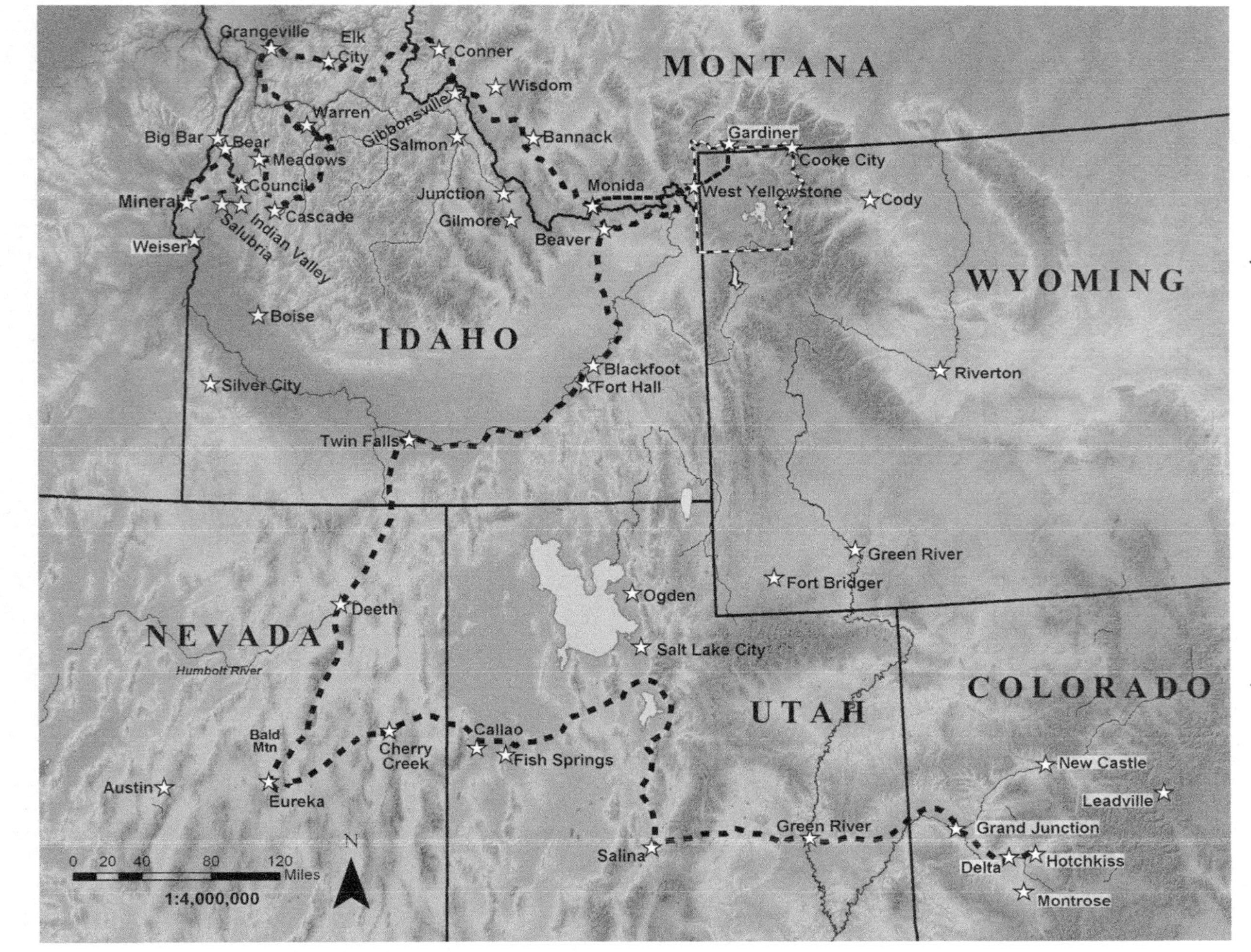

Map 1.
Ben and Lu Caswell's route from Hotchkiss, Colorado to Mineral and Big Bar, Idaho (wide dashes). The narrow dashed line between Monida and Gardiner, MT shows a portion of the route taken by Dan Caswell and Wes Ritchey from Gardiner, Montana to Idaho. The remainder of their route overlies part of that of Ben and Lu, as described in the text.

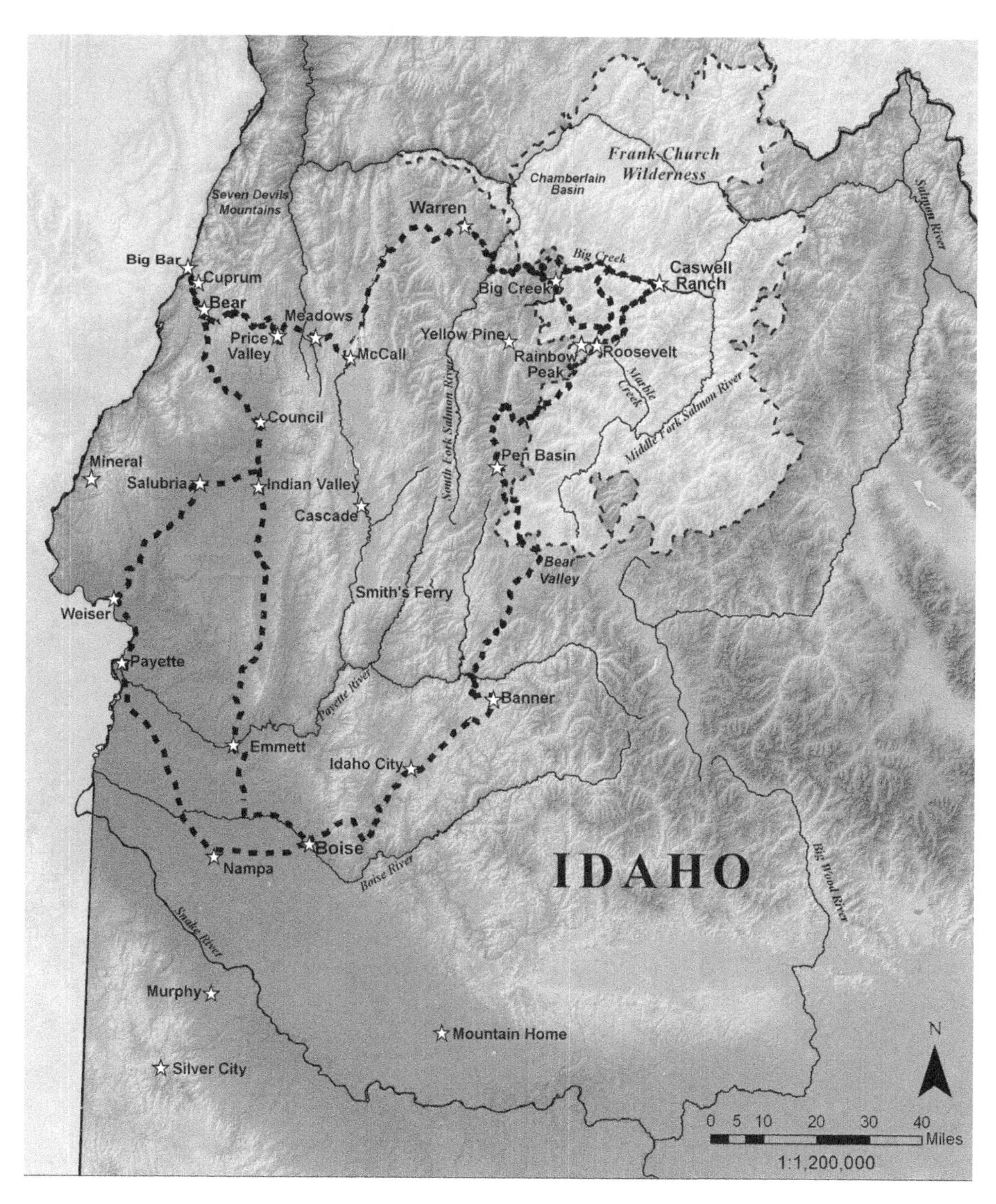

Map 2.
Main Caswell routes in Idaho after reaching Big Bar. Routes within Big Creek Country and out to Warren are shown in greater detail in Map 3.

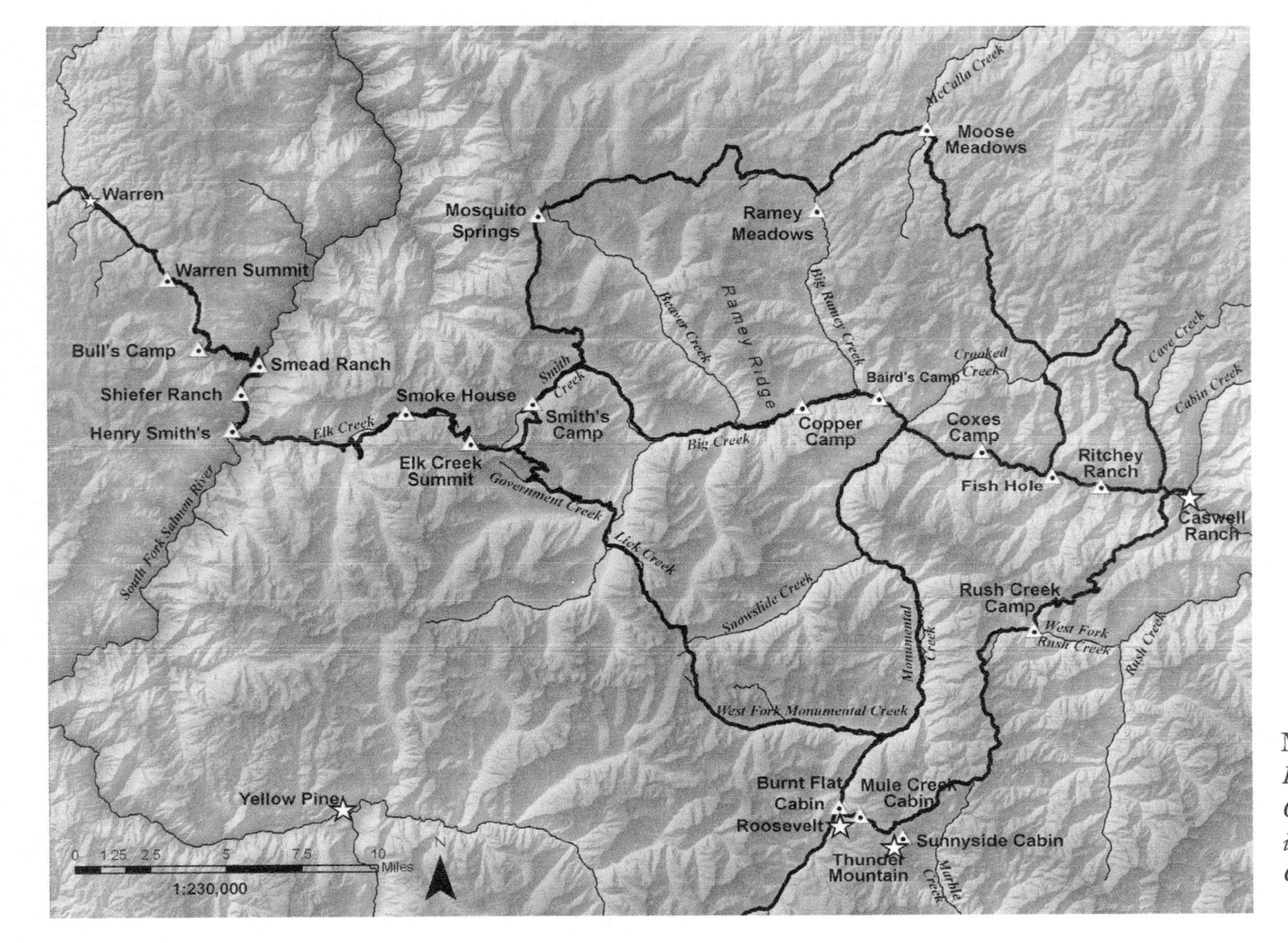

Map 3. *Principal Caswell routes in Big Creek Country, Idaho.*

PART I

Introduction

In the summer of 1894 two Caswell brothers, Benjamin and Luman, found gold in the rugged wilderness of central Idaho in a place they called Thunder Mountain at the head of Big Creek Country. Later they were joined by their brother Daniel, his friend Wesley Ritchey, and a "silent" partner Arthur Huntley. Most of the major gold discoveries in Idaho and adjacent states were made in the 1860s. The Caswell find was unusual in part because it occurred three decades later. After several years of further prospecting and strategic preparation, word of their find became public and, when several of their claims were sold to a group of investors headed by William H. Dewey in November 1901, the news ignited one of the last gold rushes in the United States. Thousands of folks stampeded into the area to seek their own fortunes: some to prospect, some to mine, and others to "mine" the prospectors and miners. Although the bonanza was short lived and never amounted to much, it had a lasting impact on the people, the region, and the state. This is the saga of Luman Caswell, his brothers, and their two partners; how they came to prospect for gold in the young state of Idaho; the lives they led and trails they traveled during their quest; and what became of them afterward.

In a long day's drive, I can haul a trailer-load of horses from my home in southeastern Idaho, pass through the state capitol of Boise 250 miles to the west, and be in Big Creek Country by dark. Today, at the start of a new millennium, as I transition between the early 2000s and the late 1800s, the main entryway into the area is from Cascade by road, nearly two-thirds of it paved. If I can manage to reach Boise a little after noon, I'll leave the pavement several hours

The Caswell brothers as they appeared during their time together on Thunder Mountain. Lu is on the left, then Ben and Dan. This photograph was first published in the April 13, 1902 issue of The Idaho Daily Satesman *but has subsequently embellished a number of other articles (ISHS # 73-57.18).*

later and pull in to the Smith Creek trail head that leads to Cabin Creek just before dark at about 8:30 PM. This is a long and tiring day but no way comparable to the trek that the Caswells had to make, over a somewhat different but parallel route, to reach the same point. It is hard to imagine that a century ago, the main gateway to the area was from Warren another 70 miles further north by rutted wagon road from Cascade.

At the turn of the 20th century, Warren was a bustling frontier town and the main supply point for the residents of the deep canyon gorge along the South Fork of the Salmon river and the rugged mountain wilderness to the east. Today, it is a scattering of rundown buildings and new summer homes along a dusty gravel road. For the Caswells, travel from Boise to Warren could take as much as a week, if solely by horseback, or as little as 3–5 days through a combination of horseback, horse-drawn buggy, and train. To reach the place where I park my pickup and trailer would require another 2 to 3 days of horseback riding.

As I write this chapter my mind drifts back to a flight I made early one spring, over a century after Ben and Lu first rode into the mountains around Big Creek, to revisit the Caswell Ranch site on Cabin Creek. I'm sitting beside pilot Steve Cope as we taxi out of the Challis airstrip in a Cessna 208 and head northwest into the heart of the Frank Church Wilderness in central Idaho. Steve works to gain elevation over the contorted mountain terrain below. I've flown with him over a dozen times during the past 16 years and have become confident of his skill. He knows the topography well and navigates using familiar peaks as beacons. I too know the country, though not as well from the air, and orient more by the stream courses and trails that I have studied and traveled. Our twin targets today, as in many of our past flights, are two landing strips, "grandfathered" into the legislation that established the Frank Church Wilderness Area in 1980 and located along Big Creek. The trip will take a little over a half hour by air and will deliver me and a backpack load of gear to Cabin Creek and then proceed on to Taylor "Ranch" to drop off other gear and supplies. Taylor Ranch now is actually a Wilderness Research Field Station owned by the University of Idaho and, at the time, was under the direction of Jim and Holly Akenson.

I am a stream ecologist and professor of ecology at Idaho State University by profession. I have used this fact as an excuse for exploring remote areas of the northwestern landscape for nearly 40 years. I taught courses and conducted research on the ecology of stream and river ecosystems throughout my career. A unique aspect of my research was the documentation, through measurements and photographs, of the responses of streams and their adjacent streambank vegetation for many years following disturbance by fire. As part of this long-term research effort, my colleagues and I studied the effects of wildfire in the Frank Church River of No Return Wilderness of central Idaho on these ecosystems, beginning with the Mortar Creek Fire in 1979. Later, we initiated studies on Big Creek, located in the same general area, and conducted much of our research out of the Taylor Field Station.

I first came into Big Creek country in the summer of 1988 with a team of researchers made up of graduate students, other professional colleagues, and family members. The effort was part of a 200-mile horse and backpacking expedition that would take us from the head of Pistol Creek, down the Middle Fork of the Salmon River, and on out from the mouth of Big Creek to its high mountain origins. Along the way, we continued our research on the Mortar Creek Fire streams and initiated data collection on the mainstem and various tributaries of Big Creek as we progressed upstream. This was the year of the Great Fires of Yellowstone National Park and other large fires were burning elsewhere in the West, including the Frank Church River of No Return Wilderness. We encountered a portion of these fires and much smoke but never felt threatened. However, later in the summer, some of our study sites burned and this was to bring about our annual return to Big Creek for the next 17 years.

In the 1990's, during the course of our studies on Big Creek, I became interested in the Caswells through acquisition of an obscure set of journals kept by Luman. My initial interest was not because of their gold discoveries, which were unknown to me at the time, but because of the adventurous and self-reliant life they led in the still remote area around Cabin Creek, now located at the core of "The Frank." Several aspects of Luman's account interested me: (1) It centers around Cabin Creek, one of the tributaries of Big Creek we had studied. (2) It details the earliest significant non-native human influences in the area prior to its designation as a wilderness. (3) It provides a fairly complete description of homesteading life and the emergence of a fully operational and largely self-sufficient ranch over a period of nearly a decade. As my awareness of and infatuation with their lives grew, I wanted to know what motivated them, how and why they came into the region, why they left their seemingly idyllic lives on one of the last frontiers, and, once I realized they had made a major gold find, how their lives changed after they became "rich."

In my research and initial writing of this book, I was immersed in the lives of the Caswells and their two partners for over 6 years.

In my mind I have ridden with them from their ranch midway along Big Creek to Bear, at the edge of the Seven Devils mountains, halfway across the state of Idaho and back. I have trudged with them for days on snowshoes to the outpost of Warren, a once booming mining town, to purchase supplies, check the mail, and engage in a heavy dose of socializing as an antidote to the confinement of winter. I have followed along with their pack string on an exciting journey from Thunder Mountain to the fledgling state capitol of Boise to pick up supplies and transport them back to their placer mine. I have labored with them digging ditches, hauling logs, building fence, cutting hay, and planting a garden and countless times have gone through the details of their daily routine. We have become kindred spirits, living out the same experiences and journeying to the same places in space but separated in time by a hundred years. We have lived in parallel universes, disconnected in time but intersecting in space and, in my mind, the two have become one. Through their eyes, I have seen the Frank Church Wilderness before it was and have helped blaze its trails; I have observed what it took to scratch out a self-reliant existence in the remote mountains of the northern Rockies shortly after Idaho had attained statehood; and I have searched for gold and found it. I have come to realize that at some point in time and space we are all brothers, bound together by DNA and shared experiences and living out our lives in the twisted terrain of a real or virtual uncharted wilderness.

I remember in particular one of our stream research trips made by horseback, beginning at the trailhead on Smith Creek, almost a mile above sea level, and proceeding down Big Creek. Though it was midsummer, frost coated our tents and gear and propelled us shivering into the early morning to prepare breakfast, break camp, manty up the pack loads, and get moving down the trail—a routine repeated countless times by the Caswells and Wes Ritchey at a far distant point back in time. We rode wordlessly among the tall conifers with only the clicking of hooves on the rocks and the rumble of Big Creek to break the otherwise muffled awakening of the day. Occasionally sunlight burst through openings in the trees and wrapped itself around us like a blanket, thawing our hands and driving the chill from our backs and legs. I savored the pungent smell of conifer needles and the earthy dampness of the forest. They are much different from the dry, camphor-charged sagebrush country where I live or the area around Hotchkiss, in western Colorado, where the Caswells and Wes Ritchey began their travels to this place. As we rode, we passed several locations well-known to the Caswells, including the cabin ruins and lush meadow at Copper Camp, the ford across Big Ramey Creek, and the river crossing upstream of the entrance of Monumental Creek, now simplified considerably by the presence of a modern pack bridge. We stopped to water the horses and have lunch in the clearing on Big Ramey, then continued on several more miles before calling a halt on the sheltered flat along Big Creek, near the site Lu Caswell referred to as "Coxes Camp." We had ridden nearly 14 miles and dropped about 1000 feet in elevation since morning. The site we chose was well off the trail and had good graze and water for the horses. After watering and picket-hobbling the horses so they could feed, we pitched our tents, cooked supper, and then stowed our equipment in panniers and under canvas tarps just as darkness engulfed us. One more check on the horses and I crawled into my sleeping bag and fell asleep within minutes, exhausted from the activities of the past few days.

It was 10 AM the next day by the time we had eaten breakfast, saddled up, and headed down the trail. With the drop in elevation from the preceding morning, we began the day without frost and the temperature continued to climb as we rode along. We stopped for a traditional drink and refilling of canteens at Lime Creek and then proceeded on to the Fish Hole downriver from the mouth of Coxey Creek. At this point, our relatively routine ride became an adrenaline rush as the trail rose what seemed like a hundred feet above Big Creek and clung to a narrow ledge blasted out of the sheer rock cliff. Midway along, the trail made a sharp right-angled turn that looked to be designed to brush horse and rider off the cliff to join the fish in the hole far below and obscured our view of any oncoming travelers. The entire traverse lasted only about 20 minutes and, although I have successfully negotiated it numerous times, it always brings relief to leave this section of trail behind. In the late 1800s, when the

Caswells first began using the route along Big Creek to reach their ranch, this stretch of river was impassable and they had to make a u-shaped diversion up Coxey Creek and then down Cave Creek—a lengthy side trip we were grateful to avoid even with the extra stress involved in our chosen alternative. By mid-day the temperature was pushing 100°F, so we opted to take a late lunch and stop near the former site of Wes Ritchey's ranch until it began to cool off. A short nap and a soak in Big Creek were added bonuses that rekindled our enthusiasm for making the final 3 ½ mile ride to Cabin Creek, where we had arranged to meet the rest of our research team the next morning, following the arrival of their airplane from Challis. We set up camp in the lush meadow along Spring Creek, next to the former site of the 1898 Caswell cabin, and drew water from the naturally-filtered, ice cold stream just as they must have done. Our ride to this point, relatively leisurely by Caswell standards, would occasionally have been made by them on trail-hardened horses in a single day, with no extended stops along the way.

As I looked after our horses and set up my tent, I had a chance to explore the heart of the old Caswell ranch, of which no obvious traces remain, and to reflect on their life here. I would have had no inkling of the intensity of activities that transpired here over the course of a decade or of the role that the place played in history, had I not read and delved into Lu Caswell's account of those times. But now I was able to picture quite vividly the position and silhouettes of the ranch house, storehouse, and other outbuildings, and the locations of the orchard, "kitchen" garden, and main fields holding acres of different crops—from potatoes to different kinds of grain. The meadow where we camped had been painstakingly cleared of rocks and irrigated with water from Spring Creek. The low hill to the south of this field, which now sheltered our camp as it had the ranch house in previous times, once supported stands of oats and wheat augmented by water drawn all the way from Cow Creek at the head of the present-day airstrip. Now only a sparse mixture of native grasses, invasive weeds, and sagebrush occupy the place where the crops once grew. Secretly, I am grateful that the ranch and its occupants are no longer here and my companions and I are blessed with the opportunity to pause for a short time in this peaceful place and encounter it much as it must have been before the state was first settled. But my modern-day wilderness experience is equally enriched by the knowledge of what took place here over a century ago and by the subtle reminders of that bit of history that, for those who know where to look, are still here to enjoy. I believe that these monuments to the early pioneers are every bit as appropriate to present "wilderness" as the artifacts of native Americans or the absence of roads and fences. They all serve to enhance our perspective of history and help us come closer to our roots.

Colorado Interlude

1880s – 1902

In 1853, William Caswell (age 23) and Lavinia Sophrona Rouse (age 17) married and made their home near his parents outside of the newly established township of Gilford, southeast of present day St. Paul. While in Minnesota, William began working as a carpenter and this remained his life-long occupation. He and Lavinia had five children before leaving the state, the last of whom Luman Grant Caswell was born in June 1867.

Luman was still a baby when the family moved to Michigan. They settled in Volina Township, Cass County, near where Lavinia had been raised and several of her siblings, including her youngest sister Ann Phillips, were living. Ann and William Phillips' last child, Bertha, eventually married William and Lavinia Caswell's second oldest son Daniel.

Lu was only 8, when his pregnant mother and 2-year old brother died of German measles. This left his father to care for Lu, his two older brothers Alvin Benjamin (14) and Daniel German (10), and 3 ½ year old sister Melvina. With the help of neighbors and relatives, the now middle-aged William, struggled to hold the family together over the next three years. During this time, he met Maria (Coleman) Cook, whose husband Lucius, a local farmer, had died a few years earlier leaving her with five children. William and Maria were married April 17, 1878; she was 40 and he was almost 50. By then, Maria's three oldest daughters were off on their own but her son William and daughter Maggie joined the Caswell household. The next spring, William and Maria lost a set of twins at birth but in December 1880 a final son, Cortland, was born.

Within a few years after William and Maria were married, Lu and Ben and Will Cook set off on their own. Ben left first. By 1880 he was residing with John and Mary R. Hall in the Russell Mining District of Gilpin County, Colorado. John Hall was a miner and

Ben was a laborer, presumably assisting John. Russell Gulch, in the heart of the district, is about 35 miles due west of Denver. It lies just south of the mining camps of Central City and Black Hawk, where the first gold lode in Colorado was discovered in 1859. It probably was here that Ben first developed his skills at locating and panning for gold and observed the use of extensive sluice systems for concentrating it. At the same time that Ben was in Colorado, Will Cook (age 16) was working in Sharon, Washtenaw County, Michigan as a servant/farm laborer for the William Lockwood family. Lu left home four years later, when he was 17, and went to work on a farm in Livingston County, Illinois. Reportedly, Maria never got along with the original Caswell children so Dan remained at home to "look after" his sister Melvina.

It is not known for certain what motivated Lu's father to pull up roots and move to Colorado but it probably had to do with opportunities for employment and free land. By 1885, William and the entire Caswell family and Will Cook were back together in Delta County on the western side of the state. The Ute Indians were removed from the area in the autumn of 1881 and the land had recently been opened for homesteading. It is quite likely that Ben was the first to have gotten wind of the availability of free land around Delta and wrote home about it. This would have enabled William Caswell to move the remainder of the family into the area during the surge of new settlers, development of farms and towns, and the expansion of the Denver & Rio Grande Railroad (D&RG RR) into the region.

On the western slope of the Colorado Rockies, where the Uncompahgre River joins the Gunnison, a verdant delta thousands of acres in extent was formed from eons of erosion and a sharp change in gradient. Until 1881 this rich and productive bottom land was occupied by the generally peaceful Ute Indians. In that year the native peoples were moved to a reservation in southern Utah and soon afterwards the vacated area was opened to US citizens for homesteading. The choicest areas, those along the river and other naturally watered locations, were claimed first and a town quickly built up to support the settlers' needs. Coincidentally, the plat of the original townsite resembled a triangle, the shape of the Greek letter

The "Colorado Caswells" except for Melvina. Left to right: William (father), Courtland, Benjamin, Maria (Coleman Cook; William's 2nd wife), Luman, and Daniel. Photograph actually taken 15 years after they arrived in Colorado and had moved on to Idaho (August 22, 1900 by Meyers Studio, Boise)(ISHS # P1987.26.13).

delta. Thus, though initially called Gunnison, the town's name was changed to Delta in 1882. Delta soon became the county seat for a new county of the same name. By mid October 1882 about 50 houses and a railroad station were in place.

Northwest of Delta, 50 miles further downstream, the Gunnison River meets the Colorado at the "grand junction" near the Utah border. The Colorado River originally was called the Grand and its valley Grand Valley. Upstream from where the Gunnison and Uncompahgre meet, the Gunnison River eroded nearly vertically 1730 to 2425 feet into very hard rock to form Black Canyon. No other canyon combines such depth and narrowness (1300 feet rim to rim at the "Narrows"). Shortly after the Gunnison emerges from this extensive "impassable" section, it is joined by its North Fork.

In 1853, Captain John W. Gunnison entered the area in search of a route for a transcontinental railway. Although the route he followed lost out to one along the Colorado River, it eventually became the path by which the Denver & Rio Grande Railroad expanded westward through Colorado to Salt Lake City, Utah. Capt. Gunnison led his party over Blue Mesa and forded the river named in his honor near present day Austin, Colorado.

In August 1874, while directing the construction of a toll road from Saguache, Colorado to the Animas River valley, Enos T. Hotchkiss discovered silver along the Lake Fork of the Gunnison River. A mining camp soon sprang up that quickly developed into Lake City, Colorado, which Enos helped found. After he sold out, the mine was renamed the Golden Fleece and he proceeded west to the Uncompahgre Valley. Enos explored the area and camped near the mouth of the Uncompahgre in 1879. From there he proceeded up the Gunnison, crossed near Austin, and continued on across Rogers Mesa to the valley of the North Fork. He returned in 1881 to clear land and prepare material for a house. The next year, in response to the opening of the region for homesteading, many settlers came into the North Fork Valley. The settlement soon was called Hotchkiss. The Ouray Times for January 14, 1882 stated that ". . . building is going on as rapidly as material can be had." This provided tremendous opportunities for skilled carpenters such as William Caswell and his sons.

William Caswell, with his wife and children, settled in Delta County, Colorado prior to the state's 1885 census. They probably arrived by train in Delta and resided there temporarily before moving on to the Hotchkiss area, 25 miles to the east, in 1886. There they all initially participated in farming and ranching. William and his oldest son Ben filed on adjacent 160 acre homesteads located about 4 miles west and a mile north of Hotchkiss. From an historical perspective, their property, on Rodger's Mesa, is only a couple of miles northeast of the junction of the main Gunnison River and its North Fork where the Gunnison and Hotchkiss exploratory parties had entered the area years before. The land initially was undeveloped but the family labored to prepare the soil for planting and secure water for irrigation from Leroux Creek via the Allen Mesa Ditch and a wastewater ditch from the Heister ranch that came to be known as the Caswell Ditch.

These were hectic times, with the influx of settlers, breaking of ground for crops, development of irrigation systems, and building of numerous homes and commercial and public buildings. William worked primarily as a carpenter and the boys tried their hand at a variety of jobs that fortified them with skills that were to serve them well in the future, including carpentry, farming, irrigation, mining, and working in a sawmill. Luman worked for his father near the town of Delta in 1885 and then went to farm on Allen Mesa (no longer recognized as separate from Rogers Mesa) near Hotchkiss when the family moved there in 1886. Luman later worked on a section crew and as a track walker for the Denver & Rio Grande Western (D&RGW) Railroad thanks to Will Cook.

By 1887, Lu and one or both of his brothers began to range more widely in their quest for income and adventure. Based on their travels and the towns mentioned by Lu, it appears that they mainly worked on the western branch of the Denver & Rio Grande during this time. First they worked in the vicinity of the Leadville mining camps, then nearer to Hotchkiss at Cimmaron on the Gunnison River. Dan marked grade for slope-staking engineers when the D&RG narrow gauge railroad was being located on the route between Gunnison and Crested Butte along the Taylor River, one of the main headwaters of the Gunnison River. In April 1887, Dan and Lu went by train to Buena Vista, on the Arkansas River about 35 miles south of Leadville, to pick up their checks. They then went north to the end of the spur line at Red Cliff and walked to the Grant [Grand] River settlement.

At this time the D&RGW RR was extending its line from Red Cliff, down the Eagle and Grand Rivers and up Roaring Fork to Aspen and also on down the Grand River to Grand Junction. The mines at Aspen and Leadville were booming and attracting most of the available workers. To keep crews at work on the railroad, contractors were authorized to raise wages and award special allowances to critical construction units. From the settlement on the Grand, the brothers went down the Grand River to Glenwood Springs, past Storm King Mountain, and on to New Castle, where they worked in a sawmill from July-September. Lu worked as a railroad tie cutter and as a ratchet setter in a sawmill. They went back to the Gunnison River in the spring of 1888 and then returned to New Castle. Finally, in January 1889, shortly after Ben relinquished ownership to his homestead, he and Lu left Colorado. Dan eventually followed suit, after working a few more years for the railroad in the vicinity of Delta and Colorado Springs, but would not see his brothers again for nearly 10 years.

In the late 1890s, William, Maria, and the remaining two children, Melvina and Cortland, also left Colorado and moved to Manchester, Texas. Melvina returned in autumn 1899 to marry Clarence Higgins and homestead outside of Hotchkiss near where the Caswells had lived. They purchased the northwest 80 acres of the Caswell homestead in 1901 and remained in the area a short while longer. But, by late 1903, the entire family would reunite in Idaho.

Idaho Odyssey

1889 – 1893

Lu Caswell was in Leadville, Colorado, an active gold camp, in 1887. He and his brothers probably were bitten by the gold bug about that time (though Ben may have succumbed earlier) and infected by the chronic disease they would carry the rest of their lives. The main outbreak of this "gold fever" erupted two years later when Lu and Ben left Colorado and headed for the towns of Austin and Eureka, Nevada "to get in on the mining." However, on reaching Eureka they had a change of plans and, rather than continuing on to Austin, turned north to Idaho. When the two set off in January 1889, it is unlikely that they ever intended to end up in Idaho, but chance and the search for gold would eventually propel them there. By the end of their journey they would travel roughly 2000 miles, through parts of five western states (Map 1).

In preparation for leaving Hotchkiss, they probably loaded their wagon with their belongings and supplies for the trip the night before and, in the early morning light, hitched up the team. In addition to a pair of draft horses and their lead horses, they had several others, including a 2-year old named Babe that Lu rode all the way to Idaho. Ben, an accomplished teamster, drove the wagon. After bidding farewell to their father, step-mother, brother Dan, sister Melvina, and half-brother Cort, they left their parents' homestead and followed the road to Delta along the North Fork of the Gunnison. At Delta they crossed to the north side of the main Gunnison River and, paralleling the Denver & Rio Grande Western roadbed, continued to just upstream of where it joins the Grand River. There the brothers crossed the Grand on the recently completed (1886), one-lane Fifth Street Bridge and entered the town of Grand Junction.

From Grand Junction they continued westward on the Salt Lake Wagon Road (and the North Old Spanish Trail), crossed the Colorado border, and headed into Utah Territory. For most of the remainder of their trip to Eureka they would be traveling through

Desert and badlands were predominant features along Ben and Lu's route between Hotchkiss, Colorado and Salina, Utah, as seen here west of their crossing of the Green River (photograph by author January 2009).

arid country with limited sources of water for themselves and their horses. In preparation, they probably carried extra water but that also would be limited in quantity. Another likely strategy was to adjust the length of their day-to-day travel in order to overnight near a water source; often this meant going 40 miles or so in a stretch or doing without. Fortunately, because of the time of the year, they did not have to contend with the summer heat and therefore would not have had to travel at night. In addition, they would have had some snow available at the higher elevations. At one point they stopped to get water at what turned out to be a private well. Only the team and lead horses had drunk before the Caswells learned that they would have pay for the water at 7 cents a bucket. So they drove around the mountain to a snow bank and melted snow for the remaining horses. Years later, Lu told his daughter Louisa "It is hard to give horses melted snow water at first unless they are real dry, but they'll come to it after a while."

On reaching Green River, they were able to get their wagon and horses across on a ferry just upstream of the railroad bridge. Instead of continuing to follow the D&RGW RR route to Salt Lake City that went northwest up the Price River, they opted to proceed west to Salina before heading north. Though over 70 miles longer, the Salina route offered several distinct advantages. It followed an established wagon road over terrain generally more gentle and at lower elevations and avoided Price Canyon and mountainous country on either side of the divide between the Price and Spanish Fork rivers, likely impassable in the dead of winter. From Green River, the wagon road crossed the northern part of the San Rafael Swell, a huge anticlinal uplift. Although missing the Swell's rugged interior, the trail across nevertheless was steep and tortuous, with winding, narrow defiles and steep cliffs crowding in on them. From there, the trail carried the travelers on a relatively easy course along the wide, well-watered floor of Castle Valley, and then crossed the Wasatch Plateau to Salina. After reaching Salina (about 2 weeks and 272 miles from home), they turned abruptly north to follow along the broad Sevier River Valley. The well-watered segment between Salina and Lehi had been settled by Mormon pioneers in the 1850s and contained a number of settlements, where they may have obtained supplies. After about 30 miles, at the entrance of the Juab Valley, the wagon road left the Sevier River and continued north to the town of Nephi, with the towering 11,928-foot Mt. Nebo dominating the background, and a few miles later crossed an almost imperceptible divide into the basin of Utah Lake. The gentle gradient and relatively featureless landscape north of Salina left no lasting impression on Lu or Ben until they arrived at the "foot of the Wasatch Mountains," alongside Utah Lake.

Their route passed along a narrow strip of land between the eastern shore of Utah Lake and the base of the Wasatch Mountains. At the north end of the lake, near Lehi, they connected with the old Pony Express (1860-1861)/Overland Stage route and again turned west. Use of this byway had diminished substantially after completion of the telegraph line in 1861 and the Transcontinental Railroad further north in 1869, followed almost immediately by the cessation of the Overland Stagecoach service. It still remained an important means of travel across central Utah and Nevada when the Caswell brothers came along 20 years later. From the time they reached central Utah until the end of the journey, the pungent camphor-laden odor of sagebrush, crushed beneath their wagon's wheels and horses' hooves, frequently filled the air and perfumed their clothing.

A day's journey from Lehi, they reached Five Mile Pass (407 miles, about 3 weeks from Hotchkiss), west of Fairfield (old Camp Floyd) and the start of a 135-mile stretch of desert, populated mainly by sagebrush, rabbit-brush, and jackrabbits. Somewhere along their route before reaching Cherry Creek in Nevada, they went through a place Lu called "Bear Flat," which he described as "an awful desolate place, a mucky dirty quagmire," and "Rocky Springs." Also, from Five Mile Pass to Cherry Creek they would seldom see another human other than at a few isolated ranches. The desert crossing to the mouth of Overland Canyon was mostly flat and dotted with a number of wells and springs, including Fish Springs and Willow Springs (Callao), associated with the former Pony Express and Overland Stage stations and located at intervals of 10-25 miles.

After leaving Callao near the western edge of the desert, Lu and Ben encountered a series of mountain ranges and interspersed broad, flat valleys in what is known formally in geological terms as the "Basin and Range Province." However, rather than passing over the mountains in the conventional sense, the route wound its way through them by means of a series of relatively low-lying passes. The first set of mountains they encountered was the Deep Creek Range, which they passed through by going up Overland Canyon, crossing Clifton Flat to Ibapah in Deep Creek Valley on the western border of Utah, and then crossing over to Antelope Valley in Nevada, where they would have passed by the Tippett sheep ranch and probably stopped for water at Antelope Springs. Next, they passed through the Schell Creek Range to the small settlement of Schellbourne, at the edge of Steptoe Valley, across which they traveled about 10 miles to the town of Cherry Creek, situated at the foot of the Cherry Creek Mountains. Following the discovery of silver nearby in September 1872, Cherry Creek had followed the boom-and-bust cycle typical of most mining towns. By the time the Caswells arrived, Cherry Creek was well into its second bust and had a population of only about 350 compared to a peak of about 7800 in 1882.

From Cherry Creek, they continued west to Ruby Valley and crossed over the Ruby Mountains, through the first of two Overland passes, then proceeded across Huntington Valley and through the Diamond Mountains via the second Overland Pass and down Telegraph Canyon to Diamond Springs at the foot of the mountains. At this point they turned south, for the first time in their journey since leaving Hotchkiss, and followed along the western edge of Diamond Mountains about 30 miles to Eureka. According to Lu's recollections, after leaving Cherry Creek, they "went to the 'Wells,' a stage station on the road to Ureka, Nevada. Stopped for water and went on through to the saw mill camp."

Eureka had been a center for the production of silver-lead ore and at one time ranked second only to the Comstock Lode in total production. It had grown rapidly from its beginnings in the mid 1860s and by 1875 was the second largest urban area in Nevada and, with the completion of a connector link to the transcontinental railroad 80 miles to the north, a hub for stage coach transportation and the distribution point for goods throughout the area. Three years later the population peaked at 9000. However, by the time the Caswells reached it, the town had seen an extended period of decline as the ore body became depleted and lead and silver prices faltered. In fact the worst year up to that point was the year the Caswells arrived, when the value of silver plummeted after the federal government stopped using silver as a monetary standard.

One can imagine that their tactic, upon arrival in Eureka, was similar to the way one might approach a fishing expedition into unfamiliar country. The brothers would have immediately visited information hot spots like the livery stable, general store, and saloons to learn where the best prospects might be. Then they set off in the most promising direction to determine if any likely sites were as yet unclaimed. This was a time-consuming task requiring hard work and equal amounts of luck and skill. In this case, they apparently learned that Big Bald Mountain was a promising site and left Eureka soon after arriving. As Lu recalled, "We noticed the town was full of Chinamen, dressed in broadcloth. They would stare at you as you drove by. One of the biggest mines in Nevada shut down there in 1889 because of silver devaluation. The white people left."

Bald Mountain is located on the southern end of the Ruby Mountains, only a few miles from where they recently had crossed the first Overland Pass on their way to Eureka. On the road to Bald Mountain, they met an Italian wood-cutter packing wood on burros to the summit above Eureka. The wood probably consisted of pinyon pine, Utah juniper, and mountain mahogany and was to be used for making charcoal, which was essential to the smelting process. The Italian wanted to increase his pack stock and engaged the Caswells to "trade" horses with him. Lu recalled that "Ben sold a bay stallion for $125 and gave him a brown mare that was played out. I traded him a sore footed colt and a small saddle plus $7.50 for a California saddle. Ben urged me to [go ahead with the deal] but I hated to give up that much money. That talked with me."

They finally reached Bald Mountain and stayed about two weeks. While there, they met the "Whiderkind boys," who had a quartz mine with which they needed help. They hired the Caswells to haul dirt from their "diggins" up to a spring at the head of a gulch and separate out the gold by flotation. However, the work paid only $1.50 a day, which Lu and Ben thought was too little, so they abandoned a promising ore-bearing ledge Lu had found and moved on. Lu eventually learned that this ledge later turned out to be good and was still being worked profitably in the 1940s. Although they had no way of knowing it at the time, they actually had been standing on a mountain of microscopic gold; by 2007 the Bald Mountain mining district had produced about 2 million ounces of gold and was still active.

It appears that the "Whiderkind boys" (Wunderlich?) alerted the Caswells to promising prospects further north in Gibbonsville, Idaho, because that was Ben and Lu's next major stop after they left Bald Mountain. They continued on from Bald Mountain, probably along the eastern edge of the Ruby Mountains, and passed between them and Ruby Lake/Marsh, which Lu described as "nine miles long and three miles wide, just a swamp with slew [slough] grass called tullies [tules] all around and springs all around the valley, feeding into it. The whole valley, [was] just a shallow lake. The wild life there was alive with all kinds of waterfowl by the thousands. When they flew they would darken the sun. I killed a goose and a blanket of wings filled the air." At the upper end of Ruby Valley, they likely crossed the Ruby Mountains by means of Secret Pass and a few miles later arrived at the small settlement of Deeth.

Deeth, Nevada was located along the transcontinental railroad line at the junction of the westward-flowing Humboldt River and the Marys River, entering from the north. It served as the supply center and shipping point for the mining country of Charleston (Mardis), Nevada and the Bruneau Mining District (Idaho) to the north and for the beef and dairy cattle areas of Starr and Ruby Valleys (Nevada) to the south. Deeth was formed in 1869 with the arrival of the Central Pacific railroad. In 1880 the town included a post office, saloon, railroad section house, warehouse, and water tower. By the time the Caswells arrived, a couple of hotels, a livery stable, and a mercantile had been added. Probably at Porter's mercantile, they stocked up on food, including one hundred pound sacks of flour at $1.50 apiece, because they expected the price would escalate the further away they got from the railroad line.

From Deeth, they proceeded cross-country over the low-lying sagebrush hills until they reached a cow camp on the Marys River. Then they went on up the river 30 miles (parallel to present highway US 93) until they crossed a low divide into Idaho Territory and the headwaters of Salmon Falls Creek, which they followed downstream until they intercepted the old Oregon Trail near present-day Twin Falls. In Salmon Falls Creek, they saw their first salmon, which Lu described as being so plentiful that it looked like one could walk across the creek on their backs. They had a great time harvesting the fish with hook and line and even shooting them. One huge salmon Lu shot was so big that, when he put the muzzle of the gun through its gills and held it up with the gun on his shoulder, the fish reached clear to the ground—a full five feet. They filled up on salmon until they couldn't stand to take another bite.

On reaching the Oregon Trail, the two brothers turned east and proceeded along the south side of the Snake River, passed Ross's Fork (old Fort Hall), and stopped at Blackfoot, where there was only an Indian Agency at the time, and where they stayed overnight on the meadow just below town. At this point they briefly joined what was known as the "Gold Road", heading north to Montana. This was the old Ben Halladay Overland Stage route that ran north from the Transcontinental Railroad station at Ogden, Utah to Helena, Montana. At Eagle Rock (present day Idaho Falls) the road crossed the Snake River on a toll bridge and continued north through a sea of sagebrush in a parched land, where they saw lots of pronghorn antelope.

The exact route and order of events after Ben and Lu left Blackfoot and crossed the Snake River until they reached Elk City weeks later is uncertain. Probably they followed the Gold Road for a while longer, most likely to the town of Beaver Canyon, before diverging to the east to the Henry's Fork of the Snake. Lu stated that they stopped at "Henders" [Henrys] Lake. Ben's mare gave birth to a colt there so they stayed about three weeks to rest up and let the colt get big enough to travel. From Henrys Lake, they apparently returned to the Gold Road in the vicinity of "Beaver Springs on the Snake River," where they met an unsavory character Lu referred to only as "Old Pete," who tagged along until they reached central Idaho. From Beaver, they may have continued west on the Pacific Ocean side of the Continental Divide and proceeded to the Lemhi River valley, where they intersected the route followed by the exploration party of Lewis and Clark in 1803 to the Salmon and Bitterroot River valleys. More likely, they crossed over the Continental Divide into Montana soon after leaving Beaver and followed a route that passed near the old Montana territorial capital and gold mining center of Bannack and continued on to the Big Hole Basin.

North and west of their crossing, the country was one of rolling hills covered with bunch grass, much different from the sagebrush covered hills they had encountered on the Idaho side of the Great Divide when they had come through on their way to Henrys Lake. This route would take them along the foot of the Beaverhead Mountains and west of Bannack to a stagecoach road that ran between Dillon, Montana and Gibbonsville, Idaho. Lu probably was referring to this portion of their trip when he said "From there [the southwestern Montana border] we went through miles and miles of cattle country with fences on both sides of the road. Swell grazing country and lake country." The gentle terrain continued to the Big Hole Pass on the Montana-Idaho border, where they re-crossed the Continental Divide back into Idaho. It did not prepare them for the abrupt change in gradient they encountered there. Almost immediately they were met by a series of sharp switch backs that dropped them 1800 feet in 3 ½ miles and then dropped another 600 feet as the road met Dahlonega Creek and followed the stream another 5 ½ miles into Gibbonsville. The first part of the road reportedly was so steep that drivers tied trees to their wagons and stagecoaches to assist in the braking and some of the passengers got out and walked over the worst places. The descent to Gibbonsville must have been a difficult and harrowing one because it convinced Ben and Lu that they would never get their wagon back out! Instead, they sold it to a rancher and used the leather from the harnesses to rig pack saddles they made to carry their belongings.

Gold was discovered in the area immediately adjacent to Gibbonsville in 1877. Aided by British investment and the construction of the wagon road up Dahlonega Creek to the Utah & Northern Railway terminal in Dillon, Montana, the town thrived for nearly 20 years. The population is estimated to have reached 1500-2000.

After leaving Henry's Lake and briefly crossing the Continental Divide on their way to Gibbonsville, the Caswells encountered a dramatic change in vegetation and landscape, seen here as their route passed through the Big Hole area in southwestern Montana (photograph by author September 2008).

There were nearly 100 buildings, including a bakery, butcher shop, blacksmith shop, church, drug store, granary, livery stable, postoffice, printing shop and newspaper, six to eight saloons, two hotels, doctor and dentist offices, and numerous residences. In short, the Caswells could find virtually anything they needed or desired there except, it seems, an attractive job or a promising unclaimed gold prospect.

The brothers, still accompanied by "Old Pete," soon moved on and in doing so may have proceeded from Gibbonsville by going back up Dahlonega Creek and over Big Hole Pass with their pack string. However, it is more likely they went up the North Fork of the Salmon River instead and there first encountered what Lu meant when he referred to "the old Lewis and Clark route to the coast" by which they (briefly) arrived back in Montana. This would have been the same route that Lewis and Clark followed in 1805 after they reached the junction of the North Fork and Main Salmon River and would have skirted the Continental Divide along its western edge rather than actually crossing over it. From Gibbonsville, this route went north another 14 miles to the summit on Lost Trail Pass before crossing into Montana and descending to the Bitterroot Valley.

There was a tolerable wagon road up the North Fork River as far as the Achord Ranch on Pierce Creek, where it then degenerated into a rugged track known as Jerry Fahey's Cut-off, along the western slopes of the valley. This continued up the North Fork, then up Moose Creek, crossed over Lost Trail Pass and down into what was called Ross' Hole, and on to Gallogly hot springs. Near the present village of Conner, probably is where they struck what Lu referred to as the "Bitter Root Trail branch of the Salmon River" and proceeded west on the old South Nez Perce Indian Trail through the Rocky Mountains, which roughly follows what is now known as the "Magruder Corridor." This trail took them to Red River and on to Elk City. The distance from Conner to Elk City, likely the most rugged of their whole trip thus far, is about 130 miles. Though the terrain was difficult, the trip itself apparently was uneventful, for only a few outstanding aspects stuck in Lu's memory over the years. "The trip, outside of a little game, remained just a trip."

On Mineral Hill they met some prospectors and camped with

them. Lu recalls that there was "Good feed and water. Stayed one day but flies were so bad we had to build smudge for the horses so they could eat. One of our smudges got into some timber by following a log and we had to cut a strip and build a fire break to cut it off. We fought fire for a couple of hours. Pulled out of there and found that twenty men had gone ahead of us about three weeks before." They followed their tracks and eventually caught up with them.

Along the way, they lived off wild game they shot and met up with a big Irishman named Joe Poynton, who accompanied them all the way to their winter quarters. Lu also recalled that "When we got down the Red River into a big meadow, there were forest fires all around us." This suggests that they were there in late summer. "The fire got so bad it drove us bag and baggage down to the river. I built a go devil or toboggan and piled [our] stuff onto it. Pulled it along on horseback with the saddle horn. The wind swapped right around and, although jumping ridges from one to two miles apart, it burned itself out." At the meadow, the brothers were able to lose Old Pete and never saw him again.

Elk City had a population of about 500 at the time the Caswells stopped there. Gold was discovered there in May 1861 when 52 men from Pierce set out to prospect on the South Fork of the Clearwater River. Prospecting south of the Clearwater was prohibited by an 1855 treaty with the Nez Perce Indians, but the discovery of gold to the north at Pierce in 1860 caused the men to ignore the treaty. By August, 1000 miners were living in Elk City and by September over $1 million in gold had been recovered. Like most mining booms, this one was short lived, but was followed by sporadic revivals, including one (1884) only a few years before the Caswells came through.

Ben and Lu camped for the night on a creek bottom, about 3 miles below Elk City, before making their way on west to Grangeville, where they restocked their supplies. Grangeville lies on the eastern edge of Camas Prairie. They must have been encouraged by what they saw there because a few years later (1893) Ben would return to the area on his own and spend about a year on the Clearwater River. After leaving Grangeville, they headed a few miles south through Mount Idaho (the seat of Idaho County at the time) and followed along the old Melnor Trail further south to Florence before dropping down to the Salmon River. Lu recalled that in this stretch they "Went down the mountain 3000 feet [in elevation]". They crossed the Salmon River on a suspension bridge that cost them 50 cents per horse and that Lu claimed was about 100 feet above the low water mark. This probably was the primitive bridge built in 1867, called the Wire Bridge, that crossed the Salmon River at Meadow Creek and was suitable for pack trains. According to Lu, "the pack train was plenty spooky. . . . [The bridge] swung so hard it threw the horses from one side to the other but they couldn't get out because the guard rail was high enough. By leading each one over, this way they couldn't rear up." After crossing the Salmon, the brothers likely made their way up Carey Creek and climbed over Studebaker Saddle, continued on past Corduroy Meadows on Lake Creek, and proceeded south down Lake Creek to Warm Springs (a.k.a. Resort & Burgdorf) near the town of Warren, Idaho.

Earlier, on the Red River, they had heard a rumor of a mining stampede on the East Fork [of the South Fork] of the Salmon River. Since they were now in the vicinity, they apparently decided to check it out. Lu later recalled, "Going over Logan Mountain (southeast of Warren, near present day Yellow Pine) we met the bunch of men who had caused the gold stampede. Three young fellows. They were told by 'Three Finger Smith' that their gold was twenty dollar diggins, but it proved to be false. While there we examined the country all around but proved to our satisfaction there wasn't anything to amount to anything." Coming down off the mountain, they camped one night at Hot [Warm] Lake and then moved on to the bench below Yellow Pine Basin. Lu said, "Next morning we were on the move again. Stopped at Yellow Pine Basin to prospect. Found some value but was too low to pay but stayed over two days to look around some more. Came out to Long Valley [on the North Fork Payette River] and camped at [what would later become known as] Cascade, our turning point. Cut across to Salmon Meadows and on to Seven Devils. There wasn't anything at Seven Devils we wanted to tie to so went on to Mineral where we wintered."

Tempted By The Devils

The Seven Devils Mountains form a band 8-10 miles wide and about 30 miles long on the eastern edge of Hells Canyon of the Snake River. Somewhere along their route Ben and Lu got wind of the fact that mining activity had heated up in the area just south of the Seven Devils near the town of Mineral, about 125 miles south of Grangeville, and they set off in that direction (Map 1).

Mineral, Idaho was a small settlement at the union of the North and South Forks of Dennett Creek, about 3 ½ miles before it enters the Snake River (site now of Brownlee Reservoir) and 19 miles west of Salubria, Idaho (near present day Cambridge). At the time the Caswells arrived, the town consisted of three hotels, four saloons, two general mercantiles (one with a grocery store attached), two livery stables, two butcher shops, an assay office, a barber shop, a blacksmith shop, a red light district, and a number of residences, in addition to the postoffice. A smelter was located below town and there were about 1000 inhabitants in the vicinity of the town and smelter.

Lu and Ben spent the winter of 1889-1890 in the area around Mineral. First they made camp above the John Dennett [Dennit] Ranch on Dennett Creek and built a cabin. Lu said, "We had heard at Mineral that the smelter company advertised for a bid on a hundred cords of wood. That looked like our meat for we had spotted a patch of timber above our cabin site. Could get the wood by building a road to it. We put in two bids at 50 cords each and got both bids as no one bid against us. Then we had to build three miles of road on the side of the mountain in order to get to it with a wagon. After we got the road built, mostly of dirt, we started our timber cutting. I cut wood and Ben hauled. We rented one team and bought a wagon. We delivered nine cords and the company shot us down. Not being acquainted and strangers we couldn't hold them to the contract and they knew it. . . . Had to let the wagon go back. A loss of twenty dollars. Then we bought a supply of groceries which took all but $200 of the bank roll. As the game all left Mineral Creek we had to move to Sturgal [Sturgill] Creek and built us a dug out. Stayed here until spring. With spring, we learned our cabin had slid down the mountain in a snow slide. . . . Glad [we] were at Sturgal." In an ironic twist, they ended up working for Dan Kurfit that spring under his contract for supplying the same mill with 100 cords of wood. Then they headed back toward the Seven Devils.

Later in the year, they moved to a flat on the Snake at the mouth of Allison Creek known as Big Bar. They settled there for winter quarters (probably 1890-1891) and ended up making it their home for three years. About that time also they made friends with Arthur O. Huntley, who had moved to the Seven Devils country in 1888, became familiar with the Big Bar area, and had a ranch on nearby Indian Creek. In addition to ranching, Huntley was involved in mining, logging, and lumbering. A. O. was midway between Ben and Lu in age but he seems to have bonded more closely with Ben, as evidenced from their future relationships.

A. O. had been on Indian Creek for only a year or two before the Caswells arrived. He was friendly, likeable, industrious, and already becoming well-established in the area. Like the Caswells he had struck out on his own at an early age and was highly independent. They appear to have hit it off well together from the start. He provided them with a local connection and shared with them his familiarity with the country and local residents. It probably was Huntley who told Ben and Lu about the site at Big Bar along the Snake River in Hells Canyon where they might settle and winter their horses.

The Caswell brothers filed a homestead claim at Big Bar and the land deed was signed by Ben and witnessed by A. O. Huntley on November 27, 1890. Big Bar offered several attractions: a mild climate (1800 ft elevation), a place to live and raise crops, pasture for their horses, placer mining for gold in the Snake River and other nearby streams, and proximity to Seven Devils country. In addition, there were opportunities to work for A. O. when he needed help haying, herding cattle, shoeing horses, and the like. Over the next few years Huntley would have ample opportunity to get to know Ben and Lu well, to gauge their personalities and work ethic, and to observe their ability with horses, knowledge of prospecting, and broad practical skills. He later wrote that Ben and Lu ". . . remained around [the area] and worked for me at odd times for several years." A. O. was relatively well-educated, probably much more so than the Caswell brothers, and therefore was an invaluable source of help to them.

Ben's claim was a "possessory land claim." It was located on the lower half of Big Bar and was about ¾ of a mile north of a cabin owned by John Eckles. The southern boundary of the Caswells' claim abutted the northern border of Eckles' ranch. The cabin the Caswells occupied was about 300 yards northeast of the junction of their southern boundary line with the Snake River. Dave Lewis, who would later become a "neighbor" of the Caswells on Big Creek, also had a claim on Big Bar (filed July 17, 1893) in the vicinity of Allison Creek, about a mile north of Eckles Creek. Apparently neither Ben nor Dave "proved up" their claims, having moved on to Big Creek country.

The town nearest to Big Bar at the time of the Caswell's arrival was Bear, which was large enough in 1892 to gain a post office. Bear was 28 miles northwest of Council and 4 miles southeast of Huntley's Indian Creek home. In 1897, another town named Cuprum was established next to where Huntley lived that saved about 8 miles round trip on a steep, winding road to obtain supplies. Both Bear and Cuprum are at the southern end of the Seven Devils mining district. The Caswells probably visited Bear regularly for groceries and other necessities and on these trips met and struck up a long-term friendship with the Warner and Smith families residing there.

The Warner/Smith families settled in the vicinity of Bear in June 1890, about the same time the Caswells came into the area. Amos E. and Phebe Warner had 11 children including twin daughters Ada and Amy (who married Clarence E. and Frank J. Smith), Joe, Charles, and Amos A. Amy and Frank lived on the stage road between Huntley's and Council and their place served as a way station for freighters and travelers, providing both meals and lodging. They operated a general store, livery stable, blacksmith shop, and freighting service in addition to homesteading their ranch. Amy also was the first Bear postmaster, starting in 1892. Frank died of blood poisoning in July 1897, following an unfortunate accident, a short time after the birth of their fifth child. The Warners and Smiths proved to be talented, enterprising, and tenacious; in retrospect it seems unfortunate that none of the Caswells married into the family.

Arrival at Big Bar essentially marked the end of Ben and Lu's trek from Colorado to Idaho, with the setting down of roots, however tenuous at first, and the beginning of some semblance of permanency. The year was 1890 and on July 3 Idaho became the 43rd state in the Union, with an initial population (88,548), slightly more than one for each of its 83,557 square miles. Presumably Ben and Lu used the following year to get established on their homestead and become familiar with the immediate area. The November 6, 1891 edition of the *Idaho Citizen* noted that "A. O. Huntley and his partner, Caswell, were down from the Seven Devils . . . after supplies," indicating that they were prospecting to the north in the Seven Devils Mountains. However, by 1892-1893 the Caswell brothers were ranging more widely in their search for gold and on one occasion they "Cut across Salmon Meadows and camped at Salmon Creek [Little Salmon River] 1892-93." In 1893, Ben left for a year on the Clearwater River in the vicinity of Grangeville. However, Lu stayed in the Big Bar/Bear area, doing mining, building, and assessment work on claims they were trying to establish ("prove up").

Into the Bush

1894

Ben came back from the Clearwater in 1894 and, in early summer, he and Lu "headed for the mountains." They rode east from their residence on Big Bar to Warren, Idaho, then followed an established trail to the edge of Big Creek country (Map 2), where they had heard that gold had been found off and on over the years. The Big Creek Mining District, covering upper Big Creek, and the Alton Mining District, covering the Ramey Ridge area of Big Creek, had been established in 1883 and 1885, respectively and some success had been obtained near Profile Summit along the upper edge of the Big Creek basin. In its October 24, 1890 issue, the *Idaho County Free Press* in Grangeville had reported that "The new discoveries in Monumental district are the most important that have been made since the discovery of Alton district. The Monumental mines are located on Big Creek, a tributary of the Middle Fork of Salmon river, and fifteen miles below the Alton district." However, the remoteness and rough terrain of the region had prevented major development of the discoveries and there had been the fear of attack from hostile Indians.

After gold was first discovered in Idaho in the early 1860s, outsiders, mainly Euro-Americans and Chinese, flooded into the territory and encroached upon the lands of the Native Americans. This led to increasing numbers of hostile encounters between the two groups, culminating in the Nez Perce War of 1877 and the Bannock War of 1878. Following the purported murder of some Chinese miners on Loon Creek in 1878, the U. S. Army initiated a new campaign in 1879 against the Sheepeater Indians. The Army encountered several old abandoned log cabins within the area during the course of the 3000 miles traveled by several detachments of soldiers during the Sheepeater Campaign but no inhabitants other than Native Americans

were found. However, slightly further west along the South Fork of the Salmon, the mining settlement of Warren and several inhabited or recently abandoned ranches and mine sites were encountered. Although the Sheepeater Campaign was largely a "protracted excursion in ineptitude," it removed the Indian threat

The Caswells panning for gold on Thunder Mountain. Also shown are a rocker and part of a flume (From an Oregon Short Line RR promotional brochure. ISHS # VF-Thunder Mountain).

from the area that later was to become the River of No Return Wilderness and facilitated its exploration and settlement by gold miners and homesteaders. Thus, by the time the Caswells ventured into the area, almost 15 years had passed since the last hostile encounter with Indians. Still the memory of the Indian presence remained a psychological barrier to incursion into the area for many local residents and it took outsiders like Ben and Lu, not so constrained by the past, to have the audacity to venture in.

The two brothers planned to spend several weeks in the area getting a feel for the country and prospecting for gold. By now they were experienced prospectors familiar with the finer points of panning, the use of sluice boxes and rockers, hydraulic mining, mercury, blasting, and related matters. Ben and Lu were in search of "placer" gold, gold that has eroded out of bedrock and deposited near the surface in sands and gravels. It is recovered as nuggets or granular "dust." Most early mining was done this way because of the small amount of capital required. In the early stages of prospecting, when only small amounts of sand and gravel sediments need to be processed, large pans are used to separate out the gold. The processing of larger amounts of material employs the use of rockers or sluice boxes. In placer mining, the loosened sediments are shoveled into pans, rockers, or sluice boxes and washed with water to separate the heavier gold from the sand and gravel. Placer mining also may involve "hydraulicking," where the banks of sand and gravel containing gold are washed away with high pressure hoses before sluicing. The sepa-

Hydraulic mining for gold on Thunder Mountain. Above: Dan Caswell operating a hydraulic "giant"(ISHS # P1987.28.1). Left: The Caswell brothers on their Mysterious Slide claim (Photograph courtesy of Stewart E. Taylor).

rated gold is further refined by hand picking, additional panning, and the formation of an amalgam with mercury. The Caswell hunt for gold followed this time honored sequence: extensive panning until suitable yields of gold were found, then rocking and sluicing of material from within the stream bed, finally expanding outward to off-channel deposits by means of hydraulicking ("piping").

Gold remaining in its parent bedrock occurs in seams or veins, called "ledges," and is known as "lode" gold. Most lode gold is found initially by searching for surface exposures of quartz. Often the quantities of placer gold and the nature of nuggets (rough or smooth) can provide valuable clues to the location of the "mother lode." Lode mining requires excavation (generally subsurface involving tunnels and shafts) and crushing of the parent rock (often in large amounts, i.e., tons, using stamp or roller mills) before separation of the gold by hand, the use of vibrating tables, amalgamation with mercury, and/or smelting. Thus lode or "quartz" mining often is both labor and capital intensive, requiring a large work force and a group of rich investors, and often needing considerable development of facilities before financial returns are obtained. Since these are beyond the means of most prospectors, they generally work mainly the placer claims and sell their lode claims either before or after further exploration and harvesting of the veins. In time, the Caswells and their partners would follow a similar procedure.

Warren is nestled near the head of what once was a broad meadow, at an elevation of 5903 feet, a few miles shy of the rim of the steep canyon bordering the South Fork of the Salmon River. Gold was discovered there in the fall of 1862 by a group of men led by Jim Warren a short time after the best sites at Oro Fino and Florence, 30 miles north on the opposite side of the Salmon River, had all been claimed. The population was 660 by the next summer, peaked around 1500 in 1865 and then fluctuated over the ensuing years as the fortunes of the miners rose and fell. Though no longer the seat of Idaho County or the roaring town it was during its heyday, Warren in 1894 was still a thriving settlement and the gateway to the mines and homesteads along the South Fork and the largely uninhabited wilderness or "bush" country beyond.

Early-day Warren, Idaho facing southeast. Warren Summit is the notch in the mountains at left of center in the background (Idaho State Historical Society [ISHS] # 1263).

The townsite is oriented northwesterly along Warren Creek at a point where Bemis Creek, Slaughter Creek, and Smith Creek enter. A wagon road came in from the north, where the former courthouse still stood on a hill overlooking the town. To reach Warren Summit and the edge of the South Fork canyon, one had to pass down the single main street past two mercantile stores, two saloons, boarding houses, the Warren Hotel, homes, a brewery, blacksmith shop, livery stable, butcher shop, and post office.

The Caswells probably stopped in town for last minute supplies and to tap into the local wisdom about the country that lay ahead and the prospects for finding gold. They rode southeast over Warren Summit, switchbacked over 3000 feet in elevation down the precipitous trail along Pony Creek to the South Fork of the Salmon River about 12 miles from Warren. At the mouth of Pony Creek, they rode past the Smead Ranch where Amasa D. (Pony) Smead (age 64), and his Native American wife Mollie (age 36), had lived and raised their eight children. A mile and a half further, they crossed the South Fork of the Salmon on a pack bridge established in the early 1870s. Construction of the bridge was an important step in opening up the country east of the river.

Ben and Lu continued upstream along the east bank to the Smith Ranch at the mouth of Elk Creek. The ranch had been started prior to 1872 by Sylvester Scott Smith. Smith was one of the first to reach Florence, Idaho in the 1860's, where he obtained a substantial amount of gold before moving on to Warren. The accidental discharge of his shotgun left him with the nickname "Three-Finger." He also was the sole survivor of an encounter with Indians in 1878 and in 1889 discovered gold beyond the Alton District on a tributary to the Middle Fork of the Salmon. It was word of Smith's discovery that had sent Ben and Lu on a fruitless diversion to Logan Mountain and Yellow Pine flat before continuing on to Mineral. Sylvester died 2 years before the Caswells passed by in 1894 and the ranch was taken over by Henry, one of his sons. From the Smith Ranch, at an elevation of about 5000 feet, the trail climbed up Elk Creek to the summit, making a 3630 foot gain in 10 miles. The U. S. Army had a camp a mile up Elk Creek during the Sheepeater Campaign 15 years earlier. Two miles below Elk Summit the Caswell brothers passed the location where the "Smokehouse," an overnight stop for mail carriers and other travelers, would later be built.

At Elk Summit, the trail went down Smith Creek to its juncture with Big Creek. Smith Creek was named after Pringle Smith, who discovered lode gold up the North Fork of the creek in the 1880s but later abandoned the claim. In 1891, Charles Werdenhoff took it over, developed it as the "Achilles Mine," and, in the early 1900s, built a 30-stamp mill on the site. Placer gold was not found in Smith Creek in sufficient quantities to warrant the filing of claims until 1901. A few miles further the Caswells passed Beaver Creek entering from the north, where James Hand had located a claim in August 1893 he named the "Golden Hand Mine."

Ben and Lu intended to go up Big Creek past the meadows (upstream of present day Edwardsburg) but got lost in a hail storm and ended up in the vicinity of where Monumental Creek enters Big Creek at a popular stopping site known as Copper Camp, where they spent two days. Pringle Smith had located a mine at Copper Camp in

1889 and was actively developing it. Rather than go back to the head-waters of Big Creek, they proceeded up Monumental Creek. As they worked their way upstream, past Snowslide Creek and West Fork of Monumental, their efforts began to intensify, stimulated by the increased "color" remaining in their pans and a small gold and silver nugget. However, as they passed a small tributary entering from the east the amount of color dramatically dropped off, causing them to believe that the source of the gold lay further up the little creek, which Ben named Mule Creek because the jumble of rocks along its edge reminded him of an overturned pack mule of Old Pete's. That summer, frequent thunder and lightening storms lashed the area above Mule Creek, impeding their work and slowing their progress upstream, so much so that they came to call the mountain "Thunder Mountain, The Jealous Guardian."

In spite of the storms, by mid-August they had reached the head of Mule Creek, several miles from Monumental Creek and "20 miles from Copper Camp." They had identified and named several promising quartz exposures (Blue Bell Lode, Summit Mine) and placer sites (Thunderbolt, Sulphur Slide, Burnt Flat) and needed to return to Warren to file claims on them. Stream flows had dropped markedly during the summer, severely limiting their ability to pan for gold. They also lacked proper equipment and were running short of supplies. In addition, they needed time to find a place much closer to their new claims than Big Bar or Warren where they could overwinter and provide pasture for their horses.

They reached Warren and filed their first claims August 22nd with Charles Bemis, a local saloon keeper and gambler, acting as recorder. In addition to Ben (A. B.) and Lu (L. G.) Caswell "from the bush," the claims listed A. B. Rombauer of Butte, Montana and Johnie Folley. It is not known how the latter two men were involved. The brothers did not stay in Warren long because they were out of cash and had collected little gold.

Ben and Lu left Warren for Big Bar to gather up equipment and other belongings before returning to Big Creek country. They also stopped by Indian Creek to visit their friend A. O. Huntley and borrow $50 for supplies to carry them through to the next summer.

They made it back to Warren by the 3rd of September, when they filed an additional claim (Mule Creek Placer). It is noteworthy that the Caswells were not the only ones with an interest in Big Creek at this time. For example, Dave Lewis reportedly settled on Goat Creek, a Big Creek tributary, in 1894. Also, an article in the September 7 issue of the *Idaho County Free Press* noted that J. M. Eakin, E. O. Eakin, D. D. Stephens, two Gamble brothers, and J. Nelson from Nez Perce County arrived in Warren with 15 pack animals loaded with 7,000 pounds of freight (probably considerably more than the Caswells put together). "These gentlemen are en route to Big Creek, some 50 miles beyond, where they will spend the winter mining. Mr. Eakin was in that country two years ago and found good placer ground on the Big Creek meadows. They take a complete equipment of provisions and mining supplies and will make Warren their headquarters." Thus, the Caswells had good reason to want to remain near their new find over winter.

After the brothers returned to the site of their discovery on Mule Creek, they had a lot of work to get done before winter set in, including erecting their main camp, whipsawing lumber, and building sluice boxes. In addition, on the way in, they had stopped at Miller's Camp before reaching Warren and obtained 50 yards of hose and a nozzle, to use in hydraulic mining, from friends by the names of Richardson and Larsen [probably Andrew and Peter, brothers of Ben's future wife]. So, they also needed to convey water 400 feet from three little lakes to the ground to be worked with the nozzle. Later that fall, the Caswells located another place only a day or so from their claims, in a sheltered valley of Big Creek, much lower in elevation and with plenty of grass for their horses. They chose a site on a large flat along Big Creek near the mouth of Cabin Creek but on the opposite bank. Here they erected a crude, one-room cabin. Lu wrote that they "Spent the winter deer hunting, lion hunting and trapping."

The 1894 cabin was built of un-peeled logs and chinked with mud. It had a single door facing south, a small window along each side, and a double roof covered with sod. The cabin was small, hastily erected, poorly situated, and unsheltered from the sun and wind, but it served to get them through the first winter. The 1894 cabin was abandoned in less than a year in favor of a more suitable site on the other side of Big Creek. Though lacking shade and some distance from water, the 1894 site provided them with a full 360° view. Directly across Big Creek, the rocky, tan slopes of Vinegar Hill rose up to meet the skyline and a little further to their right, on the opposite side of Cabin Creek, the grass-covered slope of Horse Mountain dominated the view. The flat, which encompassed both sides of Big Creek, was a broad flood

Cabin Creek as photographed in the early 1900s by Lu Caswell (ISHS # MS2/437.10). View is looking northeast from the Canyon Creek trail (north is in the upper left corner). Big Creek, flowing generally from west to east, is just out view at the bottom. The S-shaped stream entering from the east (right) is Spring Creek and the white objects near its mouth are buildings of the 1898 Caswell cabin (Elkhorn Ranch) site. The ridge just to the south of Spring Creek leads to Horse Mountain, which is located off to the right of the photograph. The tributary upstream of Spring Creek is Cow Creek; Cabin Creek bends off to the left (and out of view) at this point. The lower, southeastern flank, of Vinegar Hill appears on the bottom left of the photograph.

plain supporting dense stands of willow and other shrubs and broad expanses of lush grass that could be harvested for hay.

Vinegar Hill was named during the 1879 Sheepeater Campaign as a result of the encounter between the Indians and the pursuing U. S. Cavalry. The soldiers rode into an ambush a few miles downstream at the "Gooseneck," where two of them were wounded. The Cavalry then withdrew to the meadow below Vinegar Hill and the next day retreated to what they believed to be a more defensible position on the Hill. However, the location lacked water and the Indians pinned them down and set fire to the grass. The soldiers escaped after abandoning most of their equipment and supplies but the bitterness of their experience led to the name Vinegar Hill. Lu does not indicate an awareness of this historic event in his subsequent diaries but in 1897 he told C. W. Ritchie (who was field checking a map drawn by W. R. Brown, an officer who served during the campaign) that "they found a lot stuff the military left." Later residents of the area also claim to have recovered a large number of items left there by the soldiers.

Hay meadow on Cabin Creek Flat at the mouth of Cabin Creek (Photograph by Luman Caswell December 28, 1901 courtesy of Stewart E. Taylor). Big Creek enters from the top center (west) of the photograph and flows along the left (south) side of the meadow. Cabin Creek flows from the right (north), just behind the hill traversed by the wagon road, and joins Big Creek along the southern edge of the meadow, well upriver of the haystack.

PART II

Prologue

Luman G. Caswell's Diaries

Between January 1895 and October 1903, Luman Caswell kept an account of his daily activities, and many of those of his brothers and associates, on the frontier of central Idaho. The annual events of their lives were molded to fit the cycle of the seasons and the unique weather conditions of each day. The diaries capture the nature and rhythm of their seasonal activities, the routine and variety of their days, and the labor and fullness of their lives on a year-to-year basis. Though parsimoniously written, the entries over this 9-year period are remarkable for the detailed view they provide of a self-reliant lifestyle in what was to become the largest remaining wilderness area in the contiguous United States. The diaries also document the Caswells' initial discovery of gold on Thunder Mountain, the start of one of the last big gold rushes in the country, and the early impact it had on the lives of the brothers.

Luman Caswell was not much of a diarist in the literary sense of the word. His "diaries" are actually a series of shirt pocket-sized notebooks (he referred to them as memorandum books) in which he routinely made brief entries about the day's memorable events. These were entered as cryptic notations that were intended primarily as a record and reminder for Lu of when these events occurred and not as a formal journal. They also provided him with a source of data for future reference and a reminder of things accomplished in the context of time and place. Lu's entries expanded over the years as he came to better appreciate their utility and as the number and complexity of activities in a day expanded. For the first 5 years of the diaries the whole year of notations is quite short, often the equivalent of a typed line or less per day and amounting to 4 to 11 single-spaced typed pages per year. The remaining diaries, especially those for 1901 and 1902, have fewer missing days or periods, and the daily entries are more detailed, in keeping with the increasing number of activities. By their nature, the diaries have left much open to interpretation, inference, and piecing together and this has been my challenge in preparing them for publication.

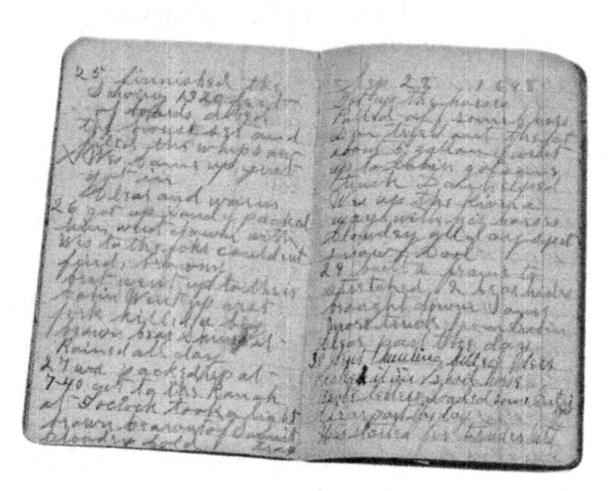

One of Luman Caswell's diaries and two pages from it (Photograph by the author).

The notebooks are for the most part well worn, with soiled covers, and probably were carried through the day rather than left in the cabin or Lu's saddlebags. The entries are in cursive, generally with a pencil and often are smudged, making reading difficult. In addition, as was typical for the time, Lu was a creative, largely phonetic speller. Thus translation of the diaries into a typescript must have been a tedious and daunting task undertaken by his daughter Louisa Caswell Hensler and by Ava (Darnielle) Lutteman (the latter in 1943 at the behest of Napier Edwards), neither of whom was directly familiar with the country, life style, or events being documented in the original accounts. The transcriptions themselves contain a number of errors, both of translation and spelling, as well as corrections of

Lu's spelling. In addition, the treatment is not consistent between transcribers.

The cryptic and unorganized individual entries do not make for easy reading and so I have extensively summarized the information, interjecting Lu's own words, as has seemed appropriate. The summarizations represent my best effort to recreate the flavor and richness of the experiences and provide a context for them, while at the same time maintaining accuracy and providing continuity and readability. I have added date (month) and location headings to improve clarity. Lu's words are set in italics and my paraphrased portions, comments, interpretations, and supplemental information are in regular font. Quotation marks are used to identify quoted material from other sources identified in the Bibliography, including Lu's autobiography, and terms used in an unusual way.

It will be helpful to know at the outset of the diaries that during the course of their time in Big Creek Country, the Caswells, like Robinson Crusoe, occupied multiple residences, some of them sequentially and others simultaneously. They also established several different routes, both within the interior of the area and to important supply and contact centers on the outside at Warren, Bear, and Boise. Within Big Creek Basin, they quickly developed two focal points: one on Thunder Mountain where the mining took place and another about 4500 feet lower in elevation, around Cabin Creek, where they maintained themselves and their string of horses (Map 3). Warren served as their principal gateway to the outside and was an important supply center, but Boise was where they redeemed most of their gold, made most of their major purchases, and negotiated the sale of their claims. Boise, the state capitol, was an important business center, stagecoach stop, and railhead. Bear was familiar to them from when they lived at Big Bar. Their friends the Smiths and Warners were there and their silent partner A. O. Huntley lived nearby.

The 1895 Caswell cabin on Thunder Mountain near the Golden Reef claim (Photograph courtesy Stewart E. Taylor). The interior of the cabin is shown in Figure 1, page 2.

1895

Cabin Creek (January 1 – May 12)

On January 1-2, 1895, Lu made his first known diary entry at Cabin Creek and recorded a foot of snow, followed the next day by rain. By February the snow is over 2 feet deep but by March 22 all the old snow is gone from around the flat near the cabin, even though it continues to snow periodically through April. Ben and Lu spend some time prospecting along Big Creek and trapping bear. Other men are in the area too. Sometimes Lu refers to them simply as *the boys*. Others are noted by name, e.g., Johnie [Folley?] and Frank Murphy, Nelson, Bob Grenell, Brown, and Dutchman (Dutch George). Lu notes that Johnie and Frank started for the South Fork of the Salmon on February 28 but had to turn back because of deep snow at the head of Cave Creek.

Thunder Mountain (May 13 – August 5)

On May 13 the two brothers head back to their camp on Monumental Creek. The route they take (Map 3) is up Canyon Creek (which could be accessed across the river from their cabin) to a camp on the West Fork of Rush Creek and then on to their camp at the head of Mule Creek, where they arrive on May 16th.

The remainder of May through the 5th of August they are busy alternately prospecting, mining, sawing lumber for sluice boxes, and building a cabin. Lumber is obtained through a process called "whip-sawing." This requires that a pit be dug and a staging built over it or that a raised scaffold be built. Logs are cut and rolled onto the stage, squared up by cutting off the slabs on four sides, and then marked off for sawing into boards. To operate the saw, one man stands on the log and another is in the pit. A good day's work would average 200 feet of boards.

Golden Reef, site of the Caswells' principal gold discovery, with Thunder Mountain in the background (Photograph from Luman G. Caswell's album, courtesy of his grandson Stewart E. Taylor).

On June 3rd, they *cleared ground and packed down* [sluice] *boxes. Piped off shelf.* In other words, they hydraulically remove the overburden from the underlying bedrock. In this case, they then pass the slurry produced by piping through a sluice with water they divert from Mule Creek. On the 12th, they *cleaned up* the sluice boxes. Cleaning up involves further refinement by panning the gold retained in the apron and riffles of the sluice. Then they saw lumber for two days and make and set up more boxes. On the 17th, they *Started piping but* [the water] *would not run thru boxes.* On June 20th they survey-in a ditch and spend the next 8 days digging it. At the beginning of July, they build a foundation for the boxes and off and on for a total of about 8 days *ground sluiced.* On the 13th, they *sluiced out the last* [i.e., they cleaned out the last of the gold from their sluice boxes] and the next day record a yield of 10.31 ounces of gold (before it is melted down to remove associated impurities). Most of the gold they obtain is fine-grained "dust," though occasionally they find larger "nuggets." During this time they also *prospected bedrock, sunk hole to bedrock,* and *cleaned up bedrock.*

On July 16 and 17, *Ben prospected for ledge.* On the 17th, Lu unceremoniously announces that Ben had *Found it.* This presumably is the Golden Reef, their first major claim. Next Ben builds a rocker and packs it up to their claim. A rocker consists of a combination washing box and coarse screen, a slack canvas apron under the screen, and a short trough with one or more riffles, all mounted on rounded supports or "rockers". One or two shovels full of dampened gravel are placed on the screen in the box and water is poured on the gravel while the box and trough are rocked from side to side like a baby's cradle. Water is added until the gravel is washed clean of material fine enough to pass through the ½ inch diameter openings of the screen. Then the remaining material in the box is inspected for nuggets before being dumped out. Most of the gold collects on the apron; the riffles catch any gold that gets by. The more riffles, the more complete the recovery of gold. Over the next 17 days, they prospect and operate the rocker. But for three solid days at the end of July and the 2nd through 4th of August they *Rocked all day.* On August 1, in particular, they *Struck a rich pocket.* On the 5th, *Ben cleaned up plate* [of the rocker] and they, *Got ready to move* [back to Cabin Creek]. The gold probably was concentrated using mercury (quick silver) because on July 28, Lu records that he *Went to cabin for quick.*

To Warren, Bear, and Boise, Idaho (August 8 – September 29)

The brothers stop briefly at the Cabin Creek cabin before heading out on August 8th. Their route (Map 3) takes them to Chamberlain Basin, then on to Elk Creek and Warren Summits. Soon after, they strike the Warren Wagon Road (Map 2) and proceed to Secesh meadows and Payette Lake. The road from Secesh Pass to Payette

Lake includes ten fords across the torrential Payette River, all of them over two feet deep even in the driest season. In the vicinity of the Lake, they split up, with Ben going to Boise to get the gold assayed and Lu going to Huntley's. Ben receives $245.75 for their summer's efforts and spends some on a used rifle, flour, and rubber ("gum") boots for the both of them. When he returns he can't account for about $120 of it.

This is the first known evidence that Ben is less than forthright even with close associates, that he is vulnerable to the temptations facing most miners, and that he does not manage money wisely. This particular episode, though seemingly small in amount, will cost the brothers dearly. With limited funds for supplies to carry them through the next mining season, they are not able to repay Huntley the $50 he had loaned them previously. They strike a bargain with him that they will give him equal interest in their claims, if he will erase their debt. Huntley jumps at the deal and eventually receives about $70,000 in "interest" that the brothers otherwise would have had for themselves. On the other hand, in Huntley they got an external advisor, a satellite base of operations, and a valuable go-between.

They leave Huntley's on August 31 and stop at Bear. The next day they shoe their horses at Frank Smith's, then go on to Price Valley near present day Tamarack on the headwaters of the Weiser River. The remainder of the trip is rather leisurely. They stay several days at Bill Irwin's, then reach Summit Meadows on the Warren Wagon Road on September 9. They lay over several days at Little (Upper) Payette Lake waiting for the rain to abate, get to the head of Ramey Creek on the 22nd, camp at the forks of Cave Creek on the 27th, and are back at Cabin Creek by September 29th.

Cabin Creek (September 29 – December 31)

After they return from Huntley's, Lu is busy around the ranch for the remainder of the year. Ben helps out a lot, especially on jobs requiring an extra hand like haying and sawing wood, but he is away much of the time too. The only visitors Lu notes during this period are the *Trapper Boys*, who stop by on two occasions in October and bring their horses and a gun for him to repair. In early October, Lu and Ben cut hay for the horses (likely with scythes), stack, and fence it for use during the winter. To make the cabin more hospitable, Lu also builds a bed and grub box; makes a chair, table, broom, and mouse trap; bores out a tub and vinegar keg; digs a root cellar; cuts and hauls wood; and washes and patches clothes.

Interestingly, Lu mentions that he *fixed road* (November 1), *fixed up wagon*, (finally finishing it on November 27) worked extensively *to repair chimney* (November 10-17), and *went to old house and got nails and table* (December 16). These entries suggest an existing road and means of conveyance prior to the Caswells' arrival in the area. Reference to a considerable amount of time spent on the *repair* of a chimney also suggests that the cabin they are living in is different from their 1894 cabin and indicates that it is a pre-existing building that already was in place when they arrived. There are two known photographs of their cabins at Cabin Creek: one labeled "1894" and another "1901," which actually was occupied in 1898. Neither of these cabins has a stone chimney. The only known cabin site in the area with evidence of a foundation for a stone fireplace is on a small bench above Cabin Creek on its west side just as the creek spills out onto Cabin Creek Flat. Associated with it there also are signs of two root cellars, a rock retaining wall, and an irrigation ditch which also supplied another terrace uphill from the cabin site. This location later is occupied by Archie Bacon and his family after the Caswells sell out in 1906. The reference to the "old house" probably is to the cabin they built in 1894 but soon vacated. Adelia (Routsen) Parke, whose family lived at Cabin Creek for a year (summer 1910-1911) states in her book *Memoirs of an Old Timer* that two partners had occupied the place prior to the Caswells but the partners quarreled over it and one murdered the other. Also, the fact that the tributary to Big Creek was known as Cabin Creek further suggests previous occupancy.

Ben is away from Cabin Creek a lot. He goes up to the Rush Creek camp on October 11 and probably goes to the Thunder Mountain claims, getting back to the ranch on the 25th. The next day he starts to the South Fork of the Salmon River. On November

3, Ben comes home and brings a saw. This apparently is a two-man whipsaw for cutting planks from logs because for the next two days they . . . *sawed lumber all day*. Ben came home again on December 11, possibly for the first time since Lu had gone (with him?) up to Monumental Creek for a few days on November 6.

Throughout the fall, they hunt and trap extensively to augment their cash income through the sale of hides and furs and to provide food. Bears seem to be especially highly prized, probably for their hides and tallow, given the disproportionate amount of time spent trapping them and the relatively few caught. The Caswells kill a lot of deer, skin them, wash the hides to remove the blood and dirt and make them flexible, grain the hides (i.e. remove the hair together with the "grain" or epidermis, usually done by liming), put them to soak to remove the alkali, wring them out, dry them, and dope them (by this Lu probably means the actual tanning process). They probably also eat a lot of venison. Later the hides are packed out to Warren and sold. In mid-December the first Bighorn sheep show up and Lu kills a ram and puts up its hide. A few days earlier, Lu noted that a . . . *wolf howled the first time*. About the time the sheep arrive, their dog Jip gets sick and dies about ten days later, possibly from the medication Lu was giving him. Lu also works on his gun and cleans and loads a lot of cartridges.

1896

Camp Creek (January 1 – June 2)

January 1896 at the ranch is ushered in with a foot of snow on the ground but by mid-month there is almost a week of rain, sometimes mixed with snow, all of which serves to restrict activities. In addition to routine tasks, (e.g., washing and mending clothes, tending traps, cutting wood, and working on hides), considerable time is devoted to hunting (mostly deer and Bighorn sheep) and trapping or related tasks such as loading cartridges or working on guns. Quarry also includes: beaver, coyote, duck, grouse ("chicken"), mink, fox, and bear. Pringle Smith and Ira Beard [Baird] and *the Trappers* come by for extended visits. Ben makes short trips away for tools (like a saw and pick) and to check traps and a more extended trip to accompany the Trappers when they go home. Lu works on a sled, fixes a bed, checks on the horses, and tends to the hides.

In February, the horses Bird, Bolly, and Trix are sick and need attention. Smith comes down and he and Ben go hunting and trapping for mountain lions; later in the month Ben kills one on his own. Lu kills a bobcat and shoots at two coyotes. He also starts trapping beaver. The brothers cut down three trees and build a skidway and windlass to roll logs up to saw. Lu spends almost a week making several aparejos (part of the rigging for a packsaddle) and repairing another and, in March, he makes several packsaddles. In mid-March, Ben heads out for Mule Creek and likely uses his snowshoes for part of the trip.

Pringle Smith and Jim *McCally* [McCauley] come down to visit on several occasions in March and April. McCauley has a cabin in the Moose Meadow area of Chamberlain Basin. McCalla Creek is named after him. Other visitors are Ira Baird and his partner. In late January, Lu notices that his dog Queen is in heat and on March 26 she has ten pups. One of these is given to Baird, when he visits in mid-April, and the rest are given to Smith just before Lu closes up the ranch for the summer. Lu spends several days fishing in April and May and catches whitefish, bull trout, and *redsides* (cutthroat trout). On one day he catches 20 trout.

Lu makes a shovel plow, forges a cutter for it, and in April puts it to work. He *plowed upper ground* [presumably the small irrigated flat above the cabin] on the 28th and the next day *plowed lower ground across creek*. By May, conditions are suitable for a garden and several days are spent planting and fencing it. On May 11, Lu *plowed garden patch*. He plants most of it on the 14th and 23rd but adds potatoes on the 15th and 24th. During this time, he also built a fence around the garden, a task that included cutting and hauling poles, digging post holes, and setting posts. He finished on the 23rd.

Lu records that he went to the mouth of Rush Creek on May 17, but makes no mention of having encountered anyone living there. Although the snow around Cabin Creek has melted by early April, it doesn't start coming off of the high country until mid May. On May 22, Lu reports that Big Creek is rising. Fortunately, he is already thinking about heading up to Thunder Mountain and on the 25th he *moved camp and horses across river* about a mile from the ranch. On the 27th he *shut up cabin*. On the next day, *Ben came over from Monumental* to the camp across the river and they got ready to leave. It is a good thing, too, because on the 29th the bridge goes out. No previous mention has been made of a bridge.

Thunder Mountain (June 3 – July 24)

The two men head up to the summit, blazing and building trail as they go, and get to their West Fork of Rush Creek camp on June 3 and to Mule Creek camp on the 6th. By the time they arrive at their claims, they are about out of food but fortunately the cabin is well stocked. They immediately get to work on mining activities and for the next 3 days build ditch and then get *hose up ready to pipe*. They cannot reach bedrock and, after 2 ½ days of hosing, they *quit it in the forenoon* probably because they have run out of water. They spend the next few days working on trail, move to *the summit*, go to their Burnt Flat cabin on Monumental Creek, and then go back to work building ditch. Unfortunately, the ditch will not hold water and they decide to build a series of sluice boxes to run the water through. They build a saw pit at Monumental and for the rest of the month alternately saw and pack lumber and build sluice boxes. By July 2 they are back to *mining full blast*. They sluice until the 6th when they *cleaned up* the boxes. At this point, the water is very low, so they saw more lumber and put a drain gate in the *big lake*, which provides enough water to pipe for half-day stretches over periods of 2 to 4 days before they stop to clean up. This goes on through the 20th, when even the lake isn't providing sufficient water. In quick succession, they remove the sluice boxes, stake a section of water for claiming, stake the Sunny Side (another major claim area), move to Monumental, and then on the 24th to the *foot of hill on Monumental.*

During this period also, the horses wander off several times and Lu and Ben go retrieve them. Pringle Smith comes up from the east fork [of Monumental Creek?] to watch them mine and stays overnight on July 15. On July 18 Lu reports seeing a wolf.

Ben and Lu get back to the ranch on the 25th of July and work on the garden, put up hay, and build fence for about a week. They start packing up on the 2nd and on the 3rd head out to Huntley's, building trail and prospecting along the way.

To Bear, Idaho (August 3 – October 16)

The primary purpose of this trip is to connect up with A. O. Huntley but Ben and Lu first stop off in Warren to ship their hides and furs to market and in Price Valley to pick up their mail. The initial leg of their trip takes them to a place on Ramey [Meadows?] they call *Birdnest Camp*, where they have a claim. Their route takes them to camps at the head of Crooked Creek and to Moose Meadows near the head of McCalla Creek, before reaching Ramey, and then on to Beaver Creek (Map 3). At Beaver, *Ben went after float* [quicksilver], possibly from Copper Camp. They then move on to *hillside meadows*, Elk summit, and Smith Creek, before reaching

Henry Smith's ranch on August 13. They start off again on the 15th and set up camp near Warren Summit before heading to town with their shipment. The next day, they make it to Secesh Meadows, then in subsequent days move on to little lake [Upper Payette Lake], the summit above Salmon Meadows, and Price Valley, arriving at Huntley's ranch on the 20th. The next few days are spent around the ranch—cleaning up, shoeing horses, and the like. Ben makes a trip to Bear on the 23rd and the next day Huntley leaves for Boise.

There are no further diary entries until October 1, when Ben and Lu arrive back at their usual camp site at Warren Summit. However, there is a very cryptic set of entries at the end of the memorandum book, in the form of a list of daily expenses for the period August 25-30, suggesting that at least Lu also may have gone to Boise, from Salubria by train on the 25th. Huntley took their gold to the assayer's office on the 27th and returned with the $175.55 in cash. This allows the Caswells to keep a low profile, while they are still developing their claims, and prevents the spending orgy that Ben engaged in the previous year. The latter is especially important, since the small amount they earned is even less than the year before. However, it enables them to buy a year's worth of supplies.

Lu and Ben get back to Henry Smith's on October 2 and remain almost a week repairing equipment, writing letters, and shoeing horses. During that time, they make at least one trip back to Warren to pick up two packs of grub. Not much is recorded in the diaries relative to their food other than wild game and what they raise themselves. However, Lu included shopping lists and records of purchases on the pages at the end of the memorandum books that provide some additional insight into their basic diet. Flour is a major item and they use on the order of 700 pounds or more of it a year. In 1895, in addition to flour, they purchased 150 pounds of bacon and 100 pounds each of beans, dried fruit, and sugar; 50 pounds of rice; and 10 pounds each of tea and lard. They also buy potatoes occasionally from residents around Warren or on the South Fork. As they become more established, they raise most of their own potatoes and an increasing variety of other garden crops.

The rest of the trip basically reverses the route they had taken out, with stops at the forks of Smith Creek, Beaver Creek Meadows, Ramey Meadows, Elk Swamps[?], and the east fork of Crooked Creek, before reaching the ranch on October 17.

At Cabin Creek, they spend a few days digging potatoes, trapping, hunting deer, and fishing before making a quick trip up to Thunder Mountain. They split up the supplies they purchased, with over half going to the mine, where Ben is planning to stay and trap.

Thunder Mountain (October 23 – 27)

After leaving the foot of Rush Creek hill, they move to the summit and build a bear trap, at what comes to be known as *Bear Trap Saddle*. On October 24 they are at the Rush Creek camp and Lu records that *Ben killed deer. Took Cap and went back*, apparently meaning that Ben took one of their dogs and headed off alone to return briefly to Cabin Creek before heading to Thunder Mountain, but Ben is not mentioned again until November 15th. The day after Ben leaves, Lu goes to the Monumental (Burnt Flat) cabin and the following day looks for some lost horses and goes on to the *upper* cabin. He then returns to Rush Creek on the 27th and reaches the ranch the next day. Years later Lu recalled to his daughter Louisa "When I came back with the outfit I got a dose of mountain fever and just about didn't make it. Had everything to take care of, horses, saddles and camp. Had to hunt to eat. It was a rotten trip down. While riding it seemed every step the horse took would break my neck off and I couldn't walk. Even after I got to the ranch there was wood to cut as there was no wood to keep warm with."

Cabin Creek (October 28 – December 31)

Lu continues to feel poorly and feverish after he returns to Cabin Creek. He later recalled "Tried to rest but had two bear traps to spring fifteen miles away. Had to as we did not want anything to die in them. On the way back from the traps it got dark on me. I couldn't get any further. It was snowing all the time. Saw a pile of rubbish under a tree, so set fire to it. Stayed under and warm all night. Didn't make a bed or anything, just hugged the fire . . . Without that blessed fire I would have died that night."

November and December are spent hunting, trapping, cutting wood, and doing a variety of lesser tasks; for example mending shoes; sighting in guns; loading cartridges; and making moccasins, shakes, tubs, and a drawing knife. Ben returns to the ranch November 15. He apparently is lonesome and has decided not to winter on Thunder Mountain. He busies himself hunting deer, trapping, and cutting and splitting wood. He gets a lynx and a big bobcat. The brothers seem to be using poison bait a lot, possibly for the first time, and not fully aware of potential problems. On December 15th their dog Skinner doesn't return. On the 16th Lu searches for him and concludes he has run off. However, on the 19th *Ben found Skinner poisoned.*

They take turns grading the road, building a bridge, and laying in firewood. They have visits from Billy Hopkins, Bert McDowell, and Charles Degrundy and also go "down" to see George Camp and Hopkins and "up" to visit McDowell and Degrundy. On December 30, Lu makes some pies and cakes to close out the year.

1897

The year 1897 contains most of the activities of the previous year and more. Lu makes a round trip to Warren on snowshoes in late winter and meets many people whom he will encounter again in future months and years. He and Ben travel by buggy from near Huntley's ranch to Boise, make public their discovery, and return. The mining operation expands. Their brother Dan and his friend Wes Ritchey arrive in August, doubling their work force and enhancing their collective talents and capabilities. They build at least one new cabin from scratch on Thunder Mountain and work on a couple of others. They seem to always be on the hunt and seem to shoot at most of the ungulates and larger predators they see. The animals they kill are mostly for their hides and only a portion are also used for food.

Cabin Creek (January 1 – February 26)

During January they cut some special logs from which to make tubs, then cut planks for the bottoms. Charles Degrundy and one of the Hopkinses come down and Ben and Hopkins go check traps while Lu repairs Degrundy's pistol. On the 10th Ben leaves for 8 days to go to Wilson Creek on the Middle Fork of the Salmon. His route traverses rugged terrain and entails crossing the Middle Fork in the dead of winter. In the mean time Lu tends traps, makes bullets and loads cartridges, kills several Bighorn sheep and stretches their hides, does the washing, pickles some meat, catches two lynx, shoots a coyote, and fixes up the furs. After Ben's return, they cut a big fir tree from behind the cabin into thirds for making planks. They continue actively trapping for bobcat, lynx, mountain lion, fox, and coyote. At the end of January, they collect a lot of their traps that had been set across the river and the next day string them out up Lion Creek.

February is just as busy as January. Sometimes the horses are on Horse Mountain and other times they are over on Cave Creek. Besides checking on the horses and tending traps, Lu makes a sewing horse and awl and uses them to make a pair of chaps, makes and mends saddle cinches with horse hair he spins and weaves, fixes a bridle, makes a pair of boot lasts, and later (March 25) uses them to repair his riding boots.

To Warren (February 27 – March 21)

On February 17th, George Camp and Billy Hopkins come down on snowshoes, pulling a sled, to visit the Caswells. They apparently give Lu the idea of making a round trip to Warren, because a week later he is busy making a pair of snowshoes and a *man packsaddle* for his back. He finishes a few days later and on the 27th heads up Big Creek, stopping where possible at the cabins of friends. Although it is not known exactly where most of these cabins are located, their relative position in terms of the ranch and Warren can be surmised. The first two overnight stops Lu makes (George Camp and Billy Hopkins' place and Bert McDowell and Charles Degrundy's cabin) are on the east or Big Creek side of Elk Summit. Presumably the remainder are on the west or South Fork side.

Camp and Hopkins are not home but Lu spends the night there anyway. On the third day he is joined by Bert McDowell, who goes down Elk Creek with him to Charles Hopkins and Bud Dawson's cabin and the two spend two nights with them. The four men then travel on down the South Fork of the Salmon and up China Creek, to stop overnight with "Sam and Keffer." John "Bull" Keffer owns China Ranch on the Frank Smith trail, about 8 miles from Warren. Sam may be Sam Smith, one of Silvester Smith's sons. After leaving Keffer's, Lu makes two more over night stops, at Billey Dunaway's and Mit [Mitchell] Haney's, before going into Warren for supplies and returning to Mit's the same day.

There then ensues a week of visiting and dancing that enable Lu to get acquainted with a number of South Fork residents, some of whose names he records. The first dance is at Billey Dunaway's the night of March 7. Crosby (Curley) Brewer and his wife Georgia are there among others. They live along the west side of the South Fork a mile south of the bridge (Map 3). In the morning, Lu goes up to Clark Roland's and when he returns the next day, Billey is getting ready to have another dance. Afterward, Sam Smith leaves for a day to get his wife and daughters and when they return there is another dance on the 11th. Apparently because of the presence of more women, it lasts most of the night. They dance again for an hour on the 12th, then Lu goes up to Clark's for the night. When he gets back to the Dunaways' in the morning, the party is breaking up and people are heading home. So Lu goes hunting with Billy Smead and stops for the night at Ira Baird's. The 14th he stops by the Dunaways' for a shirt he'd forgotten and goes back up to Keffer's.

Lu leaves in the morning for Big Creek and camps near the summit of Elk Creek. He gets back to McDowell and Degrundy's the next day and stays a couple of days before going on to Camp and Hopkins' place, where he lays over another day and fixes his snowshoes. He is back home on the 21st, having been gone 23 days and traveled over 130 miles. Ben apparently is still around but is not mentioned in the diary until April 3rd.

Cabin Creek (March 22 – May 13)

Lu spends the rest of March on routine tasks. He repairs his riding and gum boots, saws out a lot of saddle forks for making packsaddles and dresses them out, and cuts out a packsaddle pad. He also regularly checks on the horses and gives them salt. The salt encourages the horses to drink and prevents possible death by keeping their guts from becoming impacted.

April is spent tending traps, hunting grouse and mountain rats [native pack rats], and trapping for cougar and beaver, with some of the traps over on Crooked Creek. One cougar breaks the toggle loose on a trap and escapes but is treed by the dogs and Lu shoots it. Lu finishes the packsaddles and fits them on the horses, cuts out more saddle pads, and fishes for redsides. On the last day of April, he gets the ground ready to plant and cuts potatoes for seed. May 3rd he plants carrots and *vegetable oysters* (salsify, whose roots taste like oysters). The next day, Lu notices that Big Creek is rising and after checking again on the 6th, hastily throws some things together, closes up the cabin, and crosses to the other side. On the 8th, the river drops, so he returns to get seeds and potatoes and cut off the water on the garden.

Lu finally starts for Thunder Mountain on the 10th and goes first to the West Fork of Rush Creek, then to the Mule Creek cabin, where he straightens up the cabin and cleans up around the yard, puts in a garden (beets, radishes, onions, turnips), and fences it. Ben turns water in to the ditch leading to their sluice-mining operation and presumably cleans the ditch and makes repairs as needed. On May 13th Lu *took a run up Trap Creek*, located about ½ mile downstream from Mule Creek on the opposite side of Monumental Creek, apparently looking for a place to pasture the horses.

Thunder Mountain (May 14 – July 19)

On May 14th Lu and Ben go up to "Thunder camp" (a.k.a. Sunnyside?), open up things so they can dry, and fix trail. Ben takes the horses down to Trap Creek. On the 15th they pack up and move to Thunder camp, where they saw lumber from the 16th through the 22nd. They use the lumber to build sluice boxes and construct 400 feet of flume to carry water from a ditch they have dug to the boxes. Finally, they set up the boxes and pipe some rock through them. They turn the water on but the old hose won't hold water so they make more boxes. Finally on June 9th, they *Turned on water. All behaved well. Run until dark.* They frequently are distracted because their horses keep wandering off, probably because of inadequate feed in the vicinity, and have to be rounded up.

On June 7 Lu notes that there is very little snow left on Thunder Mountain. This means that there is limited water for sluicing and that they cannot mine full time. For example, on that day they pipe only till 10 or 11 AM and then do other things. During the month they kill a lot of deer and a number of times seem to go a day or more between sluicing. On June 19th, Lu wrote *Water don't get there no more but turned it on.* To get more water from a small lake, they remove the lake headgate and dig about 20 feet of drain. *Ben sluiced out the lake about 2 ½ feet.* Ben makes a cut in the outlet of the upper lake and extends the *drain in the lake about 20 feet.* After this they run for longer intervals with the rest of the time spent cleaning up or picking rock out of the sluices. By June 25 they have sluiced enough to warrant their first cleanup of 3 riffles. They also *Changed the hose. Put down the riffles and turned on the water about 9. Run till 3 . . . . Retorted the dust. Had enough in all to ball 1 box of pistol cartridges and 7 rifle cartridges* [i.e., they are packaging, and possibly hiding, the gold in the empty cartridges]. *40 oz.* Two days later, they *cleaned up the other 3 boxes. Got about 40 oz.* Through judicious use of the water, they are able to continue mining until July 9 when they *commenced to clean up the boxes for good this season.* The next day they *clean up all the boxes but one.* And the following day, *put down the riffles.* On the 14th they *Turned on the water* [and] *Piped some gravel in boxes to cover up the riffles.* Then they *Rolled up the hose. Put it away. Sorted the stuff and put it in the shack. Washed and cleaned up. Got ready to move. Ben panned some dirt and got about $5.*

Ben and Lu must have been telling their friends about their good fortune for during the summer they have several visitors at their claims, who don't lend a hand or stay longer than overnight. On May 17, William Hopkins, Clark Roland, and Curley Brewer arrive from Copper Camp but leave the following day. On July 1, Pringle Smith and Jesse Jackson come in about 2 PM while the Caswells are picking rock from the sluices. Then, *The boys called it the 4th* by quitting work and celebrating Independence Day early. On July 4th the Caswells stake their Poor Man's Treasure claim near the head of Mule and Marble Creeks. On July 10th they stake another claim, named Gravel Point, near the head of Mule Creek, 3 miles from Monumental. It joins their Golden Reef and Poor Man's Treasure claims. Dan Caswell is included on this one in anticipation of his impending arrival.

During June and July, around mining and other tasks, the brothers build a new cabin, probably at Thunder camp below the little lake, since they already have a cabin at the upper end of Mule Creek (Golden Reef) and a tent-cabin near its mouth (Burnt Flat). The construction project gets under way June 15-18 with the cutting of house logs, clearing of ground for the structure, and the "snaking in" of the logs with the horses. They take a break from mining and work on the cabin at least part time from the 28th until July 8th, at which time they put the roof logs on.

They leave for the ranch on July 15 and make it home in two days. The day after their return, they *fill up on Big Creek luxuries* from the garden. Also, the *House got afire* but the fire apparently is extinguished without major damage because they continue to live there for another year. The next two days are spent hilling potatoes and furrowing them, building a fence up the creek, and getting ready to travel—including baling and packing up deer hides.

To Boise (July 20 – August 31)

Ben and Lu leave to go out of the country on July 20. They move first to the spring on Crooked Creek where they *Struck* [encountered] *2 hungry lads from Warren by name of Price Cherran (alias Thawhorn) and Fred.* Before leaving the next day, they *gave the boys some grub.* (When the brothers return to the ranch on August 31, they find that their cabin has been broken into and ransacked. Perhaps these are the culprits.) They camp at Moose Meadows that night. On the 22nd they go to Mosquito Springs and kill an elk; then lay over the next day and process every thing but the "squeal." On the 24th they *Packed up and went to Hell and back to Devils Lake.* Then on the 25th they make it to the forks of Elk Creek. On the way, they meet Degrundy and McDowell on the Smith Creek summit and J. P. [Pringle] Smith at the head of Smith Creek at Elk summit. The next day they *moved to mountain ranch and found* [Collins] *McIntosh and* [Bert] *Zeiber at home.* They *Laid over and gassed* with them the next two days, smoked meat, and Lu wrote letters. Ben and Mac went into town both days and got the mail. On the 29th Lu and Ben *Packed up and moved to head of Secesh* [River]. *Got some groceries and hose* [very likely from their friends the Larsen's]. Then on successive days, they move to the head of Payette Lake and then to Price Valley.

On the way from Price Valley on August 1, they stop at Bear about an hour and get to Huntley's ranch around 5. The next day, Ben and Huntley go do some work on Huntley's claim and the following day Lu shoes horses and writes letters. They ride over to Amy Smith's on the 4th to wait for the buggy they will use to go to Boise. Amy's husband Frank passed away less than a month earlier. He had stepped on a porcelain doll's head when he had gotten up in the dark to tend the baby, lacerated his heel, and died of blood poisoning soon after. They have to wait until the next day for Amy to come home but in the mean time they sharpen a sickle and fit up several pairs of horseshoes in the Smith blacksmith shop.

On August 7th Lu and Ben *Harness up the broncs and hit the trail.* They take the road past Charley Anderson's hotel and stage stop on Lick Creek, then continue on to Moser's Hotel in Council (Map 2). The next day the Caswells *Hitched up and drove to Kimborough ranch* and stop along the way at Crane Creek to give the horses a rest, going through Indian Valley in the process. On the 9th, they stop at *Big Willow* for dinner (i.e., lunch) and make it to Emmett by evening. They get an early start and arrive in Boise by noon the next day in plenty of time to take their gold dust to the US Assay Office on Main Street. It isn't long before news of their good fortune spreads. On the day they *Got returns on dust* for $772.59, announcement of their discovery appears in the August 11 issue of *The Idaho Daily Statesman.*

At the time of the Caswells' visit in 1897, Boise has begun to change from a rough frontier town to a young city befitting the capitol of a brand new state. Shortly after statehood was attained on July 4, 1890 Boise's population was 4,026 and was on its way to doubling by 1900. Amenities, either present at the time or acquired during the decade, include an electric streetcar, a municipal water system, a geothermal system for heating fashionable homes and 40 business-district customers, a natatorium (the "Nat"—a public bathing facility), public libraries, a substantial business district consisting mostly of two- to three-story brick buildings and a few wooden landmarks such as Overland House hotel (1864-1903), Central Hotel (a.k.a. Hart's Exchange), and a Catholic Church. The Caswells often stay at the Overland on the corner of 8th and Main, which, for most of its life is the business and social center of town. The Boise City National Bank, state penitentiary, state Soldiers' Home, city hall, Columbia Theatre, and an apartment complex are added during the decade. Other buildings include Frank Coffin's hardware store, Falk's Department Store, several large churches, and GAR (Grand Army of the Republic) and Masonic meeting halls. Saint Alphonsus' Hospital opened in December 1894.

August 12th is spent shopping for supplies, which must have included a new watch for Lu since subsequently his notes are peppered with exact times. They also send $100 to Portland for hose. Thus, at least half of their year's gold earnings are already committed. Only 2 ½ days after they arrived, they *Hitched up and pulled out at 8.* They return the way they came and on the 16th, arrive in Bear just after noon and visit with the Warner family. Ben takes Mary Warner over to the Gladharts.

After he comes back, he and Lu return Amy's rig, saddle up, and ride over to Huntley's. The next day they set up a saddle for him, probably a packsaddle. Ben and Lu start back to Big Creek from Huntley's on August 19, but make it only to Bear and shoe 4 horses in the afternoon. The second day they ride for 7 ½ hours from Bear to a location Lu describes only as *spring over summit.*

After Ben and Lu left Colorado on the journey that ultimately led them to Big Creek Country, their brother Dan remained in the Hotchkiss area for another 4 years. During this time he became acquainted with Wesley Ritchey, who had recently come from Illinois. Wes was an adventurous young man with a keen sense of humor, who left home at an early age and quickly learned to fend for himself. He and Dan had several things in common, including that they both lost their mothers at an early age and both their fathers were carpenters. The two soon became fast friends.

The Financial Panic of 1893 negatively affected the national economy through 1896. Five hundred banks (many in the West) and three major railways failed and 15,000 companies went bankrupt. There was severe, widespread unemployment and farm prices were depressed. Many western mines closed, as did the narrow-gauge railroads that served them. Even the relatively strong Denver and Rio Grande Railroad, for whom Dan worked on a survey crew, curtailed its ambitious expansion program and conversion to standard-gauge tracks. The economic conditions, as well as a desire for adventure, likely caused Dan and Wes to leave Hotchkiss on horseback in 1893 for Gardiner, Montana. Dan was 28 and Wes only 19. Two of Dan's uncles lived in the Bozeman area not far from Gardiner (co-founders of Bozeman: Daniel Elliot Rouse and his brother Elisha Alvord Rouse) and that may have influenced their decision to go there.

During the winter of 1893-1894 Wes cooked at the Daisy mine on Henderson Mountain outside of Cooke City, Montana, about 60 miles from Gardiner along an existing wagon road. Both he and Dan may have gone there to work in the mine or to do some prospecting on their own. They also may have had a hand in packing supplies or driving cattle to the mine. The mine closed later that year as part of the fallout from the financial Panic of 1893, leaving the two partners scrambling for work. It may have been shortly after this that Wes went to work as a cook at John Spiker's hotel in Gardiner and Dan did some survey work for roads in Yellowstone Park, based on the experience he had gained in Colorado.

They likely were hoping to find gold. In the 1860s and '70s gold had been discovered in and near Gardiner (e.g., in Bear, Emigrant, and Crevice Gulches) as well as in the Cooke City area and was still being actively sought, especially in the latter region. However, Dan and Wes apparently never struck it rich and soon had to look for other work to support themselves. They also needed a place to keep, and possibly use, their horses. They may have worked on ranches (including John Spiker or William Cody's) or for the Northern Pacific Railroad, which built a spur line in 1883 to serve the newly established (1872) Yellowstone National Park. All of the ore from Cooke City had to pass through Gardiner to be shipped by rail for processing.

During the spring of 1897, Dan received a letter from Lu indicating that he and Ben had found gold and urging him to come to western Idaho to join them and provide needed help. Lu and Ben were uneasy leaving the claims for fear they would be "jumped." Apparently, it never occurred to Dan to let Lu and Ben know that Wes was coming along, probably because he knew how versatile and adaptable Wes was. So, in the summer of 1897, the two of them collected their belongings, loaded up their six packhorses, and rode out of Gardiner heading south into Yellowstone National Park toward Norris Junction on the next leg of their wanderings.

Dan and Wes had a 550-mile ride ahead of them (Map 1). They likely followed the Yellowstone stagecoach road to the west entrance of the Park and then to Henrys Lake where they struck the trail Lu and Ben had taken earlier to western Idaho. Dan and Wes probably went directly across the Big Hole Valley and on to Lost Trail Pass, rather than going through Gibbonsville as Ben and Lu had done. But they likely followed much of that earlier trail across Idaho until they met up with the other two Caswells southwest of Warren.

On August 21st Lu and Ben run into their brother Dan and his friend Wes about 2 miles west of Salmon Meadows. The three brothers haven't seen each other for almost a decade and, when they meet on the trail, don't recognize each other at first. Lu noted, "Just as we got opposite of his six packhorses, we stopped and looked at each other" [before realizing who it was]. Lu and Ben were surprised and somewhat concerned to see Wes but Dan's decision to have him come along turns out to have been a good one. Wes is a perceptive and able worker and enjoys cooking, especially baking bread.

The four of them travel together to the ranch and then on to the diggings. From the lake, they proceed to Squaw Meadows and the next day stop at mid-day at the lower end of Secesh Meadows. On the 24th they camp on the summit east of Warren at noon, then go back to leave an order at Grosteins hardware store and to see the gold dredge that is operating nearby.

The next day they *Got up horses and brought up what we wanted to make up our load. Went down to get the load checked off. Got quick and 10 lbs of cheese. Ben and Dan fixed up riggin.*

Lu uses the shorthand of *got up horses* or *packed up* to describe a rather lengthy ritual that generally entails: (1) locating, haltering, and bringing in the horses from wherever they had been grazing during the night; (2) giving them some grain, brushing them, and putting the riding and pack saddles (or, in the case of draft horses, the harnesses) on the horses; (3) then cooking breakfast and packing up the camp while the animals are having their morning siesta. Although Lu provides few details about the contents of this meal in his diaries, it likely is a substantial one and includes coffee or tea, bacon, venison, eggs, potatoes, and sourdough bread or pancakes. This is especially so after they become established on Cabin Creek and begin raising their own garden and laying hens, making butter, and routinely baking bread. After breakfast, each horse is woken up, then cinched up, and packed. This process is involved each time camp is moved but Lu simply describes it in his diaries as "packed up" or the like. If more than one individual is present, then one might fix breakfast while the others do the packing and take turns eating. Usually, as each animal is packed, it is immediately added to the "string" in tail-to-head fashion and, as soon as all are loaded, the entire outfit moves out.

On the 26th they *Packed up and moved to within about 1 1/2 miles of Elk forks.* Then, on successive days, they move to the head of Smith Creek, stopping for an hour along the way on Elk Creek to gather balsam; move to Mosquito Springs in 7 hours; move to Moose Creek meadows in 8 1/4 hours after encountering rain and some hail for 2 h and losing 30 minutes due to lightning; and move to warm springs on Crooked Creek, starting at 9:15 and arriving at 3:30. Finally, on the 31st they get back to Cabin Creek.

Cabin Creek (August 31 – September 3)

They make only a brief stop at the ranch, where they do some fixing up on their ransacked cabin. They clean their guns and putter around some more but on September 3rd they load up five packhorse loads and head for Thunder Mountain, stopping in the afternoon at their Rush Creek camp (7 h overall but *lost 2 hours*, probably spent clearing trail).

Thunder Mountain (September 4 – 28)

They arrive the next day at the mines at the head of Mule Creek, presumably at the location of their Sunnyside camp (8 ½ h trip minus a 45-minute stop to cut out a tree that was blocking the trail). The next day, all four of them get busy cutting and hauling shakes and putting them on the new cabin, a job that consumes 5 days. Then Ben and Wes add logs and dirt to construct the double roof. Next they hew out a pole for wheelbarrow handles and build a "road" for the wheelbarrow to haul rocks to the cabin for a chimney. Ritchey and Mackey [possibly Collins MacIntosh] leave for a while. After finishing the wheelbarrow, Lu continues to work on the house for the next 6 days while the others saw 570 feet of lumber. Next they build a door and grub box, chink between the logs with mud, haul rocks, and (over a period of 4 days) build the chimney.

On September 23 they stake off and file the Gold Bug Claim that includes both Dan and Ritchey but not Huntley. Its location is described on the claim notice as being at the headwaters of Mule Creek 1000 feet west of Sunny Side and south of Poor Man's Treasure. It apparently is an extension above the Golden Reef. They ground sluice a little and adjust the location of the stakes for the claim. Their first clean-up of four boxes yields about $125 in gold. The next day (September 27) they finish cleaning up, pull out the boxes, and get ready to move back to the ranch. They set off the following morning at 9:20, take a new route from Rush Creek, and get to Big Creek at 7:45. A short while later they are back at the ranch.

Cabin Creek (September 29 – October 5)

The stop at the ranch is a bustle of activity as the four men set out to complete several important tasks before cold weather sets in and they head out to pick up freight in Warren. They haul in all of the hay on September 29th and finish stacking it the next day. Next they tear down the fireplace on the 1895 cabin (this may have been where the house fire in July occurred) and put in a new "jamb rock" that Wes had gotten from the river. Lu builds a sourdough keg and nails his boots. They are kept from leaving when Wes becomes ill, including cramps, for a week. He is still feeling rough when they leave for Warren.

Ben Caswell on the trail to Big Creek Country leading a loaded packstring (Photograph courtesy of Stewart E. Taylor).

To Warren (October 6 – 19)

They pack up 14 horses and make it to the head of Crooked Creek before stopping for the night. On subsequent days they camp at Ramey Meadows, Mosquito Springs, and Elk Creek. On Elk Creek they encounter several acquaintances: Pringle Smith, Jesse Jackson, Miligan, Miles Burston [Bourston], and Henry Smith loaded with provisions for Pringle. They reach Warren Summit by mid-afternoon on the 10th.

Entries are missing for the 11th and 12th but the men must have gone into Warren and gotten supplies because on the 13th they *Packed up 14 horses and moved to old foundation on Elk Creek.* There is 4 inches of snow when they leave Warren Summit but when they get to Elk Summit it is 6 feet deep. They push on until they reach Smith's Camp at 8 PM and stay the next day to shoe horses and dry out their bedding and tent. On the 16th they move to Copper Camp where Pringle and Henry Smith are putting roof logs on their new cabin. The next day, Lu and Dan help them by using Buck, one of the Caswell horses, to haul rock. Ben and Wes go out the trail to Monumental and probably stay at the mines, leaving Lu and Dan to take the bulk of the pack string back to the ranch. They make one more recorded stop on the 18th *at little stock ranch on Big Creek* [possibly at Acorn Creek].

Thunder Mountain (October 21? – November 20)

Diary entries are missing for October 19th—22nd, but it appears that Dan and Lu return to Cabin Creek, leave off part of their load and horses, and then go on up to Thunder Mountain. They probably stay overnight at the Rush Creek camp on the 22nd. When the account resumes on October 23, they pack up and go to Mule Creek. *Took out some grub to leave at cabin*, stay overnight, and then apparently move up to Sunnyside. At this point all four are back together briefly, but the next day Ben and Dan head off for 6 days. While they are gone, Lu gets irons ready for the fireplace and Wes bakes bread and sets traps for marten. Then they go to work on the floor and spend several days on it. They also get two sluice boxes set.

Lu works on installing the cabin floor from October 28 through November 3. Most of the time Jack has help from three others: Dan,

Wes, and either Tom Covert [Capert] or Jack Roberts. Jack has been away for over a month and just gotten back. On the 30th, he and Ben take some of the horses to the "meadows," apparently at the ranch, and return 3 days later. The weather turns to snow and rain on the 4th. Now everyone is busy simultaneously on one of three major jobs and they continue at least through the 9th. Lu works on the floor. Ben builds a saw pit and he and Dan saw lumber. Wes works on digging a cut for riffle boxes.

No diary entries were made for November 10th through 14th but all four of the partners seem to have stuck around. On the 15th through the 18th they make a couple of sets of snowshoes, anticipating that Ben and Dan will need them to get back to the ranch later. Lu makes a pair for Ben and Dan makes some for himself. On November 15th Ben and Dan go to Monumental. Wes works on the Goldbug claim and finishes up with Dan's help on the 18th. That same day, Wes and Lu go over to Jack and Tom's and leave from there the next morning for the ranch, apparently on foot. They go through a foot of snow on the summit of Lookout Mountain at noon, make it to Bear Trap Saddle at 5 PM, and find 4 inches of snow and a big brown bear in the trap. *Skinned and dressed it at 10. Kept fire all nite. Very cold. Slept some.* The following morning, they *Started from bear trap with bear hide and fat at 6. Got to river* [Big Creek] *at 8. Left packs and got it with horse in eve.*

Cabin Creek (November 21 – December 2)

November 21 – *I killed 3 bucks. Were in good fix. Wes baked bread and tried out bear fat. We got about 4 1/4 gallons* [of bear fat and] *also tried out some tallow. Wes took out cross bar in bear trap as he had starved to death. Looks like he had been there a long time.* Over the remainder of the month, they hunt deer, fix up the meat tub, and fill it with meat and 22 gallons of brine. They also take the shoes off four of the horses, build a window sash and put in a window, build the back in the fireplace (twice), make a bread board, check traps, use Jim to roll a big fir out of the gulch and cut some of it up, and change barrels on the needle gun. There has been no mention of Ben or Dan since Lu and Wes got back to the ranch on November 21 but an entry on December 1 reads *Wes baked and Ben hauled some wood.*

Thunder Mountain (December 3 – 7)

They leave for a quick trip to Thunder Mountain on the 3rd. Diary entries are again absent for December 4-7. By the 8th Lu and Wes are back at the ranch but Ben and Dan are still on the mountain.

Cabin Creek (December 8 – 31)

Over the rest of December, Lu and Wes haul in several large logs. Wes sets and checks mink and squirrel traps and hunts sheep. Lu soaks hides, tans buckskin, fixes up buckskin pants, fixes a case for his clock, skins a mink and fisher and stretches their hides, and takes the shoes off the rest of the horses. Ben and Dan come down on the 19th, on foot, and get in around dark. They have left their packs at the head of the canyon so the next day Lu goes up with the horses to collect them. Now all four are together at the start of an extended spell, in relatively close living quarters, with an abundance of manpower. Lu and Wes continue on as they have before the arrival of Ben and Dan. Wes bakes and bakes. Ben makes a candle out of bear tallow, digs a hole, and soaks three elk hides in brine. Dan goes hunting with Lu, cuts out a banjo stem, helps grain hides, and makes a maul. Lu makes a fallow saw and uses it to cut saddle timber and a pair of crooks for a sled to haul wood. The year closes cloudy and cold.

1898

Cabin Creek (January 1 – May 9)

With the coming of the new year, "the boys" continue through March the winter round of activities at Cabin Creek begun in December 1897. Most tasks extend over several days or weeks, not only because they require a great deal of physical labor but also because they have to be fit around a myriad of other pressing jobs. It is amazing how much work is accomplished during a period when they might otherwise be expected to sleep-in late and hang around a warm wood stove much of the day.

The January-March period, while the four men remain together, provides a unique opportunity to examine the way the work was apportioned among them and to discern their individual talents. Recognizing that it was Lu who kept the diaries and would have focused on his own contributions, one can still get a feel for the aptitudes and energies of each of the four frontiersmen from an inventory of their individual accomplishments during this period. They all hunt and trap to some extent and collectively kill more kinds and numbers of animals in one season than most modern hunters do in their entire lifetimes. A relatively large proportion of time is spent trapping mountain lion and they are remarkably successful, though not nearly as much as attributed to the legendary Cougar Dave Lewis, who is claimed to have killed over 500 cougars in the Big Creek area in the early 1900s.

According to Lu's diary entries, they seem to take turns setting and checking the traps. In addition to mountain lions, they catch otter, mink, skunk, coyote, and bear. They hunt grouse, deer, elk, and Bighorn sheep and save the hides of all but the birds to be grained, soaked, and tanned for later sale. Some of the horns they collect are used to make stirrups and the antlers are used to make knife handles. At least once during the first three months, at various times they all mend clothes and repair their shoes and gum boots. Most of them wash clothes once or twice.

Many of their noteworthy individual accomplishments during the first three months of 1898 are given here and are not included in the more detailed month-by-month account that follows. During January, Lu loads cartridges; makes a buckskin shirt, moccasins, gloves, and mittens; fishes; builds a span of bridge; makes some soap; mends a pan; fixes a crow bar; puts a handle in a shovel; makes extractors for a needle gun; and saws out a pair of snowshoes. Some of the things he makes in February include a sled, packsaddle, sourdough keg, mouse trap, and roofing shakes. He also dresses up a saddle, mends rigging, and makes a hair cinch and a pair of horn rings for a bridle; repairs or replaces handles on assorted tools and cooking utensils; and mends hobbles and snowshoes. In March, he makes several more packsaddles and pads, some keepers for bridles, and a pair of stirrups fashioned out of Bighorn sheep horns.

During this same period, Dan makes gloves and moccasins and half-soles his gum boots, finishes a banjo, ornaments a couple of bridles with elk eye-teeth, and takes his saddle apart and oils it. He also bakes bread and makes a buckskin shirt, a Dutch oven lid, an aparejo, a novelty dancing girl, a pocket knife, and a hammer handle.

Wes helps Lu and Dan with assorted tasks including sawing wood, making shakes, and smoking meat. He regularly bakes bread, cooks, and occasionally makes a pie. He also makes a pair of mittens and several pairs of gloves, a pair of stirrups out of sheep horn, and a knife handle.

Surprisingly, Ben is referred to the fewest number of times and evidences the fewest number of talents and aptitudes. In addition to participating in several of the group tasks, he is recorded as making gloves, stirrups for his saddle, a cinch hook, a pair of pinchers, and a horn knife handle. He also takes a few extended horseback trips on his own, including one up river in March on which he takes along a couple of extra horses. Ben also is mentioned only a few times during the autumn of 1898 and the non-mining period of 1899, although always in friendly terms. Perhaps Lu takes Ben's services for granted or Ben is saving himself to do the mining.

During the winter of 1897-1898, the men's personality differences must have been magnified by the confined living conditions and other

The 1898 Caswell cabin on Cabin Creek (July 10, 1901) (Photograph courtesy of Stewart E. Taylor).

close contact because the four of them never spend an extended time together again. Probably as a result of this tension, Lu begins another cabin in February 1898. Lu's work on the new cabin at the ranch intensifies in March, with help from the others and an occasional visitor. The roof is completed and the cabin nearly finished by early April. Then other things take priority and the exterior doors aren't put in place and the new stove installed until September. By November 1898 he and Dan are pretty well settled in the new home. The cabin is eventually adorned with an antlered elk head, giving rise to the title "Elk Horn Ranch." Ben hereafter mainly occupies one of the cabins on Thunder Mountain, either on Mule Creek or, increasingly, at the new site at Thunder Camp (Sunnyside). Wes links up with Bert Zeiber and together they build their own cabin on the Thunder Mountain claim Wes receives from the Caswells and begin mining, although he continues to provide considerable help to the Caswells.

January

Wes cooks New Year's dinner. This gives Lu time to finish the sled he's been working on and use it to haul three loads of wood. The next day, Wes goes to check their traps and takes the dogs Cap and Fuss along. He sees lots of mountain lion sign and *Cap went after something.* [Wes] *found a lion at the sheep carcass which caused the death of Fuss. Wes shot* [the lion] *off the dog* [but] . . . *left him in the box trap. Dan went over and got lion.* Wes had another encounter with cougars near the end of the month (January 28) when he *Found 2 lion kittens at trap just above house. Got them both then went over to bait and got another big one at carcass. Chained up 1 kitten lion to play with* and killed the other, which Ben later skins. That same day Dan and Lu go down and hunt *all afternoon for poisoned coyotes but did not find any.* The next day Wes goes to check the traps again and it is noteworthy that Lu's entry states *Wes went to traps on Cabin Creek* because this is the first mention of the creek by name in the diaries.

Another new location is mentioned on the 30th when Lu notes that he and Dan *Went down to Browns.* This probably is Brown's Basin, located a few miles down river from Cabin Creek. While there, they *Cut timber for 4 packsaddles* [and] *1 man saddle* [i.e., backpacking frame].

Ben and Dan started for Copper Camp on the 2nd but turned back because of weather and trail conditions. They set out again on the 11th and require a full (10-h) day to get there. Presumably they spend the next 3 days socializing before returning the 15th.

February

With 1 ½ inches of new snow on the 3rd, the snow depth is now 4-5 inches. During the month, Lu takes horses over to Cave Creek with Ben and later takes salt to them. He also teams up to whipsaw over 750 feet of lumber.

Several days during the month are spent working on the new cabin. The project shows evidence of long-term planning and begins counter-intuitively with whipsawing of lumber for flooring and gathering of materials for the roof. They cut out 160 feet of lumber, haul in a tree for ridge logs, and cut up logs into "bolts" for making shakes. "Bolts" are short (18-24 inch long) sections or rounds of logs cut serially along a tree trunk. Shakes are then split off vertically along the flattened (cut) face of a bolt using a froe. Bolts can be split up into firewood too using a maul or axe. Dan and Lu also set four posts for a windlass at the building site.

March

Tom Capert comes down from Thunder Mountain on the 13th and stays until April 2. On the 17th, Tom and Ben take their horses upriver. A notable entry regarding some of the partners' "trapping" tactics and their implications is made on the 19th when Lu notes that *Ben found another deer carcass killed by lion. Filled it with stryct-nine* [to try to poison the cougar] *and 2 eagles took bait.*

A considerable amount of time again is spent working on the new cabin. On the 8th and 9th Lu and Ben cut 10 roof logs. Then on the 10th and 12th Lu makes over 800 shakes and on the 13th and 14th he gets up the horses and hauls shakes and roof logs to the building site. On the 15th Lu *Hauled last of shakes and cut some logs to tie shakes down.* The next day he *Snaked in balance of logs for cabin. Hewed down 3 of the big logs.* Lu and Dan worked all day on the cabin on the 17th and Ben and Wes helped in the afternoon. Lu and Dan work on the house pretty much full time from the 22nd through the 29th, with occasional help from Wes and Tom. On the 26th they get the roof logs all on and the next day they *Hauled in some logs for gable.* Dan and Lu are still working on the cabin when the month ends.

April

During April 1-2, Ben, Wes, Tom, and Lu go to Copper Camp and J. P. Smith, Jackman, and Jessie Jackson arrive a few minutes ahead of them from the South Fork. *Layed over and spun yarns.* Lu returns from the Copper Camp trip on the 3rd while *The boys Ben, Tom and Wes put packs on their backs and pulled up Monumental* on the way to Thunder Mountain. Ben stays there until May 6 before returning to Cabin Creek. He clearly appreciates the importance of getting to Thunder Mountain as early as possible in order to take advantage of the water provided by runoff from melting snow for their placer-mining operation. It also is evident that in the short time since he met Wes, Ben has become comfortable enough with his personality and work ethic to have Wes come along instead of Dan. They must have had quite a few stories to tell when the two contingents met up again. Lu later wrote, *Ben, Wes and Tom was 5 days coming from Big creek meadows. Got in at mines 5th day of April and worked all but 3 or 4 days of April.*

Dan had stayed behind to care for the ranch and dig a cellar. As soon as Lu gets back, he and Dan begin working on the cabin again. They work on it all day from the 4th through the morning of the 8th, finishing the roof on the 6th. Then they stop because of more-pressing tasks.

The snow is gone from around Cabin Creek and the ground warm enough for planting by early April, so Lu and Dan get started on a garden. In the afternoon of April 8 and into the next day, they plant lettuce, radishes, and onions. On the 10th, they plow in the morning with Buck and Jim and, in the afternoon put up fences and burn the brush along the creek. The next day Lu spades the garden and Dan finishes burning brush, then Dan spades the rest of garden on the 12th. They take off a few days to go on a prospecting trip on lower Big Creek but resume spring cleanup and gardening activities on the 16th when they *burned off meadows and finished putting in garden below house. Grubbed some on potato patch.* They finish clearing the potato patch and plow up the turnip patch and get it sown on the 18th. The potato ground is plowed and most of it planted from the 20th through the 24th. The next day, Dan puts in the cabbage. On the 26th, they *planted some potatoes in old garden and some in creek garden.* Then, on the 27th Dan sets out the last of the plants except for some carrot and corn seed they plant during the first week in May.

Their prospecting trip takes them to some country not mentioned elsewhere in the diaries. They are bound for the vicinity of Soldier Bar, a high, narrow bench on the opposite side of Big Creek, where Pvt. Eagan died and was buried during the Sheepeater Indian campaign. On April 13 Lu and Dan *Packed up and came down to Impossible creek* [present day Cliff Creek]. *Set bear trap.* 14—*Killed a deer and moved down to mouth of Flat* [Goat] *creek. Took in* [Payed a visit to] *Soldiers Bar. Struck* [dug] *a prospect hole. Moved up to flat* [probably the hanging bench on Flat Creek] *and sunk another hole and went up creek.* 15—*Dug a hole, tried 3 pans. We packed up and went across* [Big Creek] *to Soldiers Bar. Explored it and panned several pans. Packed up and came home at 5 o'clock.*

In and around finishing up the garden, Lu and Dan start getting ready to go to Thunder Mountain for the main mining effort up there. Big Creek begins rising notably from melting snow on the 15th and, after another week of increase, Lu starts to worry about getting their horses and gear across. They round up the horses and on the 26th move those of Jack, Tom, Wes, and Dan across the river. *It is getting muddy and packed things up to move across.* These activities continue but generally amount to "two steps forward and one step back" because the horses come back and have to be taken across again the next day and the camp fixed up and fenced this time. But on the 30th the *outfit* is on the Cabin Creek side once again.

May

In addition, to getting the horses and supplies favorably positioned, the two brothers seem to be waiting for Ben to show up. They fill in the time by hauling in wood, going fishing, and trapping go-downs (the local name for ground squirrels). Lu secures fish by angling, setting lines, and shooting. They catch a mix of redsides and whitefish. On the 7th Lu sets four fish lines and catches a trout measuring 22 inches and weighing 3 ¾ lbs. On the 8th he shoots five whitefish and catches four more. Also on the 8th, he *Struck pay dirt on Camps Bar.* This could mean that he found gold there because the next day he notes *Represented* [marked out a proposed claim] *the Salted Surprise and staked it . . . brought over some tools from cabin.* Since this claim is on the opposite side of Big Creek from Cabin Creek, the latter part of the entry indicates that Lu retrieved some tools from their old 1894 cabin and brought them back to their current living quarters.

The river is down on the 2nd so Lu splits up the grub again and takes it across the river. Ben comes home from the mine on the 6th then takes a day off to go prospecting on Cave Creek, where he spots two elk. Lu bides his time by going fishing and Dan brings in Jack's horses again. On the 8th, they get up their horses and get ready to move across the river.

Thunder Mountain (May 10 – July 12)

Starting in May, Lu in particular does a lot more traveling in 1898 than in the previous few years, usually in the company of at least one brother and/or Wes. Most of the trips are "local" including new routes directly along Big Creek from Monumental Creek to the ranch and via West Fork of Monumental Creek to Warren (Map 3). There is a lot of travel from Thunder Mountain to *the meadows*, meaning Big Creek Flat at the mouth of Lick Creek near present day Edwardsburg but possibly the grassy flat at the mouth of Cabin Creek.

View up Mule Creek valley from Burnt Flat Cabin site with Thunder Mountain in the background (photograph by author August 2009).

Ben and Wes went to Thunder Mountain about the time that work on the Elkhorn cabin ceased in early April and attention at the ranch shifted to planting a garden. Now, when Ben comes back to the ranch for a brief stay in early May, Wes remains behind to watch over the claims, and then Ben, Lu, and Dan arrive for a couple of months of hard work on Thunder Mountain. They seem to be picking up where they left off in 1897 and, though not stated explicitly, much of the activity appears to be in the area of their Sunnyside claims and possibly also the Golden Reef site.

Lu, Dan, and Ben arrive on Thunder Mountain on the 11th and, the next day, set up a filter made at the ranch earlier in the year and get it going. It appears to be part of their mining operation, though its specific use is not clear. Perhaps it is a replacement for the screen in a rocker. On May 13th Dan and Lu go up and fix the flume, Ben goes after tools and grub at the Mule Creek cabin, and he and Dan shovel out the head of the flume boxes. They work on riffle boxes for the next two days, get them all set, and build a scaffolding for the flume boxes. Then Ben goes over and has Jackman start the water into the ditch. A week later Dan installs head boxes in front of the riffles and Wes gets some time to go prospecting on his own. Besides Jackman and Wes, Bert Zeiber, Mit Haney, and [Henry?] Smith are on the mountain in the latter half of May prospecting and staking claims.

The Caswells divert water out of a small lake near the head of Mule Creek and, from the 26th through the 29th, go back to hydraulic mining or "piping," and pass the slurry through the flume and over the riffles as in the past. Water is in limited supply, so they run for short periods of time and then switch to other tasks, like patching hose and rolling and pounding rock, while waiting for the supply to build back up. They "roll rock" to move aside boulders and other large pieces of rock, too large to be carried along by the water and obstructing access to the finer, gold-bearing material. The more promising pieces of rock, which appear to contain gold, are pulverized with a hammer or "pounded" to facilitate recovery of the gold.

June

The four men continue piping and rolling boulders during the first five days of June. On the 3rd, the pipe gets choked up and they have to turn off the water. Their horses have been missing for days and have evaded several attempts to find them. But on the 4th *Jack Roberts and Ben came in with boys horses.*

On June 6 Lu *Made a head box for little lake* and on the 7th *Put in headgate in lower lake.* Also on the 7th they *Commenced to clean up in afternoon*, continued through the next day, and on the 9th *Finished cleaning up. Put down riffles. Got 6 1/4 lbs. or 100 oz.* They rolled out rocks and piped again on the 10th and 11th, started the second cleanup on the 12th, and finished the next evening. The "clean up" in the flumes is concentrated by the usual panning process but they also use a furnace, heated with charcoal produced on site, to further concentrate the gold. They make the charcoal by digging a pit, filling it with wood, and slow burning the wood underground to restrict the supply of oxygen. They start it going on May 23rd and later "dig up" or remove the overlying soil from the surface of the pit to expose the "coal."

On June 16th they *Sluiced off bluff. Took up floor over bluff. Bert brought in a good prospect off of Thunder mountain* and the next day Lu *Went up to Sunnyside to show Bert his lines and measure them. Bert staked a claim.* Earlier, while on Sunnyside, Lu had gathered balsam and on the 19th, h*e put some balsam on* [the horse] *Bobs crippled shoulder* and continues to treat it for some time afterward. *Fixed up around house and made a broom* [out of wire grass]. *Ben did some work on ledge and staked some claims.*

From about June 20th on they don't do much mining though they do prospect, file claims, and work on existing ones, including Gold Bug and Gravel Point. Ben and Dan also work on the flume and scaffold from the 21st through the 26th. A flurry of other prospectors are in the area to file claims or to "look around," including Miles Burston, Hallahan, Palvin [?], Pringle Smith, Joe Thomas, Van Meter (a partner of Henry Smith), and *Wordenhoff* [Werdenhoff]. Also in this same period, Dan, Wes, and Bert Zeiber are prospecting and staking claims and Bert is building a cabin.

Lu continues work on the Sunnyside cabin begun the previous year. He makes a bunk and bedstead on June 21st and cases the middle doorway on the 23rd. On the 27th he builds a cupboard, after previously sawing out 84 feet of boards in 5 ½ hours with Ben and planing them, and makes bars for the windows on the 30th. On July 5th Lu put shakes on the house. Ben split enough more to finish and on the 9th Lu put the bars, he had made previously, on the windows.

July

At the start of July, Dan and Lu begin to construct a cut in the lake outlet. Lu and Wes continue the job and finish it 2 days later. In the mean time, Dan and Jack [Roberts?] leave for the ranch and Ben, who has gone to the meadows on June 29th with Jack, returns along with Mit, Henry, and Joe. It seems that Dan must have continued on from the ranch to Warren (see below). On July 7th Ben starts off to *Big creek flats.* He returns on the 9th but almost immediately packs up and starts through to the meadows.

According to their Assay Office records, the Caswell brothers (Dan?) turned in some of the gold from the year's mining efforts on July 6th in Warren and the rest on the 22nd. The proceeds from both of these transactions are split among the three brothers. According to Lu's diary, on the 18th they *Went to town received returns on dust. 65 oz.* This must have been in addition to the 52.36 and 83.39 ounces they are recorded as having brought in on July 6th and 22nd, respectively. These three transactions amount to $2490 and are close to the total of $3000 that *The Idaho Daily Statesman* reported (April 13, 1902) they had earned for the year. In either case, it is 2 to 2 ½ times what they had made during the previous 3 years combined! This is their first real money and they use it to catch up on some long-deferred "luxuries," like dental work, as well as more-frivolous treats.

The Caswells also are able to stock up on needed supplies, both for the mines and the ranch, and acquire a considerable amount of pipe for expanding their hydraulic-dredging operations on Thunder Mountain. As a consequence, most of the remainder of the year is spent bouncing back and forth between Warren, Thunder Mountain, and Cabin Creek as they transport pipe and other supplies.

To Warren (July 12 – August 12)

On a pack trip in mid-July all three brothers and Wes ride to Warren directly from the mines on Thunder and take a route that courses up the West Fork of Monumental Creek to Lick Creek, then down Lick Creek to Big Creek Meadows, and from there up Government Creek to Elk Creek Summit (Map 3). On the return trip, they leave off many of the supplies they purchase in Warren at the cabin(s) on Thunder Mountain but then continue on to the ranch by way of their West Fork of Rush Creek camp.

July 11th is spent in preparation for the trip. *Shod horses. Packed up lion hides and furs. Fixed up saddles, got ready to move. Jackman and Henry and 2 other fellows came up.* The next day, they *Had quite a time saddling up* but get started by 9:45 AM and get in a full 12 hours on the trail. On the 13th, Lu *Fitted up some shoes. Shod horses and got ready to move. Went out and killed a fat buck.* The following day, they set up camp in mid-afternoon at the head of Snowslide Creek, a tributary of Monumental Creek. They make another early stop the next day to take advantage of the good grass on Big Creek Flat. The "long bench" campsite on Elk Creek is reached just before 5 PM on the 16th and the next day they stop briefly at Jack Shiefer's and then Bull Keffer's before going on for another 3 ¾ hours to set up camp above Warren. *Gave Bull Keffer and Jack some meat.*

They discover that the biting flies are thick and devote the next day to finishing setting up camp and building a brush pile for the horses to get away from the flies. The rest of the month and the first three days of August (16 days total) are occupied with going back and forth from camp to Warren almost every day, purchasing supplies and treats, and visiting with friends. Lu also writes out five notices and has three of them recorded. Lu's itemized supply purchases range from a box of screws for 75 cents to clothes, two camp kettles, carbolic acid, castor oil, and a bolt of canvas. He also buys 25 cents worth of candy, a small package of Mastiff tobacco, and two memorandum books of the type he uses for diary entries, and spends 75 cents for three cigars, 10 cents for gum, and 25 cents for nuts. He picks up 4 pounds of rosin and one of sulfur, probably for dosing the horses, and six sheets of sand paper, a gallon of linseed oil, paint, and brushes for the cabin. Wes and Dan both have several teeth filled. Dan trades horses. Ben buys six sets of horseshoes. McIntosh, Pringle Smith, and Werdenhoff stop by for visits. Dan visits Tom Neighbors and Tom later reciprocates. Ben goes to Nagles' Hill and Lu stays overnight at Billey and Ida (Smead) Dunaway's.

On the 22nd Lu goes down to Dan and Maggie (Smead) Leech's, for a visit then returns to camp and assembles two saddles. The following day, he notes *Went to town. Spent 40 c at bar Got 14 feet of canvas. I went to the* river [South Fork] *with Mary* [probably Mary Eagan, whom Lu refers to again in the autumn of 1899]. 24—*Came home, drove in horses and worked on aparijo* [aparejo]. 25—*Worked on aparijo, went to town in eve.*

June 28—*Ben, Wes and I went to town to settle up. Divided the money. Got some grub.* Later, the *Idaho County Free Press* (August 19, 1898) reported that the Caswells left Warren ". . . with a pack train of 12 horses loaded with supplies purchased from Henry Grostein. Caswell paid him over $1,300 in gold dust. Caswell also gave Grostein one hundred ounces of gold dust to send to the Boise assay office."

August

Dan and Lu go to town on the 4th to make up the loads and don't get back to camp until 7. The group leaves from Warren Summit the morning of the 5th and makes it to Elk Creek before stopping for the night. Bert Zeiber apparently is traveling with them and he *got some potatoes and onions at Bulls.* According to the August 19, 1898 issue of the *Free Press*, one of the Caswells (probably Ben) told a crowd in Warren that he had panned out dirt that yielded $8 to $10 per pan. "When questioned about the extent of the pay ground, he invited all the men to follow him, stating that there was plenty for everybody. During the day of their departure dozens of miners and prospectors followed. As the news of the strike spread, men from the camps near Warren took the trail for the new Eldorado, and hundreds are now there."

The return route is similar to the one they took going out, with overnight stops at the head of Smith Creek, Big Creek Flat, Snowslide Cabin, and the mouth of the West Fork of Monumental Creek. They use the West Fork camp as a staging site to divide up the "grub" and other "stuff" for the mines and the ranch. On the 10th they pack supplies up to the mines and return to the West Fork. Wes, Bert, and Bert's brother Fred move up Monumental Creek to the Caswells' camp at the mouth of Mule Creek. The next day, Lu, Dan, and Ben apparently head up Milk Creek, then camp early in the afternoon at the West Fork of Rush Creek where they meet up with Pringle Smith and Jackman. They all apparently travel to the ranch the next day and find *Everything looking well. 4 outfits camped on Big creek.*

Cabin Creek (August 13 – 16)

During a brief stop at the ranch, Jackman helps haul hay for a day and then gets ready to pull out for Thunder Mountain, so they settle up with him for his work and Dan and Ben help him shoe his horses. The brothers put up the rest of the hay and Lu builds a fence around it. Lu also mends rigging, makes an aparejo and cinch, and shoes horses. Interspersed around the various other activities, he finds time to kill a few "chickens" (grouse) and Dan weeds the garden.

Thunder Mountain (August 17 – 21)

They pack up 14 head of horses and go through to the forks of Monumental Creek by way of their Rush Creek camp. The *burrow man*, a packer who uses mules, apparently has brought in a load of supplies and is waiting at the forks for the Caswells to arrive. The following day, they load up the supplies and get to the mines before noon. A number of their acquaintances are already camped in the vicinity, including Clark Roland, Dan Leech, Pringle Smith, and Jackman, and the next day Miles Burston and Billey come up together and join them. Meanwhile, the Caswells put a headgate in the lower lake and finish digging the cut to bring water to it. Wes and Bert, who have been working on their own cabin and have it roofed, come up for a visit.

To Warren from Thunder Mountain and Return (August 22 – September 4)

On August 22, Lu heads out, along with his brother Dan, Dan Leech, and Clark Roland, to go to Warren for supplies by way of the West Fork of Monumental Creek. They stop for the night at Snowslide basin and the next day make it to Elk Creek in 9 hours. After a short (3 h) ride the following morning, they stop at the mouth of Elk Creek and set up camp. This is an improbable location to leave their packstring before going into Warren but they may have done so because of a fire on Pony Creek or limited horse feed between Elk Creek and Pony Creek. In the afternoon, they go to town to make up an order at Hall and Woods' store and spend the night. *Cost $3.40 for feed all around. Got some tricks.* They get back to Elk Creek on the 25th and the next day *moved to old Bulls ranch* [closer to Warren] *to change range for horses. Ben went to town.* On the 27th they move most of the horses up to Summit flat (3 h) and then go to town and pack up a stove for the new cabin at the ranch. By the time they get back, the horses have scattered and they hunt for them until 11 PM. The next day is spent bringing in the horses and making up the pack loads in town. They pack up on the 29th and finally get on the trail at 11. *Had a row with Susie* [pack horse]. *Busted the pickles. Got to Bulls at 1:30. Camped and got some potatoes. Fixed up pack and got 100 lbs. of salt.* On the 30th they get ready to leave for Thunder Mountain. Pringle Smith, Jackman, and Bull all help and they get to Smiths camp at 5, after an 8 ½ hour ride. Along the way they *had a wreck,* suggesting that some pack loads may have fallen off and/or that one or more of the packhorses went off the trail. It snows until 10 the next morning, delaying their start until 11:30, but they still get to Big Creek Flat by 1:30.

September

On the 1st they make it to the forks of Monumental Creek in 7 ½ hours and the next day arrive at the cabin after another 3 ½ hours. Over the next two days, Lu cleans his guns and putties up a window, while waiting for Charley Meyers to come in with a load of supplies for the ranch. Charley arrives on the 5th and leaves the load at the forks of Monumental. The next day Lu and Fred Zeiber go down to the forks and Lu gets the stuff ready to pack.

Cabin Creek (September 6 – 9)

After a long day, Lu arrives at the ranch late on September 6. The following day, he stops by the new cabin, sets up the stove and starts to build a grub box. Earlier, when Lu was on Thunder Mountain, he ran into Miles Burston, Jim Stanton, and Jack Milligan and on the 3rd watched them leave for Warren. But on the 7th they stop by the ranch on their way to the Middle Fork of the Salmon and on the 13th will meet again on Thunder mountain. The day after they leave, Lu finishes the grub box, polishes the stove, and hews out the door sills of the cabin. On the 9th he makes a door and gets it hung and the cabin closed in.

Thunder Mountain (September 10 – 26)

Lu is back at the mines on September 11th. On the way, he meets Wes and Bert at Bear Trap Saddle where they bait the trap and set it. He also sets a box trap on Trap Creek. However, his primary purpose for being on Thunder Mountain is to saw lumber for riffles. Lu must have help with this endeavor but the names of the other participants are not given in his notes. He does however make note of others prospectors who are in the vicinity about this same time, including Johnson, Haney, and Sterner and the returnees from the Middle Fork Burston, Stanton, and Milligan. Lu spends the 12th getting the saws ready, while Ben goes hunting. *Gummed whip saw also filed cross cut.* Then he digresses another day to help Wes set up bear traps and to post a claim notice on Poor Man's Treasure. But, on the 14th, a log is cut, put on the skidway, and slabbed down. Over the next ten days Lu and his unknown partner saw out lumber including 152' on the 15th, 290' on the 16th, 230' on the 20th, and 120' on the 23rd. On the 25th he *Finished sawing 1320 feet of boards. Wes came up.* Lu starts back to the ranch on the 26th: *Got up Sandy, packed him and went down with Wes to forks. Went up west forks. Killed a big brown bear and skinned it.*

Cabin Creek (September 27 – 30)

We packed up at 7:40 and got to ranch at 5 and took a light brown bear out of summit traps [= close to 9 ½ hours again, including stop for extracting the bear]. The next day Dan rendered the bear fat and got about 5 gallons. He also *helped Wes up river a ways with his horses.* Apparently Lu has begun moving things into the new cabin because he notes: I *went up to cabin and got some truck.* On the 29th they *Built a frame and stretched 2 bear hides. Brought down some more truck from cabin.* 30—*Went hunting, killed a deer and packed it in. Shod horses and wrote letters. Loaded some cartridges. Wes started for Thunder Mountain.*

October

To Warren (October 1 – 13)

At the beginning of October Lu gets ready to go to Warren, apparently for the primary purpose of posting letters, as only a relatively short time is spent in town. He leaves in the afternoon of the 2nd and only makes it to Coxes [Cox's] place on Acorn Creek before stopping for the day. Other stops on subsequent days are made at Pringle Smith's Copper Camp, *long bench* on Elk, and Bull's. He leaves Bull's on the morning of the 6th, gets to Warren 4 hours later, and apparently spends the night there. The following day, Lu sends off orders for $5.50 worth of seeds and a spring for a pistol from Montgomery

Wards. He also mails 15 letters before returning to Bull's. He leaves Bull's the morning of the 9th and camps below the beaver dams on the west side of Elk Summit at mid day because of rain. On the 10th, he rides for 8 hours, passing through 6 inches of snow on Elk summit before stopping at Smith's camp at 3:30 and laying over the next day to dry out. He leaves Smith's and gets to Cox's at 2:15 after a 6 ½-hour ride. The next day he leaves at 8 and gets to the ranch at 11. *Cleaned and sighted guns and shot them a few times.*

Cabin Creek (October 14 – 16)

By the time Lu returns, Wes and a man named Frank are at the ranch with Dan. Lu helps Frank chase down a Pinto horse and sees him off at noon. Over the next 2 days Lu polishes the stove, digs some vegetables for Wes to take to Thunder, and visits with Cox. On the 15th Dan and Wes bring in an elk they shot and the next day Wes comes by for the vegetables on his way to the mines.

To Warren (October 17-29)

The purpose of this trip is to meet up with Ben, who apparently is coming in with a load of supplies. On the way to Warren, Lu is joined by Smith at Copper Camp. After they reach Bull's on the evening of the 19th, Lu sends his horses back with Smith, leaving him afoot until Ben arrives. There are no entries from the 20th through the 25th but on the 26th Lu notes that he had stayed at Iola, a mine near Warren Summit, waiting for Ben, who returns that day. Lu and Ben start for the meadows on the 27th and Lu records the activities of several other packers who are busy getting supplies in for the winter: *Jack Milligan, Jim Stanton, and Miles Burston packing over for themselves. Meyers gone to Yellow Pine for Charley* [Werdenhoff]. *Shafer packing for James Hand.*

Lu and Ben apparently split up at the meadows with Ben going to Thunder and Lu to the ranch. Lu camps on Smith Creek on the 28th then stops briefly at Copper Camp the next day before arriving home in the evening and noting *Dan gone hunting*. On the 30th, Dan apparently still hasn't returned but Cox comes down after his burros and goes home the next day. After Cox leaves, Lu *Got up Babe and went up to Dan and Wes camp. Stayed all day waiting for them. Came home.*

November

Thunder Mountain (November 2 – 6)

Dan returns November 1st, he and Lu leave on the 2nd, and spend the night at the forks of Monumental Creek. The next day they go via Mule Creek to Thunder Mountain for some unexplained purpose, stop at Bert Zeiber's for dinner, and return to the forks. On the 4th they go to their Rush Creek camp on the West Fork and build a cabin. Constructed in only 2 days, from start to finish, it has a dirt floor and clearly is not the quality of most of their other cabins. They finish at noon and are back at the ranch by 6:30.

Cabin Creek (November 7 – 26)

During November, Lu and Dan finish moving into the new cabin. They polish the new stove a third time and haul down more items from the old cabin, including Dan's trunk, a sawhorse, and a tub. They also spend time early in the month getting ready for winter, hauling in a load of hay and putting potatoes, cabbage, and carrots into storage. On the 21st, the river freezes over and 2 inches of snow fall with more the next day.

The impending cold and snowy weather also is an incentive to finish getting the second layer of the double roof on the cabin. On the 10th and 14th they fell "shake trees" and spend the next several days sawing off bolts and splitting out shakes from them. They continue making shakes and putting them on the roof at least through the

24th. Generally Lu splits off the shakes and Dan nails them on the roof. On the 22nd Lu cuts a saw log and Dan trims it up. The next day he makes a bedstead and puts up kettle shelves. Wes now has his own place about 4 miles upriver and on the opposite side of Big Creek from the ranch, probably on Buck Creek. However, he visits several times during the month and Dan occasionally reciprocates. When Wes leaves after visiting on the 23rd, he invites Dan and Lu up the next day for Thanksgiving. *Had a good dinner. Bert came down from Thunder and Cox came down. We came home and I split shakes.*

Entries are absent for November 25 through December 31. As the interval begins, Lu and Dan are at Cabin Creek, Wes is at his ranch, and Ben probably is on Thunder Mountain.

Burnt Flat (Mule Creek) Cabin (on right) built in 1899 and outbuildings (made with the charred logs from the Flat) (from the Earl Willson collection ISHSLA #66-74.276).

1899

The recorded account for this year is one of the most incomplete, with more than 5 months of entries missing. The year must have been even more hectic than 1898, judging from the large gaps in the account (when Lu must have been too busy or too tired to write) and from the glimpse into their activities provided by the existing portion.

According to Lu's autobiography he makes a trip in January or February to get some guns and gum boots from Warren, while the others are working on pipe on Thunder Mountain. Lu has a difficult trip in 2 feet of fresh snow, on untreated snowshoes that keep packing up with wet, sticky snow. Two companions, Richardson and Dawson, accompany him on the return trip as far as Logan Creek [Big Creek Flat] but do not break trail or help in other ways even though they each are only carrying 20-pound packs, while Lu's weighs 75. Lu injures his feet in the process and barely makes it home.

Cabin Creek (March 11 – April 22)

When the journal resumes in March, Lu and Dan are at the ranch and Wes at his "ranch" further up Big Creek. Ben has stayed on Thunder Mountain to protect their interests there. The routine is very similar to the year before. They are continually trapping and hunting as this is important for obtaining cash for needed supplies. Apparently they have learned that, after graining the hides, they need to stretch them, a fact that may have cost them when selling hides the previous year.

The first entry, on March 11, records that Dan has killed a Bighorn ram above Cave Creek and brought it in. This apparently motivates Lu to make a knife for graining sheep and elk hides and to hoop a big tub and fill it with melted snow water for soaking them. By the 25th, they have grained and put hides of 5 sheep, 2 deer, and an elk through the brine to soak. The elk hide is of special note because it is the last of only a relatively few times that the taking of an elk is mentioned in the diaries. The final step is to wring out the hides and "put them through the frame." On the 27th, Lu notes *Put 3 hides in frame. Dan sewed them in and I wrung them.* This step apparently is repeated more than once (e.g., *Put 4 hides through frame for last time.)* but is completed on the final day of the month and appears to involve a total of 10–12 hides.

On the 12th, Jim Stanton and Fred Zeiber come in from Thunder and then go "home" to Ritchey's place up Big Creek. Some time prior to this Wes joined forces with Fred and his brother Bert to work the Mysterious Slide group of three claims that Wes has been given by the Caswells. Later, on the 22nd, Wes and Fred leave for the claims.

Besides making four pairs of stirrups from sheep horns, and "fitting up" six pair of horse shoes during March, Lu performs other horse-related tasks. He works on the packhorse "riggin" and makes some pack saddles and an aparejo pad, which he stuffs with hay. He also makes some chains and fixes up enough straps to make seven pair of "side line" hobbles. Periodically, he brings in the horses and gives them salt.

During the month, Lu makes mention of "Bens house" and "the other house." Presumably, both of these refer to the former (1895) main cabin but indicate that Ben may prefer to stay there when he is around. Lu also makes first mention of blacksmith "tools" and presumably has a "shop" in which to use them. One of the things he makes is a 4-tine spear, for capturing fish.

On the 24th, Lu observes: *Rained all night. Little creek* [Spring Creek] *running past the house* [i.e., the water was over the banks of the creek]. Not only is he made aware for the first time that the little creek can flood its banks as a result of snow-melt runoff but also that the ground has thawed enough that they can start digging post holes, setting posts, and putting up fence. Dan starts the process off on the 28th. Lu also is reminded to check on the stored potatoes. On the 29th *Dan went up to cabin and found potatoes rotting. Went up to pit and opened it up. Sorted potatoes and covered it up again.*

April

At the end of March and first 4 days of April, Lu and Dan whip-saw lumber and construct a porch on the new house. Lu gathers up the traps on Cave Creek and by the 13th he and Dan are in the final stages of preparing hides for the season.

During April, Lu and Dan take on three main projects that proceed more-or-less simultaneously: fence construction, digging a new ditch, and tilling and planting crops. Dan takes the lead on building the fence and is assisted by a couple of visitors. Lu assumes responsibility for the ditch.

The location of the fence is not given but its construction extends from March 28 to May 14 and Lu accounts for at least 120 post holes being dug in the process. Harvey Taylor comes down from Monumental Creek on the 2nd and helps Lu saw lumber for a day. Then, on the 4th and part of the 5th, he helps with the fence. Cox arrives from upriver the day Taylor leaves and works on the fence for about 6 days. Most of the holes are dug by the 6th and then posts and poles are hauled and put in place. Dan works on the fence on his own after Cox goes home and finishes on the 14th.

Cox shows up again on the 12th, staying overnight, and on the 20th he gets 100 pounds of vegetables and a packsaddle tree. He may leave the area soon afterwards as he isn't mentioned again in the diaries. His name lives on in Coxey's Creek, Bar, and "Hole." Although not mentioned in the diaries, Lu later recounted to his daughter Louisa the following explanation regarding Taylor (possibly during the summer of 1899): "Dan and Ritchey, on the way to the mine, ran across H. E. Taylor and family at Monumental copper camp, who were pennyless and foodless. The boys took pity on them and invited them to go to the ranch. They did and one day they moved in on me. Three children, Claud 13 years old, May 11 and a baby two years old. Mr and Mrs Taylor and all their worldly goods on two broken down horses. Mr. Taylor didn't stay but left family for three months while he went outside. He was one of the worst liars alive and made his living that way. She cooked for us and stole us blind. When they left they moved out food and other stuff which took five horses to carry."

Lu starts preparing to construct the ditch by making a lot of stakes on the 8th. Over the next 3 days, he surveys and stakes out its route, which leads onto a "bench." There is an elevated flat or bench just southeast of the new ranch house that they are preparing to irrigate from upper Spring Creek by means of this ditch. Lu starts digging on the 13th, shifts to plowing to loosen the ground the next day, and then shovels and plows and digs to the end. He builds about 25 yards of ditch on the 16th, getting water running through the upper part late in the afternoon, and completes the entire job on the 18th.

Tilling and planting in April are restricted to getting the grain in. From the 9th to the 12th about a half acre or more of wheat and oats is put in and from the 17th to the 19th about an acre of oats.

Hike to Warren (April 23 – May 4?)

In spite of the difficult trip he made at the beginning of the year, Lu decides to make another trek to Warren on foot and snowshoes in the Spring. After patching up his "manpack" the day before, he leaves at 6:20 AM April 23 and makes it to Copper Camp by 6 PM, having traveled about 22 miles. The next day he has to repair his snowshoes and doesn't start till noon, travels only about 11 ½ miles and stops about a mile above Smith's camp at 4:20. The third day he leaves camp at 5:25 AM and has a long day, hiking 27 to 30 miles in about 12 ½ hours. He stays that night at Bull Keffer's. The next morning he gets to Warren and remains there another day and a half until noon on April 28, filling his time with touring the Iola Mine east of town, writing letters, and visiting. On his way home Lu again stops "at Bull's;" this time a snowstorm keeps him there for 2 days. He helps Bull with numerous tasks in addition to "just visiting."

May

Lu hits the trail again on the morning of May 1st and makes it to Henry Smith's place at the mouth of Elk Creek, in time for dinner. After another 3 hours of hiking, he camps at the upper end of "long gulch" and builds a fire. On the 2nd, he *Started at 5:15 and got to* [Elk] *summit at 11. Took lunch at 2. Camped at Smith creek about 6.* The next day, Lu makes it to Copper Camp in 4 ½ hours and runs into Wes, who probably has come down from Thunder Mountain. At this point, there is a 4 ½-month gap in the diary. It had taken Lu a little under 12 hours to go from the ranch to Copper Camp on the way out. Assuming that he laid over the rest of the 3rd, left the next day, and made good time, he may have been home by the 4th.

Thunder Mountain, Cabin Creek, and Warren (May 5? – September 13)

There are no entries from May 4 through September 13—the entire mining season and then some. Dan should still be at the ranch when Lu arrives back. They still have potatoes and perhaps a few other vegetables to plant but Ben will be getting anxious for them to come to The Mountain before spring runoff ceases and opportunities for hydraulic mining essentially end for the year.

Assay receipts indicate that on August 12th the Caswell brothers deposit $406.71 in gold at the Assay Office in Boise and, in a separate transaction (the front part of the receipt containing the date is missing), another $1687.29. This amounts to about half of the $4,000 that *The Idaho Daily Statesman* (April 13, 1902) will report that they made this summer. On September 1, 1899 the *Idaho County Free Press* reported that "A. B. Caswell, the discoverer of Thunder Mountain and his brother D. G. Caswell came in yesterday with more than 200 ounces of gold taken out of their claims this season. They have twelve claims in all. They thought they had all the ground corralled, but found a mistake this year when over 150 locations were made. There are fully fifty prospectors on the ground now. There has been a meeting held in that section and a district organized. W. Richey will be recorder." Though the *Free Press* is published in Grangeville, Idaho, it likely got its news from Warren.

On December 29 the *Grangeville Standard* noted that the "Caswell Brothers in 42 hours work with a hydraulic cleaned up 30 pounds of gold this season. When this clean-up was made there was no water except melted snow. They had made their preparations and kept their pipe going day and night. There are 12 ounces to the pound, Troy, thus their clean-up amounted to 360 ounces."

Apart from the assay receipts, there is no known record of a trip to Boise or who made it. The gold may have been sent there from Warren for them. Clearly, the trip to Warren on August 31 involves at least Ben and Dan and they apparently go on as far as Cuprum or Bear to buy cattle (see below). Conceivably, they could have been in Boise prior to that. Evidently the partners reinvest some of their earnings to buy hydraulic pipe and other mining supplies and, at this point, are frantically working to get the pipe and other items into the mining site before snow closes the trail.

To Warren from Ranch and Thunder Mountain (Three Trips: September 14 – November 12)

September

Lu makes four trips to Warren during the autumn, three of them included in his account for the year. When the entries resume on September 14, he is setting off on the second one. Apparently he is alone at the ranch at the time and his brothers are traveling outside of Big Creek country, perhaps to Boise. Wes's location at this point is unclear.

Lu has a late start from the ranch and gets only to Baird's cabin the first night. He makes it to Smith Creek the next. On the 16th, he takes a *new trail up other fork of Smith creek.* The next day he gets all the way to Warren Summit by mid afternoon. Dan and Ben have arrived the night before. *Brought 2 cows, 2 calves, 2 horses.*

They are much too early for the load of pipe they have come to pick up and, though they don't realize it, have about ten days to kill. For the most part, they occupy the time by chasing after their horses; writing letters; buying groceries and other "truck" in Warren; lounging around camp; visiting with the likes of Pringle and Henry Smith, Clark Roland, and Jim Stanton; and working on rigging for the packsaddles. The pipe finally arrives about noon on the 27th.

They load up what they can, get the rest the next day, and move it all to a place Lu calls "Cabin flat," where they lay over another day and wrap the pipe in burlap for packing on the horses.

October

They finally get under way on October 1st and make it to the forks of Elk Creek amidst rain and snow. The following day, they reach Elk Summit after 4 3/4 hours, where they encounter about 6 inches of snow. They continue on to a site Lu calls "Sunnyside camp," which must be somewhere along Government Creek. On the 3rd they reach a stretch of dead and downed timber on the way up Lick Creek and are forced to cut trail for the balance of the day. On the 4th, Lu reaches the "hillside camp" on the West Fork of Monumental Creek at 4 but has to go back a mile to meet Dan, who is lagging behind. Lu also notes cryptically that *Ben got poison on him.* Presumably this was on himself and was mercury.

They reach Thunder Mountain around 1 the next day and unpack the horses. Lu and Ben immediately head back for another load and reach Warren Summit on the 10th. In the mean time, Dan and Wes take 5 pack loads and head off to "the meadows." [Note: this next trip is erroneously placed at the end of 1898, instead of 1899, by Lu in his autobiography and Babbitt 2002:88.] After setting up camp in 2 inches of snow near the summit, Lu and Ben spend the rest of the day and all of the next in Warren. Lu gets his mail, writes letters, and fills out mining notices and the two of them get some oats and grub. On the 12th, they start getting ready to leave and bring 15 loads of pipe and groceries back from town along with "Mrs. Egans horses." According to census records the next year, Mary Eagan is a widow who runs a boarding house in Warren with the help of her Chinese servant Ah Soon. She is 39 and has a child that does not live with her. Apparently Lu is on friendly terms with Mary, though the extent of their friendship is not known. One of her horses is an old mare and Lu frequently refers to it as such. Lu returns to town, deals with some more correspondence, fills out another notice, and meets up with Tom Neighbors, who has come up with a wagon to haul part of the load over Elk Summit for them and meet them in the vicinity of Government Creek. At this point all of the Caswells' horses are unshod.

Ominously, all of this dawdling around is pushing them closer to the heart of the snowy season. They finally get underway on the 13th and rendevous with Neighbors on the South Fork at their usual camp above Shiefer's. The next morning, Lu and Ben get underway ahead of Neighbors. On the way to their next camp at the beaver dams on Elk Creek, it begins to snow and by the time they reach the summit the next day, it is about 2 feet deep.

Lu and Ben head down Government Creek to Big Creek Meadows. Initially, they stay over for a day at the Meadows to dry out their bedding and wait for Neighbors but then are forced to wait another day because of a snow storm. On the third day, they are held back all morning because of rain but finally leave at noon and start up the Lick Creek trail to their burnt timber camp. It rains all night at their camp but snows on Lick Creek summit. The next morning on the 19th, they start over the summit into the West Fork of Monumental Creek but run into another storm with 2 to 3 feet of snow on the ground and have to turn back. Getting their string of horses turned in the deep snow must have been a horrendous task. They backtrack to the Meadows, head down Big Creek, and make it to Copper Creek, about 3/4 mile from Copper Camp, by the evening of the 20th. They are running low on food and have not been successful at hunting. They lay over again to dry out on the 21st and Ben goes down to Pringle's place at Copper Camp and gets some flour, baking powder, and horse shoes. They shoe three horses but then run out of nails. However, their string of bad luck changes when Ben kills a fat doe. They sleep-in the next morning and go only about 4 miles on the mushy trail but make it to Baird's cabin before stopping again. Now they are within a mile and a quarter of the mouth of Monumental Creek. Ben stays at the cabin, while Lu takes three packhorses and their loads, along with Mrs. Eagan's roan mare and Huntley's brown colt, and goes on down Big Creek with supplies for the ranch. At Placer Bar, Lu finds Tom Neighbors camped but makes no mention of what became of the load he was hauling for the Caswells. When Lu arrives on the 23rd after a long day, Dan is digging the cellar.

The day after arriving at the ranch, Lu heads back to Monumental Creek, with horse shoes and nails, to meet Ben and haul pipe up to Thunder Mountain. He stops for dinner with Neighbors before continuing on. Lu and Ben stay at Baird's cabin for several days shoeing horses and making other preparations before leaving on the 28th and reaching their Mule Creek cabin on the 30th. The next day, Lu and Wes, who apparently has been on Thunder for some time, return to the ranch to spend a couple of days. This time when they arrive, Dan is putting up hay.

November

On the fourth and final trip to Warren, Lu travels alone. Wes stays behind to help Dan with ranch work. Ben apparently remains at the mines. Lu camps the first night at Baird's, then stops at Copper Camp to pick up Pringle Smith before riding on to the Smith Creek Camp. The next day they make it to the Forks of Elk Creek for the night and, after stopping at Bull's for dinner, get to Warren by 6. Lu stays around for two days writing letters, while Pringle records notices for him. Lu also records one for Pringle. The notices are mailed to Al W. Talkington, the county auditor. Lu has taken on the responsibility as the first deputy recorder in the district, hence his record keeping, but he eventually turns the job over to Harvey Taylor.

Lu starts back at noon on the 8th but is plagued all this day and the next with a fierce headache. He stops the first night at Elk Creek ranch and the next at the forks of Elk Creek, where he shoots a 2 ½ foot long salmon. On his way past Copper Camp to Baird's the next day, he leaves off a number of things for Pringle, including carrots and potatoes that he buries to prevent their freezing. He also gets Pringle's guns, either to work on later or for safekeeping. He arrives home shortly after noon the following day.

Cabin Creek (November 13 – 15)

Lu has only a few days before he heads off again. He mends two pair of snowshoes, writes out another notice, and files a crosscut saw for Dan and Wes. However, most of the time is spent working on a wagon for Bull and it is nearly finished by the time Lu leaves. Dan and Wes spend their time cutting and hauling logs.

Thunder Mountain (November 16 – December 5)

Wes accompanies Lu on this trip. They take two packhorses loaded with supplies for the Rush Creek cabin and for Thunder Mountain. After leaving off the supplies on Thunder, Lu goes to look for a horse that has wandered off and makes his way down to the Wickiup on the West Fork of Monumental Creek, where he stays over night with Wes. It appears they then split up and Lu goes to Mule Creek to help Ben with a cabin he is building on their Burnt Flat site. Lu gets there on the 20th and they are immediately visited by Fred Holcomb for a couple of days. They put four roof logs up on the 21st and begin splitting shakes. They finish the shakes and start putting them on by the 23rd. The next day, Lu finishes the roof while Ben works on the fireplace, which he completes on the 25th.

On the 26th, Ben goes up to Thunder, while Lu gets a log ready to saw into boards. However, Ben decides he'd better use Lu's help to whipsaw lumber at the mine site for making riffles. So, on the 27th, they hike up and, over the next 6 days, cut some trees, make a saw pit, and saw out 138 pieces of riffle timber.

December

Lu starts back on the 4th but stops for lunch at Harvey Taylor's cabin before spending the night at the Wickiup. He gets home after a trek of a little over 7 hours. *Brought horses down and shot an otter. The boys* [Dan and Wes] *had cellar done and barn ready to roof.*

Cabin Creek (December 6 – 8)

In the short time Lu is back at the ranch, he files a saw, copies several notices into the official ledger, makes a wagon wrench and two lug chains for the wagon, and replaces the handles on an axe and a maul. He also sets up the gold scales and weighs out some samples. During this same spell, Dan and Wes haul logs. On the 8th Lu pays Wes $38 for 1 ½ months work on the ranch.

Hike to Warren (December 9 – 19).

Lu is back only 3 days before he and Wes strike out again for Warren. They leave their snowshoes behind but think better of it as they get closer to Elk Summit and borrow some of Pringle's when they reach Copper Camp. By the time they near their second camp site on the 10th (at the first crossing above the forks of Smith Creek) they encounter a foot of fresh snow and Wes dons his snowshoes. The next day, Lu records that they *Came from crossing at Smith creek to about 2 miles below fork of Elk creek. Bucked from 6 to 20 inches of snow. Had a narrow escape of getting covered in a slide.* This is a bit of an understatement! They actually had gotten buried in an avalanche. Wes was able to dig himself out and then got Lu out.

On the 12th, they stop at Degrundy's for a couple of hours to visit before leaving after dinner. Babendorf and Brewer are in the process of constructing a toll bridge across the South Fork at Curley Brewer's place, 1 ½ miles upstream from the one at Shiefer's. Lu and Wes stop for a while and help put stringers across for the bridge before going on to Bull's for the night. In the morning they go on to Warren but stop first for dinner at the Iola Mine. They spend the rest of the day and the next two in Warren "writing letters and waiting for the mail." This is how Lu usually explains time spent in Warren when not purchasing goods. However, that hardly seems compelling enough to hike and snowshoe for over 4 days one way! Of the day they arrive, he wrote *Had quite a time at Mrs. Egans in eve.* And of the next day, *Got to like Miss Thomas. Had a good time.* Clara Thomas is a single 28- year old dress-maker in Warren. Beyond these entries there are no indications of his activities in town other than the usual.

It is not clear what becomes of Wes after they reach Bull's, as he is not mentioned again for the rest of the year. Some of Lu's notes indicate they are going back to the ranch together, for example: *Bill* [Borden] *to help us pack our stuff. Packed up our 2 loads and left Bulls at 7. Camped at Beaver dam at 4:30.* But then on the 17th, it seems Wes is nowhere around: *Bill Borden and I put 2 loads on our back at 7. Got to* [Elk] *summit at 10:20. He went back. I took* [both] *loads and came to 1 mile below forks of Smith creek, got there at 4:30.*

The remainder of the trip is uneventful. On the 18th, Lu goes through 18 inches of snow at the mouth of Smith Creek but gets to Copper Camp at 3:30 and stops for the day. On the 19th, he *Put away things and started for home, got to mouth of Monumental at 11. Saw a big gorge* [i.e., the river was plugged with piled-up ice] *at Big creek. Got home at 8. Very hungry, you bet.*

Cabin Creek (December 20 – 31)

As the year ends, Lu and Dan, spend a relatively leisurely time at Cabin Creek and Ben apparently is at Thunder Mountain finishing the Burnt Flat cabin and working on riffles and pipe. Lu builds a water box for the grindstone, mends clothes, splits wood, hunts deer and sheep, and makes sauerkraut and pickles among other things. The previous year, Lu had gotten a new wood stove for the cabin. On the 27th, he finally gets a sheet of tin under it to protect the floor. Based on the number of loaves of bread Lu later records baking at a time, this must be a full-size wood cook stove. Some of the things Dan does are to cook, mend his boots, and work on his saddle. Together they store the cabbage in the cellar, thresh out 6 sacks of oats and the wheat, and share Christmas dinner. Lu clearly is not happy at first that Dan and Ben have brought in cows to the ranch. On the 29th, he writes *Dan took after cows. I don't have anything to do with cows.* However, in later years his attitude softens and he becomes their primary steward.

1900

As the new century begins, only Lu and Dan are residing at the ranch. There is a striking difference between Dan's contribution to ranch operations compared to Ben's past involvement. Dan is more of a carpenter and cook and takes the lead on two main construction projects. Ben is living in a cabin near the mines on Thunder Mountain. He differs in this respect from most prospectors, who overwinter at lower elevations or retreat to villages, such as Warren, or even to Boise. Winters in the high country are marked by deep snow, howling winds, and isolation. But they also can be calm and peaceful and allow time for reflection and relaxation as well as for trapping and preparation for the next mining season. Although Wes spends the mining season on Thunder Mountain, he may be one who overwinters in Warren. The winter and spring of 1900 are periods of relative peace and calm before the boys "grab the bronc by the tail" and are propelled into the world of money/wealth and politics.

Cabin Creek (January 1 – June 21)

January

There are 3 inches of snow on the flat at the start of January and by early February the river is nearly frozen over. Coyotes and owls are notably evident from their regular howling and hooting. In spite of the short day lengths and cold weather, Lu and Dan maintain a relatively high level of activity, even though the scope of the activities is limited by frozen ground and snow. There is much work to be done around the ranch house and in the woods and the livestock must be fed. One notable event occurs on the 14th when Lu records that *The old yellow granny (Old dominick hen) laid an egg. The first domestic egg on Big creek.* By March 18, she has laid 45 eggs without missing a day.

Their activities often are guided by the process of "sequencing," where the ultimate goal is achieved only at the completion of a series of properly sequenced steps, over an extended period. A case in point is the decision to haul hay from the flat near the river to the corral area just below the house. This requires a set of actions that begin on January 2nd with Dan working on the hayrack; expand to a series of fabrications and repairs to the wagon; include stacking, fencing, and then re-stacking the hay to prevent overheating; and eventually extend beyond a fortnight before the job is finished. Lu works some in the shop sharpening all of the blacksmith tools and straightening up the heads of nine iron wood-splitting wedges. Lu has acquired several pieces of new equipment and spends part of January setting them up and trying them out. He makes a case for the new gold scales out of mountain mahogany. Next he makes a shaft for the emery (grinding) machine out of an old gun barrel. Later, he works on the gumming machine, a device for sharpening large saw blades, and modifies the drive wheel before using the machine on a crosscut saw. In addition, he completes a number on maintenance-type jobs, from replacing handles to filing saws and making a pair of forceps. Earlier he had *Tried to pull a tooth for Dan but couldn't find anything stout enough to hold it.* Perhaps the forceps are for that purpose.

A major project during January and early February, is the construction of a food storehouse or "commissary" north of the ranch house, with a distinctive glass window in the door. First Lu and Dan haul and peel the logs and set up a scaffold for the whipsaw. Next Dan lays the foundation and, after a week's delay, they get the walls eight logs high. Construction resumes 2 days later with the addition of four roof logs and the roof is completed in another 3 days. Then they saw 185 feet of floor boards, install the floor, chink the walls, build and hang the door, and on February 5th move in the grub and other items.

February

In February, Lu and Dan hunt for deer and mountain sheep. In addition to eating the meat, they grain and dress the hides, use the sheep horns for ornamentation, and poison the offal for bait. Lu mounts one ram's head and hangs it on the wall and Dan makes an apparent religious icon that Lu refers to as a "sheep horn gesus." The "strychnined" bait is used to take mountain lions and coyotes for their furs but peripherally also kills a number of eagles and other wildlife. Unfortunately, the Eskimo dog of Arthur Gordon, who accompanies the mail carrier Bill Borden, also is killed.

March

Spring comes early in 1900. By March 2nd the temperature reaches 50 F at noon and the snow around the house is gone. By the 15th Wes Ritchey is able to make it in from Warren with the mail and leave 2 days later for Thunder. Thawing of the ground allows activities to shift to fence building and preparations for planting crops. The garden is expanded tremendously in variety and size and the areas planted to oats and corn are expanded. They have acquired chickens, turkeys, and milk cows which, though the eggs and milk enhance their diets, add to the work load.

A series of steps required to build a picket fence in the vicinity of the house begins on March 2 with the cutting of brace poles. The fence consists of a series of vertical posts sunk into the ground at intervals and connected with two horizontal brace poles to which the pickets or slats are nailed vertically. It is a labor-intensive type of fence both in its construction and subsequent maintenance. They cut and split rails on 3 additional days and then cut several trees and use them to split out a supply of pickets. After nearly a week's delay, they resume the process on the 14th and, sporadically over the rest of the month, mark out post holes and dig them, haul the fencing to the job site with the horses, set the posts, put on the horizontal poles, and nail on pickets. Lu makes three sets of gate hinges and installs them. On the 30th, they finish the section below the house.

Preparations for planting begin on the 12th with the sowing of tomato, pepper, and cauliflower seed in cans. Although temperatures are below freezing at night, by afternoon of the 13th the ground remains thawed and plowing can begin. The next day Lu makes a cutter for the plow, complete with clamp and other fittings he installs. Later he also cuts some poles and makes a device he calls a "planker" for preparing the field prior to planting. Planking apparently involves dragging the poles crosswise over the field with horses, to level and smooth the soil for a seed bed. Dan does most of the plowing, by choice, though Lu helps when needed. Jim, Browny, and Dan are the principal horses used for draft work at this point. Lu had tried using Mrs. Eagan's old roan mare also, but she proved too skittish. Plowing starts in earnest on the 19th and most of the ground for the initial planting is ready by the 27th, though they were able to plant some of the cold-tolerant vegetables such as onions, peas, and radishes and set out some plum trees on the 25th. Dan begins harrowing the plowed fields on the 27th and gets a little bit more done before being interrupted by a visit from Pringle Smith and Clark Roland, who arrive from Copper Camp around 3 PM on the last day of the month and stay for several days.

Near the end of the plowing, Lu sets to sharpening the picks, crowbar, cutter, and grubbing hoe to use to dig out wild rosebushes and other brush that are uprooted and boulders that become exposed by the plowing. These efforts extend over several days and culminate on the 29th with the setting out of gooseberry, currant, and raspberry starts. The following day they burn the meadow in the afternoon and Dan sows some timothy grass seed.

Lu and Dan seem to have been busy enough during the last ten days of March with the plowing, planting, and clearing of fields but they also find time to get the smokehouse going and smoke some meat. They build a furnace to produce the smoke and dig a trench to create a tunnel to carry the smoke into the smokehouse. Cottonwood is used to fuel the furnace and the completed unit is put into operation on the 23rd. As noted in Lu's entry for the day: *Skinned out 2 deer and 1 sheep and put them in smoke house. 9 hams in all and 5 shoulders.* Later Dan adds a ram and a ewe he kills. The smoker requires frequent tending for several days until the meat is done.

April

Ben and Wes come down from Thunder Mountain on the 2nd to get Dan and some pack horses. They leave after 2 days, along with Smith and Roland. After Dan and the others depart, Lu has sole responsibility for the operation of the ranch, except for occasional visitors, until late June, when he leaves for extended periods through mid-September and hired "ranch sitters" are left in charge. As a consequence of his focus on ranch operations, he is out of touch with the mining activities on Thunder Mountain. As soon as the others leave, Lu gets back to plowing and planting with a vengeance. He does so on top of the routine chores of milking, caring for the chickens and turkeys, and tending both the milk cows and draft horses. He even manages to find time for some hunting and fishing.

Getting the crops in is a big task that involves two separate teams (Jim & Dan, Browny & the Eagan mare) to harrow the rest of the plowed ground and plow the new. The wheat is planted first. Lu sows nearly 2 acres on the 6th and finishes harrowing it the next day. Then he plants the oats: first harrowing the newly plowed ground, next sowing the oats, then harrowing them in. He repeats these steps in a couple more places, finishing on the 9th with the "fall new ground." On the 10th Lu uses Browny to mark off the oats and part of the wheat and finishes the grain the following day.

Lu subsequently turns to planting mainly root crops, endive, and some peas on the 11th—13th. The root crops consist of carrots, beets, parsnips, several kinds of radishes, rutabagas, salsify, and turnips. Two days after getting the root crops in, Lu makes a hotbed consisting of a wooden frame, dug 2 feet deep, filled with manure, and covered with sifted dirt. *Brought down 3 glasses* [panes] *from other house to put over frame.* On the 20th, he plants it with cabbage and cauliflower seeds.

The primary vegetable crop Lu plants is potatoes. Preparation for planting begins with the production of "seed," a process that is fitted around other jobs (e.g., *Cut seed potatoes after supper till 10.*) and consequently extends over many days. Lu starts making seed potatoes on the 10th and finally finishes on the 25th, after spending almost the entire day at it. After plowing, harrowing, and planking, the ground is *marked off.* The potatoes are planted by dropping the pieces into trenches made by the "marker" and covering them with soil. He puts some choice seed in the house garden but most of it goes into a "patch" of a little over an acre. Lu chooses Browny and the old Eagan mare for plowing the patch and uses Browny on the marker. But he uses "Dan horse" to harrow and plank the house garden on the 26th. This in spite of the fact that a week earlier he *Had a scrap with Dan horse in stable. Tried to kill me. I reckon lots of bad luck for picking up that old knife.* He finally gets done planting potatoes about 4 PM April 29.

In addition to the other crops mentioned, Lu sets out some rhubarb, plants some sunflower seeds, and tends an existing strawberry bed. He also plants *coffee peas and vine peas* that Dan had brought over from John Eckles' place on Big Bar. Coincidental with getting the vegetables planted, Lu cleans out the ditch and gets the water running through it. On the last day of the month, he begins irrigating the onions.

May

Thunder Mountain (May 7 – 9)

On May 4th Bill Borden arrives from Thunder Mountain with the mail and what Lu terms "good news" that apparently induces him to make a quick trip to Thunder Mountain. Bill stays for over a week and, from the 7th through the 9th, does the ranch chores while Lu is away. Lu arrives at Mule Creek on the 8th. *Dan there alone. Every thing all right. 9—Packed up at Mule creek and started home. Met Ben at Monumental about 1 mile below west fork. We had a long talk about boundry of Thunder mountain* [gold ore deposits]. *Took lunch and came on to Rush creek, got here at 3:30.*

The Caswell brothers' grandniece Freda Babbitt provides some additional insight about Lu's meeting with Ben. Apparently a mining notice issued in Ada County on March 1, 1900 indicated that Thunder Mountain Consolidated Gold Mines, owned by H. E. Taylor and W. Yates, had bonded the property of the Caswell brothers on Thunder Mountain. According to Babbitt, until Lu and Dan met on Monumental in May, they were unaware that Ben had been negotiating with Taylor and had signed a contract with him that was to close on July 1, 1900. In her view, Dan stayed on at Mule Creek but ".

.. Lu was upset and went back to the ranch." This interpretation may not be entirely accurate since Lu had written in his diary on May 4th that Bill Borden had brought "good news." Also, Lu would not have known to meet up with Ben on Monumental if Borden, or one of the letters he delivered, hadn't indicated that Lu should do so. Upset or not, Lu must return quickly to the ranch to relieve Bill.

Cabin Creek (May 10 – June 21)

After he arrives back at Cabin Creek, the garden produce and grain take the bulk of Lu's effort until the third week in June, when he leaves on a series of horse packing trips. The crops he and Dan have already planted require that Lu immediately turn a substantial amount of attention to irrigating the developing plants, especially the fields of oats and wheat. However, in addition Lu continues planting and adds several cold-sensitive plants, including corn, cucumbers, summer squash, a seemingly endless number of tomatoes, and watermelon. Corn planting entails plowing some new ground and grubbing out the wild sunflowers before harrowing it. Other plantings include well over 100 Mammoth variety cabbage plants, beans, cauliflower, kale, lettuce, and additional beets, onions, peas, seed potatoes (6 gunny sacks worth), radishes, and turnips. Lu soaks the corn, peas, and sunflower seeds prior to planting. Also, mice seem to be especially attracted to the corn and peas and Lu tries to dissuade them through the use of strychnine-laced squash seed.

Irrigating is accompanied by its own set of problems for Lu to confront. For example, on June 5th he saw that the grain was in need of water and got water going on about 2 acres. *It took lots of work. Had to clean a lot of ditch besides water all plants with bucket where one could not get water to run to.* On the 6th the ditch broke again leaving him with 200 yards of ditch to shovel out the following day. On the 8th he *Got up about 3 A.M. tended water, running pretty good. Put part of water on wheat and potatoes. Planted 8 row navy beans across corn patch. Ditch broke while I was planting and had to shut it off to fix it.*

[Got the] *break fixed and 63 yards of sand shoveled out. 18 inches deep.* On the 9th he *Finished cleaning out ditch, it was filled up for 200 yards. Got water on potatoes but turned it off in eve.*

As the plants begin to grow, they require weeding and thinning, which Lu attends to as time allows. He apparently foresees that weeding will become a problem and, soon after Borden leaves for Warren on May 13th, begins making a cultivator—a project that stretches over almost two weeks. He makes the shovels out of two old plow points and grinds them down with the emery wheel. He breaks the first pair of handles and makes another. After assembly and three coats of paint, the cultivator is ready for use.

Lu has several setbacks with the garden involving cows, frost, and hail. The calf got through the fence to the potato patch in mid May causing Lu to lament *To-day has been a day of much activity building up what nature tore down for me.* Fence repair and additional fencing along the creek are required to keep the cattle from doing more damage. On May 23 a heavy frost kills most of the tomatoes and on June 10 a light frost damages the beans. But the worst is yet to come. On the 15th, *The crop is almost ruined by hail. It fell nearly 2 inches deep some as big as hazel nuts. Peas and onions are beat clean to the ground.*

To Boise via Idaho City (June 21 – July 25)

On June 19th Lu writes, *Celibrated my birthday by going fishing. Caught 6 nice ones. Huntley and a fellow by the name of Lockwood came down from the mines . . . .* This is only time that Huntley is recorded as being at the ranch—clearly something is up! From earlier communication with Ben, Lu knew that the mining activity was winding down and that they would be heading for Boise in time for the closing of the deal with Taylor's group on July 1 to purchase the Caswell mining claims.

Huntley has come to fetch Lu and to bring Lockwood to take care of the ranch. The next day, Lu shows *Claud* [Clyde] around and how to run things and on the following day, gets up Bird and Bolly, packs up his camping outfit, and leaves with Huntley for the Rush Creek cabin. The next day, they arrive at Mule Creek shortly after noon, in time to help get ready to head out for Boise on the 23rd.

The first part of the trip takes them over mountain trails for about 70 miles before connecting with the State Wagon Road at the upper end of Bear Valley Creek, a major headwater of the Middle Fork of the Salmon River. Ben, Dan, Huntley, and Lu leave with 10 horses and make it to the east fork of Indian Creek for a short rest around 5 PM, then continue on to Pen Basin, in the upper reaches of Johnson Creek, to spend the night. The following day they reach the Bear Valley road camp. From here they follow the old wagon road south but still have another 100 miles to cover before reaching Boise. The next day takes them down Clear Creek to the South Fork of the Payette River. The narrow, winding track drops 3000 feet in 16 miles. It is one of the hardest days they encounter on the way and they stop before noon for a 3-hour break before going on to the South Fork to camp for the night. In the morning they cross the South Fork by bridge and climb out of the canyon to Banner Summit. Somewhere in this vicinity, the men encounter the census-taker and are entered into the 1900 Federal census for Banner Precinct. They pass Banner, go over Mores Creek Summit, and stop along Mores Creek 12 miles from Idaho City. The next day they pass by Idaho City without stopping, reach the upper toll gate at noon, and, after a nearly 4 ½ hour break, reach the Halfway Station just after 7 PM.

They arrive in Boise shortly before noon on the 28th, having covered the 170 miles in 5 ½ days, and go straight to the Assay Office. Assay records indicate that Ben deposits gold worth $1504.20 that day and $35.52 the next. The 29th & 30th are spent hurrying around town probably getting haircuts and shaves and new clothes, ordering supplies, and even meeting with a newspaper reporter.

On the 30th, an extensive article on the Caswells' good fortune for the mining season, resulting from their interview, appears in *The Idaho Daily Statesman*. According to the article, the three brothers came to town with $5000 in gold dust, as a ". . . result of 72 hours piping on their claims. With 60 to 70 inches of water flowing for that short period they took out enough of the yellow metal so they can rest the balance of the year or spend the time preparing for next season's operations." They ". . . were prepared for a much longer run this year, but they lost three or four weeks on account of trouble with their pipes. Next year they expect to have a much longer run, and therefore, a much bigger sack to bring to the assay office here."

July

Ben, Dan, Lu, and A. O. had arrived in Boise with the expectation of closing the deal on their claims on July 1. Taylor's company was to make an additional $9,000 deposit to hold the option of $100,000 that Ben had agreed on. However, at the meeting they learned that Taylor's company couldn't get the money so forfeited the $1,000 bond that they had posted in March.

Although the loss of the sale may have disappointed at least some of the partners, it isn't evident from Lu's entries in his diary. By all appearances they proceed as planned. They make additional deposits of gold at the Assay Office amounting to $1786.52, purchase several wagon-loads of hardware and other supplies, buy groceries and order a large quantity of hydraulic pipe at the Stiens & Co. hardware store, celebrate the 4th, and take a buggy ride. Lu and A. O. even order new saddles and Dan trades his old saddle for a new one. Lu pays $48 for his and stops by the saddlemaker's shop several times to specify features he wants. He also buys a pair of big brown mares named Poll (Polly) and Deb, together with their collars and halters, for $158.

The four partners stay at the Overland Hotel. E. ["Irv"] W. Johnson, proprietor at the hotel, learns of Taylor's failure to make the deposit and tells Ben about "Colonel" W. H. Dewey, a prominent Idaho mining man who had acquired his wealth over years of dealings in the Silver City area. Dewey is connected with Pittsburgh capital and Johnson suggests that Dewey could facilitate purchase of the Caswell claims if he is interested. This gives the partners much to ponder and apparently they have not finalized a deal with Dewey by the time they leave Boise on July 10. In the meantime Huntley apparently returns to his ranch in Cuprum.

The partners try to make arrangements with a man named Merit to freight their purchases to Thunder Mountain but are unsuccessful. Instead they acquire several wagons, including one driven by a Mr. Early, to haul their load. They leave Boise a little before noon on the 11th and stop at the lower toll gate on the road to Idaho City for the night. The next day, they get to the upper toll gate in 10 hours before stopping. On the third day, they reach Idaho City by midmorning and take a 4 ½ hour break in town before going on another 3 hours to above Hardy Flat on Mores Creek. As the country steepens, Lu helps his new team pull their load by attaching a rope to his horse Bird's saddle horn "on spike." On the fourth day Lu spikes with Bird again. The outfit stops for a break at midday on a branch of Mores Creek and gets to Mose Kempners ranch, about 1 ½ miles south of Banner. The next day, the wagons make it to the summit on Banner and take a mid-day break before descending the steep, twisting road down to the South Fork of the Payette River and crossing over to the mouth of Clear Creek, near present-day Lowman.

On the 16th, they start up the steep, narrow, rocky, Clear Creek road. At Jack Johnson's they *Got him to hitch on a team to help us to summit. Broke down a wheel about 8 miles out* [halfway to the summit; probably near O'Keefe Creek]. *Sent wagon back with Jack. Got another man* [Rogers] *who came along to help us up.* On the 18th they *Loaded up and came to the end of the wagons for us* [referred to on some maps as the "transfer camp"]. *Stopped about halfway for noon. The Deb mare of mine gave out. Too badly bruised up being wound up all nite. Hauled her load with Bird the last 2 miles.*

They lay over on the 19th. Early stays to rest his horses and shares with Rogers half of a deer he shot. Rogers is paid $10 for his help and leaves. The next morning, Early is very ill with what he thinks is appendicitis. It is decided to take Early and his wagon-load of goods 3 miles further up Bear Valley to their old camp site. There they unload the wagon and locate two prospectors who agree to help him through to Boise. After seeing Early off, they move the rest of their supplies from the transfer camp to their Bear Valley camp.

On the 22nd they put packsaddles on six of the strongest horses (Bird, Bolly, Poll, Deb, Daisy, & Shorty) and start moving the freight to Thunder Mountain. The first stop is the summit at the head of Elk Creek, between Bear Valley and Sulphur Creek. Ben goes that far with them and then apparently goes back to meet up with another load of freight. *Camped for noon on Sulphur creek and Pen Basin for the nite. Got to old camp we made coming out to Boise.* The second stop, after a long day, is Indian Creek and the following day, another long one, delivers them to Thunder.

Before leaving for Boise, Lu had arranged with a man named Dick to continue working the Caswell claims with the available water. Dick got 7 pounds (about 84 troy oz) of dust, that was worth about $1,735, and receives $100 from Lu for his labors. Lu makes it back to the ranch on the 25th after a 5-hour ride and still has enough time and energy to shoot five grouse and catch 20 fish. He seems pleased that *Everything looks pretty wet.*

Cabin Creek (July 26 – 28)

Lu has only a couple of days to get caught up before heading back to Bear Valley to pick up more freight. Claud Lockwood leaves the day after Lu returns but Charley Campbell and Bert Zeiber have come in and Bert will stay to tend the ranch. *Took shoes off Poll and Deb. Shod Babe, Lucy, Jim, Bonny, Bolly and Bird. Sent roan mare of Mrs. Egans* [Eagan's] *out by Clyde. Let him take old McClellan saddle to ride. Paid him $46* for tending the ranch. Over the next two days Lu shoes seven more horses and gets the packsaddles ready.

To Bear Valley via Thunder Mountain (July 29 – August 14)

On this trip, the Caswells seem to be improving the trail and constructing shortcuts on the route from Thunder Mountain to the Bear Valley transfer station. They apparently pick up another load of supplies and equipment from Boise that was met by Ben. This is the last recorded time, other than a trip by Ben in August 1901, that they use the Bear Valley route to Boise. The two trips in 1900 probably utilize this route because of the amount of pipe and other heavy items that needs to be transported directly to Thunder. Lu and Campbell leave Cabin Creek on July 29. They take along all of the pack horses and their packsaddles but only three are loaded at this point. They have to clear downed timber and rock out of the trail and don't get to Thunder until 4 on the 31st.

August

Wes, Dan, and Lu leave for Bear Valley August 1 with 15 packhorses, in addition to their saddle horses. They get Jonas Fuller to go along with them to help cut trail. Jonas is a Civil War veteran about 63 years old, who had mined at the Homestake Mine in the Black Hills for a number of years before coming to Thunder Mountain. His presence in the area suggests that word is getting around about the Caswells' discovery of gold. They make it to the forks of Indian Creek before stopping for the night. The next day, they scout out a new trail to Trappers Fork and travel for only 4 hours before camping again. Clark Roland comes into camp and stays with them. They reach the head of Sulphur Creek the next day and Roland leaves for Thunder Mountain. Lu and Jonas cut trail over the ridge while Dan and Wes pack up. They get to Bear Valley at 12:30 on the 5th and discover that Ben is off hunting.

On the 6th they start back toward the mines with 18 horses but, for the first of the trip, shuttle part of the load at a time to a spike camp and then go back for another before moving on to the next camp. Jonas stays at the Bear Valley camp to watch after things. They get everything to Elk Creek Summit on the first day and to Baker Summit the next. On the way to Baker Summit, they encounter an old man named Hall whose horse had gotten snagged in the belly by a sharp stick and died. They transfer his horse's load to their own packhorses and continue on. The third day, they get everything moved to Meadow Lake.

The final few days are a maze of events involving cutting new routes to ill-defined locations and shuttling back and forth to move the loads forward. They reach Trappers Flat the evening of the 10th and on the 12th they make it back to their Indian Creek camp for the night. They reach Thunder Mountain the next evening and Lu exalts that they *Got trail blazed clear through.* In the near future, this will become the initial route by which men and heavy equipment will come into the area to build a quartz mine and mill.

On the 14th, Ben shoes the sore-footed horses. They leave seven horses for Wes to go back to Bear Valley for pipe, once it arrives. Lu takes another 16 head and returns to the ranch.

To Boise via Warren (August 15 – September 10)

Lu barely has time to catch a few winks and eat before heading off on the 15th to meet a train bringing his father, stepmother, and stepbrother from Texas and go on to Boise. He saddles Jim, Daisy, Bird, Cap, and Bolly and makes it to about 2 miles above his usual Smith Creek camp before stopping for the night. At 1 the next day, he catches up with Ben and Dan coming directly from Thunder Mountain. They push hard the rest of the day and get within 2 miles of Warren Summit. With an early start, they reach Warren at 10 AM, stop for a couple of hours, and then go on to the Larsen's placer mine on Ruby Creek, near where it meets the Secesh River. Andrew and Peter Larsen and their sister Anna Marie had immigrated from Denmark in the 1890s. Anna Marie and Ben are close friends and marry within another 30 months. The Caswells reach Meadows on the 18th and stay at the hotel. In the morning they rent a rig from Johnson, drive 27 miles to Council, change horses for the next 22 miles, and get to Salubria at 10. *Found folks there since 14th.* With the push to meet up with their folks accomplished, they put up at Days Hotel and spend the next day and a half recuperating and visiting before taking a train to Boise.

They check into the Capitol Hotel and, over the next couple of days, take a buggy ride around town; go to the Natatorium; have group photographs taken by Myer; examine possible building lots for their father; and shop for "a lot of truck." On Friday the 24th, they *Went up with Ira Beard* [Baird] *and saw his sisters. Nice girls.* On Saturday Lu rents a rig and takes Stella Baird and "Pa and Ma" to the races. Dan and Ben also have women out for the day.

Late Saturday night the brothers meet with Colonel Dewey's son, E. H. Dewey, to close the deal on their claims but no mention of it is made in the diary. Between their meeting in the Overland Hotel in July and August 25, E. H. Dewey, became very impressed with the results presented by the Caswells. The younger Dewey sent a 70 pound ore specimen he purchased from the partners for $500 and glowing reports to his father and the group of Pittsburgh investors he represented. As Lu later recounted to his daughter Louisa for his autobiography, "Our lawyer representative, Mr. John Blake, drew up the contract and our option for the five claims for $100,000. Dewey stipulated that the same claims Taylor had signified in his contract, be included. We hadn't intended to let Ritchey or Dan's locations [Golden Treasure & Equinox] go. Ben's always overanxious and impulsive action cost us two valuable pieces of property. But one has to go through something like that to learn the way around in mining business."

In the late hours of Saturday night August 25, they eventually cut a deal. Under the terms of the agreement, Dewey agrees to pay $100,000 (equivalent to $2 million in present day terms) for the claims, to construct a wagon road from the state wagon road in Bear Valley to the property, and to erect a mill at the mine. Development is to start immediately and Dewey is given until 1903 to complete the deal. No down payment is required but instead the partners can continue mining until payment is made. This must have suited the partners just fine for they had already set in motion plans to expand their operation and increase their ability to extract the gold.

Lu and his half brother Cort continue to romance the Baird sisters. On Sunday, they *Visited with Beard girls in forenoon. They took dinner with Cort and I. I took Stella out buggy riding in afternoon. Had a pleasant time. Gave $1.50 for rig. Cort had Pauline Beard out to base-ball game.* Then on Monday, before leaving town, they have rings made for the women.

All four brothers and their parents catch the train to Weiser the evening of the 27th and stay overnight. Their parents leave the next day for Portland but the brothers stay until the following morning to catch the train to Salubria, where they hire Day's rig for $7.50 to Council, and stay at the hotel. They leave in the morning and, in 4 hours get to Rossi's stage station on Hornet Creek Summit, where they have lunch. They put up at Ada (Warner) Smith's boarding house in Bear that night. The next day, Lu visits her parents and buys a mare from Charles Warner for $35 before going back down to Ada's in the evening.

September

Lu, Ben, and Cort leave Bear and make it to Salmon Meadows the next day. But Dan and a friend Harry Coon go back to Council to get baggage that did not arrive by train with the Caswells. Dan and Harry catch up with them in Meadows the next day. *Bet and lost 50c on horse race. Ben run Hobson against Coons grey horse.*

They camp on Upper Payette Lake on the 3rd, spend the next night at the lower end of Secesh Meadows and, after a delay to find the horses, go on the next morning to Warren. Ben and Cort take the loaded horses to Warren Summit, while Lu stays behind to write letters and post checks. He writes six more letters the following day, orders a sewing machine, and buys some oats and other "truck."

On the 7th, they go to town for the rest of their stuff and Dan buys a mare from Tom Neighbours. Then they leave and camp above Shiefer's. Their next two camps are at the "Beaver dams" on Elk Creek and at their Smith Creek camp. Cort and Lu go hunting both evenings but Cort misses a shot at some Bighorn sheep.

The entry for September 10th is at the end of a memorandum book. Lu notes: *Packed up at 9 got to hill above camp at 6. Stopped at Copper camp 30 minutes.* There are no other known records until December 1, but from the reference to their stop for the day at the "hill above camp," one may infer that they go back to Thunder to unload some of their supplies and possibly to work on mining related activities. Wes should be there already having packed in the last of the pipe from Bear Valley.

Cabin Creek (Mid-September – December 31)

Ben and Dan probably remain at the mines the rest of the year.

Eventually Lu and Cort make it to the ranch. They may have done so soon after reaching Thunder Mountain in order to relieve Bert and look after the animals and crops. Lu may have had his hands full packing supplies for others part of the time because in a later entry to his diary on April 30, 1901 he notes *Divided up the money with Ben and Dan, received for packing last fall.* Jonas Fuller comes down in early December looking for work. Lu knows Jonas' wood-cutting abilities and general work ethic and agrees to hire him to help cut house logs. Jonas takes up residence nearby, possibly at Ritchey's old place.

December

For the rest of the year, only Lu, Cort, and Jonas are at the ranch. The mild fall weather continues through most of December with only a light skiff of snow on the ground on the 28th, followed by a storm the next day leaving 1/4 inch. The light accumulation of snow makes possible travel to and from Thunder and the completion of some last minute cleanup projects at the ranch before winter sets in. They gather and store the last of the squash (in a cellar under the house), onions, cabbage, beans, and rye seed; build a picket fence around the strawberries; fix a cellar door; cut and haul lots of firewood; make improvements to the road; and complete/initiate a couple of new projects. Notably, there is little reference to hunting, trapping, or associated activities during this time. Cort celebrates his 20th birthday during the month and provides welcome help on a number of fronts including washing clothes and helping cook.

On the first day of December . . . *Fred Holcomb came down from Thunder Mountain for the doctor book. Ben was sick abed—he thought it was mercury the cause of it.* Fred went back after an hour and a quarter rest. It is doubtful he was able to provide Ben much relief when he returned.

The main new project for the month is the construction of a pole-type shed on the north end of the house for the storage of saddles, harnesses, and other horse tack. The job also entails cutting and hauling numerous loads of logs and shake bolts to the building site and splitting out a tremendous number of shakes. Cort helps Lu split shakes and work on the shed and helps Jonas cut logs. Lu chars the posts to preserve them and sets them into pre-dug holes to serve as uprights. Next he *leveled up and cut out for ridge logs to shed. Cort peeled the logs.* By mid-month Lu is able to finish putting the roof logs on, split shakes, and get most of them on the roof. He also covers the walls of the shed with shakes, puts up a heavy beam inside, and inserts pins into it to hang saddles and harness. Finally, Lu completes the job on the 27th, except for a few shake battens, when he installs the rest of the pins and hangs the saddles on them.

Lu even manages to bake several batches of bread and some mince pies during the month. *Cort ground up meat in sausage mill for mince meat.* Probably in recognition of Cort's presence, he also celebrated Christmas, a rare event for him. *Baked some pies and a cake, roasted goose for Xmas dinner.* The next day, Cort goes with Jonas for a short visit.

South Fork of the Salmon River at the site of Shiefer's Bridge on the trail between Warren and Elk Creek Summit (photograph by author August 2009).

1901

Cabin Creek (January 1 – May 18)

January-March

Although diary entries for the first 9 days of January are absent, Lu and Cort apparently remain around Cabin Creek the whole time. As in the previous month, they probably are joined regularly by Jonas Fuller, who continues to work for Lu part-time. They occasionally are joined by Dan ("Reddy") Brown, who resides with Jonas further up Big Creek. Jonas continues to work for Lu until late March, when he and Reddy head up to Thunder Mountain. Jonas often stays at the ranch and he and Cort play cards until late into the night, a source of irritation to Lu, who is tired and wants to sleep. Dan Brown plays too but he often is away, as in January when he snowshoes to Warren and is gone for 17 days. At the end of January, all three of the card players snowshoe up to Thunder Mountain *to do some representing on some new locations.*

Jonas and Reddy come back, along with Wes, a week later, and Cort returns a week after that with Fred Holcomb. Jonas is hurting from the trip and stays at the ranch a day to rest and bathe his limbs. Cort and Holcomb return on the 14th. Cort is suffering from frostbitten feet and it is several days before he recovers.

Lu traps and hunts a lot less this year than in any previous year. Probably the Caswells' harvest of gold the previous season has alleviated much of the need to sell hides and furs to obtain cash for goods and services. Lu does continue to set out poison bait and traps for cougar and occasionally kills a deer or "coyote" with his rifle but otherwise most hunting, trapping, and preparation of hides is done by Cort. The bulk of Lu's hunting and trapping is in February. On the 2nd, he goes up to the trap on Cave Creek and . . . *shot 6 times at a kyote at long range but failed to hit him. Got awful close 2 or 3 times.* Five days later, he kills what he initially thinks is a "large kyote" but later realizes is a wolf. *Brought it home with me and skinned it out, will feed the carcass to chickens. Saw 2 together but could not get a shot at the other.* The next day he *Washed the wolf hide and Came home got dinner put the meat to cooking for chickens . . . went down in sight of the Lycks to see if any kyotes down there. One got in the trap, must of been there 4 or 5 days, and got it out, looks like lost leg.* Two days later, he goes back over to Cave Creek to salt the horses and put out bait from the front part of a sheep he kills and saves the hams to eat. When he returns to renew the salt 6 days later, he *found one* [dead] *eagle and magpie at the bait on Cave Creek.*

On the 12th, Lu and Cort have what seems to be a minor spat. Lu notes only that *Cort went up to bait trap with the old* [dead] *rooster, took after some deer and I told him not today,* [he was] *rather warm about it, so was I.* Three weeks later, Lu makes another brief reference to the incident and that's it. However, the tiff that Lu and Cort have in mid-March, while seeming from the diary entry to be minor, apparently brings to a head an underlying conflict and changes the tenor of their relationship for the remainder of Cort's time in the backcountry. On April 2nd Lu notes that Cort *asked an explanation and I gave it: which is satisfactory to him.* Little else is said but when Ben, Dan, and Wes head back up to Thunder Mountain on May 4 after a short visit, Cort goes with them and subsequently does not return to the ranch except for brief visits. He eventually goes back to Texas without benefitting substantially from the mine or the ranch. Simply by being a half brother and so much younger than his siblings, Cort seems to have been at a disadvantage from the outset. It also doesn't help that he is a latecomer to the operation and lacks the sense of ownership and dedication to hard work that Lu, Ben, and Dan have. Except for the preceding incident, the relationship between Lu and Cort seems cordial most of the time, judging from Lu's diary entries. Cort mainly works with Jonas or goes deer hunting alone and works up the hides for sale in Warren. He also helps Lu occasionally.

As usual, winter is a busy time even though there is a fair amount of snow on the ground, restricting travel away from the ranch and requiring the use of a sleigh for hauling in poles and bolts. In January, the main project is building a bridge across Cabin Creek and making a wooden wheelbarrow from scratch.

Construction of the bridge includes getting and keeping the tools in shape, excavation, building a grade, and making planks. The project stretches over about 6 weeks. On the 16th, he *went up to show Cort and Jonas where I wanted the grade built, came back and started a pick, sharpened all the rest.* Over the next four days, on increasingly frozen ground, Cort and Jonas work on the grade to the bridge approach but by the 21st the ground is frozen so hard Lu has to blast it loose. Over the next week, the grade is completed, Lu puts an extension on the wagon reach, and hauls down the bridge timbers. Then, during 4 days extending over the month of February, they get the stringers laid, add the decking, smooth up the grade, bring in the ties, and pin them down to complete the job.

After beginning work on the bridge, Lu builds a wheelbarrow. The seemingly small project takes 10 days to complete. Other activities recurring frequently in January include baking bread (both rye and "light") and pies, writing letters, feeding the horses and salting them and the cows. On one occasion, he bakes 8 loaves and 5 mince pies. Most of several days are spent writing letters, including the 14th when he *wrote letters to Arbukles and my girl.* The latter likely is Stella Baird, whom he had given a ring the previous August. He also makes a stand for a grist mill and on the 22nd *Ground the first corn in the new grist mill.* Towards the end of the month Lu has some health concerns, which he describes as *some kind of a nervous attack last night, not feeling very good today. Have not felt good for the past week, have trouble to sleep with out having nervous spells. I don't know what it is,* [suppose] *it is caused by using coffee and tobacco.* By February 4, he concludes *Believe my trouble is numbness from using tobacco.*

Beginning in February and extending into early April, Lu spends considerable time on the repair and maintenance of the horse equipment. He washes and oils his riding saddle and bridle, fixes one stirrup, mends the bridle and puts conchos on it, and "fits up" a number of pairs of horseshoes. In one spurt of activity at the end of March, he makes a number of stirrups from sheep horns that Cort found on Cave Creek. He cuts them all out and then puts them through a press, and finishes up all but one pair on April 3rd: *1 pair for Cort, 1 pair for Fred Holcomb, 1 pair for Ben, 1 pair for*

Dan. Cort's are the best. He also tunes up the harnesses for the draft horses, washes and oils the collars, makes a new neck yoke, and makes four pads for the harness backbands that he lines with sheep skin. However, most of the effort during this time is spent making packsaddles, rigging, and aparejos and repairing sundry items of tack, including britching, cinch, and breast strap for the pack horses. The aparejos take the most time. For example, in one case he makes the rigging for two horses in a day and a packsaddle (not including cutting out the saddle trees) in 2 days but apparently takes the better part of 7 days to cut out material, sew, and add sheepskin pads to make two aparejos.

A major project for March is making charcoal, which begins on the 1st with the cutting up of a fir tree. The next day, Lu digs a trench under the place selected for the coal pit and on the 3rd *Jonas and I went to work on the coal pit. Got up the team, snaked up the logs, turned them out and built the pit, covered it and got it all ready to fire at 2 o'clock.* Four days later he sets the coal pit on fire and begins tending it, almost continuously at first and then at increasing intervals. By the 11th, the pit is being checked every 3 hours at night. Sometimes they all take turns but other times Lu does it himself. On the 15th, Lu opens the coal pit and gets it *smoking good.* So good in fact that the pit breaks open, burns up some coal, and, for the next 2 days, has to be "smothered down." However, at the end of 2 weeks of smoldering, Lu *Opened the coal pit took out about 10 bushels of coal and closed it up. The fire is not all out yet. Broke good.* The next day, he *Looked after coal, put roof on it.* Following this, the coal is left alone until April 10th when they *Piled up the coal and covered it with shakes* and then, on the 23rd, *We shredded my coal.*

During some of the same interval in which the coal is being made, Lu becomes ill but keeps tending the coal pit most of the time. On March 4, he *Took suddenly ill in the night, sick a bed all day, took Indian Root Pills and hot drink of brandy and ginger. Cort and Jonas stayed in and waited on me.* The worst is over by the 6th, though he still feels very weak, and it isn't until the 10th that he is almost back to normal.

April

The beginning of April still is wintery. On April 2nd Lu writes *Snowed and blowed about all day, about 4 inches of snow on the ground. The deepest I have known in this country this time of year, but no frost in the ground.* However, signs of spring are becoming increasingly evident because the next day Lu *Heard a grouse grunt* and noted that the *Godowns are out.* By the 10th, spring is noticeably on its way and by the 16th Lu indicates, the *Hills getting green.* The chickens and turkeys are beginning to lay in earnest. Feeding and milking the cows become routine now but the milking is not without its hazards, as Lu records on April 3rd, *Old Liz liked to kick me out of sight in the mud tonight. Cranky I guess, all of a sudden. Will have to go to tieing her leg.* Milk soon is available from Liz and Pet in quantities for drinking and making butter. Pet is fitted with a bell and both cows turned loose to graze, then brought in to be fed and milked. Lu does all the milking at first but later, after Bull shows up, he is relieved of the chore.

On the 10th, Clark Roland comes in from Copper Camp with the mail and stays for a couple of days. Money Lu has been expecting arrives with the packet and he sends some of it out with an order for a syringe and a scrap book, which take over a month to come. He also stays up writing letters until 1 AM on the day Clark leaves, to have them ready to go out with him. One of the letters, containing 11 "Labor Notices" and 16 descriptions of mining locations, is for A. W. Talkington, the county recorder in Mount Idaho.

When spring finally does arrive, it comes on with a rush and Lu's efforts become focused primarily on planting garden crops and grains and associated tasks, including controlling the numbers of godowns and mice. Some of the godowns fall victim to Lu and Cort's shooting but both the ground squirrels and mice are poisoned with strychnine as well. The two men also thrash out five sacks of oats and 45 pounds of beans that have been left on the stalks from the previous year.

The growing season begins on April 10 with plowing the fields, digging up onions and other root crops overwintered in the ground, and burning the meadow on Big Creek flat. However, they also squeeze in a little time for fishing, as the "red sides" have just begun to come up the river. Also, the oat and wheat seed are cleaned up in preparation for planting. The first godowns are spotted on the 13th and Lu shoots three. This also is the day they make the first butter this spring. Cort churns it, Lu works it, and they get about 3 pounds that Lu rates as *very good.*

About this same time, Lu plants the first of the grain and some beet, kale, onion, radish, salsify, and turnip seed. The sequence of plowing, harrowing, drilling/sowing, re-harrowing, planking, and furrowing, established the previous spring, is repeated. Poll, Browny, Dan, Deb, Jim, and Suse all serve as draft horses. Poll with either Browny or Deb constitute the preferred team. Jim is rather inexperienced but is used some with Dan and does *first rate.* Suse is worked for the first time but is paired up with Browny and also does quite well. Some of the oat ground is above the house but sites for the other crops are not specified.

The Caswells' long-time friend Bull comes in from Warren on April 20th to help. A later entry (October 3) suggests that he also may have brought 13 head of cattle with him. Until now, Lu has relied solely on Cort's help and he seems to respond favorably, in spite of their earlier tiff, and continues to pitch in until he leaves for Thunder. However, Cort's contributions are limited by lack of experience, especially with plowing. The winter apparently has been hard on Bull but he shows up ready to work and his expertise as a teamster and a farmer add substantially to ranch operations.

Bull's arrival on the 20th sets off several days of heightened activity but first Lu has to examine his mail. *Came to the house with him, read my letters and then got dinner. Plowed afternoon. Bull set out strawberries, I helped him finish in the eve.* Over the next 2 days, Lu and Bull prepare the garden by the house. Lu plants his "ground cherries" and *Bull made a lot of water gages.* [Bull] *is feeling some better, guess* [he has] *been pretty badly used up.* On the 22nd Lu notes that it took him 3 hours to get breakfast and do the chores. *Bull got up Browny and his mule and worked them on the harrow and planker while I sowed the wheat. Got up Suse and Dan to drive in the afternoon. Mrs. Taylor came down, also Claud* [Lockwood], *after vegeta-*

bles, brought flour to pay [for] *them. Mrs. Taylor gave me a dog* [Mike].

Near the end of the month, they prepare the ditch for irrigation and plant cabbage, more carrots, cauliflower, collards, coffee peas, and potatoes. On the 24th, they sow the last of the grain . . . *put in nearly 2 sacks* [of wheat] *all together and 2 sacks of oats.* A frost on the 26th freezes some of the carrots and the tops of the grass. They work on a 260 foot section of ditch above the house and build a dam across a washout, clean out another section, about half full of sand, below the house, and bed the ditches with straw to keep them from washing out.

On the 29th, when Lu goes down to dig more ditch, he *Heard the boys holler on the point across the river.* Ben, Dan, and Wes have arrived from Thunder Mountain on foot to get horses and supplies, pick up Cort, and take a short break. The men probably find some time for socializing and exchanging information about mining and ranching but, for the most part, Lu and Bull keep working, with some help from the others. For example, during April 30th Lu *Divided up the money with Ben and Dan, received for packing last fall. Started the water through the ditch and went to irrigating. Bull also helped. Cort and Wes went fishing, got left. Cort irrigated some and burnt the old deer hair in door yard. Dan made 2 sinch hooks, got 4 done and cut his stirrups down,* [they were] *too wide. Ben helped me dig some post holes. Wes cooked cake and chickens.*

May-June

The group's collaborative activities continue into the first few days of May. They get the rest of the potato ground marked off and planted, some post holes dug and posts charred, and wood cut for pickets. On the 2nd Dan got things ready to go back to Thunder and Lu gave him almost all of the powder he had. On the 3rd, after Lu and Ben had been working in the woods, they *Came home and found Borden here, gave him a drink to revive him up. He was well in a minute. Had quite a bundle of papers but no letters, brought some truck, I sent for.* The next morning, Lu *Helped the boys, Ben, Dan, Cort, and Wes off for Thunder Mt. Went up as far as the bar beyond Cave Creek with them and left them. Borden went with them.*

After the men leave, Lu and Bull resume their farming routine. Bull apparently doesn't like domestic work and, at one point, Lu laments that he has *to do all my own cooking, washing dishes, milk cows, feed chickens and calves.* They continue to plow, till, and remove rocks from the fallow fields and plant beans, cantaloupe, citron, two types of corn—*yankey* and popcorn, egg plant, onion sets, peas, plum seeds, more potatoes and radishes, salsify, sunflower seeds, two types of squash—Hubbard and yellow, 50 tomato plants, and watermelon. Lu shelters the tomatoes from frost with shakes driven into the ground on their north sides. Nearly all of the crops are up by May 17th, except for a few of the late plantings like cantaloupes and citron, and the oats are nearly 4 inches high and being watered for the second time.

Their other major task during this period is to irrigate the plants. Bull introduces the idea of using furrow boards to insert at strategic points along the ditches and cause the water to spill over into the field along defined stretches of ditch. As a result, Bull makes a lot of these boards. They often are driven into the ditch bottom or secured with pieces of sod.

On May 18th, Lu notes *The river and Cabin Creek getting pretty big now.* Lu gets ready in anticipation of a trip to Copper Camp to get blasting powder and is up until 11:15 PM. He washes clothes and bathes, as he has been doing every 4 or 5 days, because of the dust. He shoes Bird and Bolley to ride and carry the powder.

To Copper Camp (May 19 – 21)

Started for the Copper Camp by way of Crooked Creek. Mike, the Taylor dog, broke the 2nd time on deer on the head of Cave Creek. That was too much, I took out the rifle and cut loose at him at 200 yds, running, brought him [down] *the first time.* Lu *Had a hard trip* that took 12 hours to reach Copper Creek. There was about 4 feet of soft snow on the summit and he *Came down a hell of a ridge to Big creek.* On the 20th Lu links up with the mail carrier. Borden had gotten in with the powder and mail the day before about 2 PM. *He went up today and got it at Beaver Creek. Helped him down from Pringle's with it, payed him 25 dollars for the trip, got dinner, gave him some grub.* Lu had taken along some milk to drink and at Copper Camp he offers some to Jessie Jackman and Pringle Smith but *Pringle declined. Packed up and came down to Monumental, had to build some trail at Crooked Creek.* The next day Lu *takes 10 hours getting home.* He *came around by Cox Creek and Cave Creek. Built a bridge, climbed a point with horses, went back, afraid the trail wasn't built. Found the* [main herd of] *horses on the head of Cave Creek, had a hell of a time getting them down. I was spilt off one bare back, fetching them off of the mountain, lost my money book, but found it . . . Put my saddle on Suse and fetched them home. Bull said it froze the night after I left, indeed the plants look it.*

A couple of days after Lu's return, Cort comes down for the powder and departs the next day. He tells Lu that there is no snow on the divides between the ranch and Thunder.

Cabin Creek (May 22 – June 12)

By the time Lu left for Copper Camp, the planting for the year had pretty well been completed except for carrots, beets, and some more tomato seedlings, which he plants the day after he returns; some cabbages, cauliflowers, cucumbers, melons, and summer squash he and Bull plant on the 28th; and more potatoes and popcorn. Otherwise the main tasks of gardening remaining are to hoe and water the plants and try to fend off frost. On June 4 they: *Went to covering the crop* [probably with straw to protect from freezing and hold in moisture]. *We got the squashes, sunflowers, tomatoes and sweet and field corn all covered. Took until 2 o'clock AM to cover the corn.* But, even then: *Quite a few things* [were] *killed by the freeze last night, most of tomatoes frozen. The field corn was covered, is all right, I guess.*

The main task on the ranch for the remainder of the summer is repairing and building picket fencing and making gates around the house and for corrals. The project is started a few days before Lu leaves for Copper Camp but resumes in earnest the day after he returns and continues to June 7. Several days of preparation are spent felling trees, cutting them into bolts, and splitting the bolts into pickets with blasting powder. After getting the pickets on in front of the house, Lu exclaims of the new fence *It makes it look good.* The finishing touches involve making several sets of hinges and gates of assorted sizes. They also get the *Old fence torn down, lugged the rest of posts and poles up to top of bench for other fence. Fixed up the old corral.*

In and around their regular chores (such as Lu cooking and baking bread and Bull now milking the cows) and other work, they still find time for hunting deer and fishing for salmon and redsides, both for recreation and food. They employ some unique methods for capturing salmon, such as spearing and shooting with a 30-30. Lu also kills two large packrats and Bull shoots a chicken hawk.

Shortly before Lu leaves in mid-June for an extended period, their routines are broken up by visits from Bill Borden and, later, by Jonas Fuller and Dan Brown. Borden arrives late on the evening of the 7th and leaves early on the morning of the 10th. While he is there, he helps Bull sprout potatoes, readies a chicken for supper, and helps Lu and Bull castrate two calves. On the 8th, while Borden is occupied with other things, Lu writes letters all day. The next day, after cutting the calves, he chats and writes more letters until 12:30 AM . . . *wrote a letter to Martin Marlin Company and sent an order and $35.00 to M.W.* [Montgomery Ward] *& Co. for plow* [and] *fanning mill* [for separating grain and chaff]. After breakfast, Lu gets up Bird and Jim and puts Borden across the river about 7 AM. That night, Jonas Fuller and Dan Brown come down from Thunder but they don't make enough noise for Lu to hear them and spend the night across the river.

The next day, Lu busies himself with some last minute preparations . . . *Mended my gum boots, fixed Bull's shoe so it wouldn't hurt. Mended my pistol scabbard. Cleaned guns, sided up in front of house to keep the calves from chewing my harness. Made out another order to Montgomery Ward & Co. for wagon wheels—wide tire, wagon spring platforms, scales, dehorner,* [and] *tooth forseps.* Jonas and Dan Brown leave for their home on Big Creek. Jonas apparently has injured himself and is having trouble seeing.

Thunder Mountain (June 13 – July 1)

The entries for the last part of June are missing. During this time Lu and Dan trade places, with Lu going to Thunder Mountain and Dan to the ranch. In the spring or early summer, the Caswells discovered a ledge that they believe will assay at $3,000 a ton. According to Babbitt "One hole that Dan opened up had gold like grains of wheat in it. Dan did not want the Dewey group to get wind of this, so he covered up what couldn't be easily retrieved . . . ." and he hopes that Dewey will not exercise his option to buy before the Caswells can harvest the gold themselves or negotiate a better price on the claims. Up until this time Dewey has not delivered on his part of the bargain to build a road into the mines and initiate improvements on the claim. On this basis, the Caswells hope that their agreement can be voided.

July

As the diary resumes, Lu has prepared a letter to let Huntley know what is going on so he may try to stop the transaction. However, Lu then learns that Dewey's crew is on its way in to begin work. This heightens the urgency of contacting Huntley and Lu rides most of the night straight through to the ranch to have the letter delivered to Huntley.

Cabin Creek (July 2 – 17)

Lu apparently hands the letter off Bull the morning of July 2nd to take to Warren (Bull is recorded as returning on the 8th) because Lu then remains at the ranch, with no apparent anxiety, until the whole outfit heads for the outside on July 18.

As word of the gold discovery spreads, the first wave of treasure seekers heads for Thunder Mountain and several tent cities spring up along Monumental Creek to meet their every need. As a result of the rising gold fever, there is an influx of new visitors at the ranch.

During the 16 days at the ranch, Lu does the chores, irrigates, thins out beets and turnips, sets out tomato and cabbage plants, and hunts deer. He also cooks until Dan recovers from a bad case of piles, in relation to which Lu observes . . . *piles are murder*. In April, Lu had indicated that he was *About to loose my Sewing Machine.* By July 2nd a replacement has arrived and he sets it up and tries it out to his liking. On the 10th he returns from a fruitless horse chase on Cox Creek to find that Ben, Wes, and Cort have arrived. Mauldin, a local resident, stops by and takes a photograph of Dan, Bull, and Lu outside of the cabin. Lu says that shortly afterward *Bolley kicked me almost a rod, crippled me up some but not serious* and, as noted on the photograph, he "losted his watch" as a result.

After the brothers and Wes are all together, there is a lull of about a week while the men wait to depart for Boise. During this time, Lu weeds and thins beets and sunflowers. Bull sows rutabagas in the corn field, does some plowing and cultivating, and irrigates. Ben shoes 5 or 6 horses. Cort and Wes chore around and cook. On the 16th, *Charley Campbell came in from Thunder Mt., brought the mail.* The final day before leaving is mostly spent hanging out. *Charley, Cort and myself went fishing, caught 13, speared 4. Charley and Cort went fishing after noon, caught 17. Bull hilled up potatoes. Dan cooked.*

To Huntley's via Warren and Then on to Boise (July 18 – September 2)

Bull is left in charge of the ranch and the four Caswells depart on July 18. It is not clear what becomes of Charley and Wes but apparently neither of them goes to Boise. The journey from Cabin Creek to Huntley's by horseback extends over a period of 10 days. The brothers generally get underway between 6 and 7 and stop by mid-afternoon. Overnight camping spots coincide with places with plenty of grass for the horses: Placer Bar near Acorn Creek, "upper camp" at Copper Creek, Elk Summit at head of Smith Creek, above Shiefer's on South Fork, Secesh Meadows, Squaw Meadows, first creek below Payette Lake, Price Valley, and Big Bar.

The first few days they are bothered by biting flies. On the third day, Bill Borden comes into their summit camp and they go to look at his ledge. The next evening, Walter Moore and Charley Meyers visit them near the South Fork bridge and Cort catches a nice mess of fish. They are about out of food and stop at Warren for an hour to resupply before going on to Secesh Meadows. Moore subsequently joins them there and travels with them for a couple of days. Walter lets them try his new Borchardt pistol and later apparently obtains some for them. At Meadows, Walter leaves for home and the Caswells make a brief stop to buy more grub, before heading to Price Valley for the night.

On the way to Huntley's, they stop to visit the Warners and Lu rides Charley Warner's new colt over to Huntley's. They meet Huntley and his hired hand John Smith on the trail and stay at Big Bar that night. In the morning, Lu saddles up the colt and goes after the horses for A. O. He notes in his usually understated way . . . *The colt pitched very hard with me. Tore my shirt.* After this little rodeo, they all return to the Warner's. While they all have been at Big Bar, Joe and Charles Warner have gotten back from nearby Kinney Creek and the Caswell bunch arranges with them to look after their horses until their return from Boise.

In the past, the Caswells have gone on the next leg of the trip by horseback or buggy but this time they take a stagecoach from Bear to Council and then catch the train, which has been extended northward from Salubria during the past year. However, in order to get passage on the stage, they lay over for a day. They get started about 7 AM on the 29th but have a bit of excitement, when the buggy bringing them from Huntley's breaks down in front of Amy Smith's. Lu's valise doesn't make it onto the stage, necessitating a trip back to Bear. The valise is recovered at the cost of a missed train connection and another half-day delay. They finally catch the train from Council at noon the next day and make it to Boise about 7 hours later. When they arrive, Lu has an interview with a newspaper reporter.

August

The main reason for going to Boise is to void the agreement with

Dewey. The Caswells and their partners engage the lawyer Richard H. Johnson to act in their behalf. Johnson recommends that they also consult with a specialist named Moore from Walla Walla and he arrives by train on August 1st. They decide to have Johnson draw up papers to invalidate their contract and . . . *notify Dewey out of Thunder Mt.* Huntley catches a train to Nampa the next day to deliver the papers to Dewey's son Edward. The following day, Saturday August 3, Edward comes to town and they all meet at the Boyd's to have *a chewing spell with him.* On Monday they have *a long talk with Lawyer Johnson about the bonds* [and give] *Moore a light bond to fight the case.* Johnson and Moore decide that forfeiture cannot be declared until November 1, 1901, the date fixed for the improvements, has passed. This essentially mandates another trip to Boise in October to deal with the issue. Moore goes home on the 6th and Johnson gets the notices made out the next day. No other mention of Dewey or the lawyers is made during this visit to Boise, although some of the partners stay around until the 17th. They would have left earlier but on the morning of the 14th, a close friend Amelia Kohnle dies and they decide to stay for her funeral on the 16th. Amelia and her husband John ran a confectionary store on Main Street called the Candy Kitchen. Their 20-year old daughter Florence or one of their female employees, may have been the object of Dan Caswell's attention.

Legal matters are not the only thing the partners attend to during their stay in Boise. They spend a good deal of time looking after the gold dust they brought along to deposit and samples of ore they are having assayed. As soon as offices open after their arrival, they take the "clean up" to the Federal Mint for assay. They also turn some ore samples over to be assayed. Assaying ore involves heating a sample until the gold reaches the liquid state and is separated off, cooled, and weighed. The results for the ore samples are then extrapolated to an equivalent value per ton of raw ore. They receive payment for the dust totaling $7,152.11 the following day and deposit it in the bank, with $1500 of Lu's going into a checking account. One ore assay that Dan gets on the *rich rock* from one of their ledges goes at an exceptionally high rate of $12,000 per ton, adding to their desire to void the contract.

Ben and Lu shop for some horses and tack for Ben and Cort to take back to Thunder Mountain by way of Idaho City and Bear Valley. Lu buys one grey and one brown mare from Myers for $170 plus a bridle and Ben buys two others, a riding saddle, two pack saddles, and some blankets. Ben and Cort leave early on the morning of August 8 and make it to Idaho City by nightfall. Ben telephones his friend Anna Larsen to let her know they have arrived there safely.

With considerable money in the bank for the first time on record, Lu makes some major purchases of equipment for the ranch. He obtains mowers, a rake, and possibly some other hardware for $160 from Fletcher Strain & Co. in Boise and has them shipped by rail to Council. The mower and rake each weigh about 500 pounds when assembled and he will have them transported from there to the ranch by pack train. The equipment will reduce the time and labor needed to make hay. Lu also buys $70 in medicinal supplies; two pairs of pants, a shirt, a hat, shoes, and other items of clothing and dry goods; a fishing rod and automatic reel; a clock; and a stag hound pup. He orders a pair of field glasses and a combination vice and drill by mail. He and Dan purchase provisions, clothes, and blankets from Falk's and hardware at "the new hardware store" and Dan gets himself a phonograph.

Not all of the time spent in Boise is devoted to business. They also partake in some recreational activities and do some socializing. Lu specifically mentions attending a band concert and a couple of horse races, taking a buggy ride, and having a bike ride, mostly early in their stay. Later, Lu visits the Bairds and arranges to take Pauline and Stella for a buggy ride on two consecutive days. His last "dates" are the day before he leaves Boise when he takes Sue Johanson to dinner and spends a *pleasant evening* with Miss Baird at the band concert.

Lu and Dan leave Boise August 18 on the 1:05 train but go only as far as Weiser. For some reason, they need to show ore specimens there to a man named Barton. They leave the next morning and arrive in Council about 1 PM, where they put up at the hotel and make arrangements with Sea Watkins to haul their freight to Warren for 2 cents per pound. Their stage arrives at 1:20 PM on the 20th and stops for supper at the Halfway Stage Station. Afterward, the stage owner Pete Kramer takes them on to Bear. They stay at Amy Smith's and spend the next two days in Bear getting ready to travel, visiting with the Warner's (*gave the girls some present*[s]. *Took the family's pictures.)*, and settling up with Charles Warner ($30) for taking care of their horses.

On August 23 they leave Bear and get to Price Valley. *Camped in a new place. Dan and I are alone now.* The next day they camp at Big Payette Lake. *Met Walter Moore at Salmon Meadows . . . Walter and I tried our Borchardts on owls, got them both, after several shots.* Lu discovers that he has left his new fishing rod in Bear so, when they stop the next evening at the head of Secesh Meadows, he writes Joe Warner a letter asking him to mail it. At Miller's camp on the way to Warren the next day, they meet Ben, who has come from Thunder Mountain (and the freighter coming with their load from Council). Miller's Camp, where the Larsen's have their mining operation, is about 20 miles west of Warren.

The three Caswells set up camp on Warren Summit, meet up with Wes, and, over the next 2 ½ days, weigh out the pack loads and ferry them up to the Summit. On August 29, they leave and get to their old camp on the South Fork. Billey Smead had promised to meet them but he hasn't arrived. The next day they camp in mid afternoon at the beaver dams on Elk Creek. *Wes went ahead and cut the logs and took out rock to clear the trail. All hands took out a big log in the creek.* Fortunately Billey shows up by the time they leave the next day. *Wes went ahead to clear trail. Ben and Dan done took their 13 head of horses, went across to Thunder Mt. Billey Smead and I took my 13 and came down Smith Creek for the ranch. Over took Wes on the road, camped at McFaddens place* [probably along Smith Creek or near the mouth of Beaver Creek].

SEPTEMBER

Wes stays with Lu and Billey and continues to clear the trail ahead of them. However, both Wes and Lu are needed to clear trail on the 1st and take just over 8 hours to reach Nicotine Bar. They reach home the next day in another 4 hours.

Cabin Creek (September 3 – 4)

Lu stops at the ranch only long enough to put away the new items, gather up some food, and get the pack string ready to travel again. Wes rounds up a couple of fresh horses and leaves right away to go *outside*. Wes is not accounted for in the diaries again until November. Billey Smead helps *Bull get in the wheat and top out the hay stack* and then gets in a day of fishing.

To Warren to Pick up Another Load of Freight (September 5 – 14)

Lu and Billey head out on the 5th to pick up more freight that Sea Watkins has packed from Council to Warren. They take 12 head of pack horses and get as far as Placer Bar the first day. On the 6th, Lu and Billey spend 7 ½ hours on the trail before stopping at McFadden's Prairie in time to shoe Bird. The next day, just beyond the head of Elk Creek, they meet up with Ben and Dan who are headed back with nine pack horses to pick up the part of the load destined for Thunder Mountain. They also meet Meyers who is *coming out to take a load of my freight.* They all camp together about a mile below the forks on Elk Creek and the next day set up camp at Warren Summit before going to town to check the mail.

The next day they *Went to town afoot, early to get Myer's load weighed out for him. Got it all ready but he didn't want to pack up. Had to prod them around for 2 hours to get them to pack up. But got them off at last. Then Dan and I made up our loads, got done at dark. We stayed in town all night with 3 horses, wrote 4 letters, stayed in Kelly's store.* However, Meyers, with his fondness for booze and cards, proves to be a difficult person to work with. In the end, three other packers, Jake Galvino, Walter Davis, and Ernest Heast, are hired to do the packing using Meyers' pack string. On the 10th Lu: *Saddled up Browney and went after the horses on the mountain above camp. Billey met me coming on in with them just before sun up. We loaded up all our freight and got back to the Summit. Ben met us in town, he had been to see his girl* [Anna Marie Larsen] *on Sea Sesh.*

On the 11th the Caswells and Billey Smead get underway and camp *above Dutch Frank's place, along side of Smith and Jackman.* On the way, they pass Meyers' outfit in camp on the South Fork, still looking for their horses. They split up on Elk Summit with Dan and Ben going to Thunder and Lu and Smead going down Smith Creek. Bill Borden also joins them on Smith Creek and they get into camp after dark. The next night is spent at the Baird cabin and the following day they make it home. *Had to go about 3 ½ miles over on Crooked Creek slope to get the horse*[s]. *Packed up and started at 10:40. Got home right side up with care at 6 o'clock, 19 miles and as rough trail as in the country. Horses feeling fine. Bull got the corn cut, been frosting.*

Cabin Creek (September 15 – October 2)

In the first few days after returning to the ranch, Lu puts away his camping gear and new purchases and sets up his new scales to weigh Meyers' load when it arrives. There is a period of accelerated comings and goings at the ranch. In particular, an unprecedented interchange between the Caswells on Thunder Mountain and Lu at the ranch, suggests that something big is up, though it never is made explicit in the diaries. However, it probably is significant that Dan and Cort do most of the traveling back and forth and that Ben sticks tight on Thunder until just before Lu departs for Boise again. Borden goes back to Warren on the 15th, followed the next day by Smead and Bull.

In addition to the Caswells, there are extended visits and multiple arrivals and departures by the amateurs working for Charley Meyers. Jake Galvino and Ernest Heast finally get in on the 20th, six days behind Lu, with only 10 head of horses. They had lost some of their packstring at the head of Elk Creek and were forced to leave four loads and Davis there. The two men start back the next day to retrieve the rest and are gone another 5 days, arriving back on the 26th. Heast and Davis leave the following afternoon after hunting their horses all morning. Jake stays around until the 29th to help Lu and go fishing. Lu has since gotten back the fishing rod he left in Bear. *I caught 4 nice ones with my new rod and Jake got one.*

Dan and Cort arrive late on the 25th with a message from Ben and leave early the next day. Apparently Ben has gotten word that enthusiastic reports about the Caswells' claims, from the mining and assay experts Martin Curran and William E. L'Harme, have gone to Dewey. This seems to assuage any anxiety Dewey might have had about the purchase of the claims and sets in motion another trip to Boise. Cort makes another quick trip from Thunder, arriving at dark on the 28th and leaving the next day. No mention is made in the diaries about what transpired between Cort and Lu but Cort must have brought word about a meeting in Boise with Dewey and the lawyers and that Ben was coming down with the horses and final advice to Lu.

Lu does get a few things done before he hits the trail again, including harvesting the last of the tomatoes and cooking a bunch up for sweet pickles. He also hauls in a grub box from the old house, installs it in the storehouse, and stows all the food. He shoots a magpie, a camp robber (Clark's Jay), a squirrel, a packrat, and a skunk that had killed four chickens and traumatized the others. Most of all he works on shelling and cleaning the peas over a period of a week. This enables him to try out his new fanning mill that must have come in with Meyers' first pack load. Other "toys" also have arrived with the pack train, including a hillside plow and a hay rake, which he sets up before leaving.

By the 30th Lu knows that he will be departing soon. Over the next couple of days, he makes preparations including washing clothes, repairing his riding boots, taking a bath, and changing clothes. In addition, he thrashes out some oats, runs them through the fanning mill, and sacks them up.

October

To Boise via Warren, Bypassing Bear and Huntley (October 3 – 26)

Ben gets in on October 2nd with all the horses from Thunder

and Lu starts off for Boise the next day, probably after they have a long talk and develop a strategy. As this trip is to work out the final details of the deal with Dewey, it would seem to be an important one but amazingly, for unexplained reasons, Ben stays behind on Thunder Mountain and Lu goes on his own. Dan (and possibly Wes) is already in Boise. Since arrangements apparently have been made for Huntley to meet Lu in Boise, there is no need to detour to Bear and instead Lu goes by buggy directly from Meadows to Council, where he catches the train.

Dan and Lu talk with Dewey on the 10th but then spend another 3 days chasing around town on assorted errands and waiting to hear back from him. In the interim, Dan buys a horse from old man Early and Dan and Lu take the horse for a buggy ride. Mr. Early fortunately survived the apparent appendicitis attack he had while helping the Caswells haul freight to Bear Valley the previous summer. Finally, on the 14th, they begin a series of meetings with Dewey, his lawyer Borah, and their lawyer Johnson that extend over the next week and apparently involve intense negotiations on both sides. Huntley comes in by train on the afternoon of the 16th to assist the Caswells in the haggling. Later Lu visits Miss Gillespy, who is the daughter of proprietors at a boarding house where he has stayed, and takes her out a couple of times, including for a pleasant time at an opera. An agreement is reached with Dewey on the 21st that involves further on-site claim authentication and verification by T. D. Babbitt, Dewey's representative. Lu and Babbitt both leave immediately: Lu by way of Warren and Babbitt via Bear Valley.

Lu exits Boise October 22nd alone, gets to Council at 12:30, and hires a rig to Salmon Meadows. He spent the next night on the Secesh and is . . . *About done up with a bad cold.* He arrives in Warren at noon the following day and continues on to Shiefer's. While he is there, Meyers comes in from Council with four packloads for Lu, and he helps Meyers unpack amidst a rain and snow storm. The next night he gets to McFadden's Prairie after dark and then has another long day to reach Cabin Creek.

To Boise via Thunder Mountain and Warren (October 27 – November 27)

Lu leaves the ranch the next day, takes two of his strongest horses (Jim and Browny), and rides straight through to the mines on Thunder Mountain. The horses are *about played out* after a hard ride on a stormy day. Lu's purpose is to secure the locations of the claims, including some that are not part of the deal, and to meet with T. D. Babbitt to verify the locations and complete the paperwork on the claims that Dewey is purchasing. As they are finishing, Bill McClure, a well-known packer and freighter, gets in with 34 pack loads of equipment for Dewey and sets off for another bunch. It is evident from this that Dewey is fully committed to the project and has shown "good faith" by meeting the deadline of the initial agreement.

November

The legal work is completed on November 1 and Lu and Ben head back to Boise to meet up with Dan, Wes, and A. O. and culminate the sale. *Ben to go across the high trail and I to go by the ranch to leave my horses there. We met Holcomb at the mouth of West Fork* [of Monumental Creek] *and him and Ben went together. I . . . Passed Myer's at West Fork. Ground freezing fast, 1 inch of snow at Thunder Mt. Snowed at the river* [Big Creek]. Lu leaves the ranch the next day and makes it to the rock flat below Copper Camp before stopping. After a long day, the final 8 miles in the dark, he makes it all the way to Shiefer's the next day. Following a late start, he reaches Warren by 2 PM . . . *met Holcomb at Long Ridge and Ben in Warren waiting for me.* On the next leg of the trip, they are joined by Tom Neighbours, Fred Hindman, and the mail carrier and stay at the way-station on Upper Payette Lake. Neighbours and Hindman leave from Big Payette Lake for Council. *Ben gave Neighbours $10.00 to pay Rivis for hay and grain at the Little Lake.*

For some unexplained reason, instead of riding the 40 miles to Council and taking the train to Boise, Lu and Ben take a new route that is 120 miles entirely by horseback! In order to save time and weight, beginning at Warren they stay at commercial lodgings and carry only a little food. Also, once they are off mountain trails at Warren, they make much better time. They have overnight stops at Rose Berry (14 miles south of Lardo and 2 miles west of present day Cascade), Smith's Ferry, and the sawmill in Emmett. After crossing the outlet of the Big lake at Lardo, they head directly south along the east side of the North Fork of the Payette, through an area known as Long Valley, then on to Round Valley and over a low divide to Smith's Ferry, where they cross the North Fork. A couple of miles below the ferry, the river enters a constricted canyon, which would have been virtually impassable at the time. So, they probably cross over the mountain to Squaw Creek and pass through the villages of Ola and Sweet before reaching the main Payette River, a dozen miles upstream of the town of Emmett. At Emmett they cross the Payette on a bridge near the sawmill, climb Freezeout Hill, and continue on to Boise. On the stretch between Rose Berry and Boise, they make especially good time and log several 30-mile plus days of 7 ½ to 9-hour duration, including mid-day stops for dinner.

Ben and Lu arrive the afternoon of November 10 on horses that are *about run down* and find Dan, Wes, and Tom Neighbours already there. Dan has been in town long enough and/or often enough that on the 11th he goes *through a course of training at his lodge, joining the brotherhood* [probably the Freemasons]. Huntley arrives from Cuprum a day later.

The final details of the transaction drag out over the next 5 days and the men spend the time completing paperwork and making various purchases. Ben and Lu both buy new suits of clothes for the signing event. The morning of the 11th they *Turned over the papers to Johnson so he could fix up the deeds. Waited there to give information til afternoon.* A day later, *Johnson got the papers all ready. Huntley came in from Cuprum, we all went to the show, but Dan and A. O. H. had a talk with Dewey over the phone.* On the 13th *Wes got $500.00 dollars down on the Misterious slide claims from Curran.* According to Lu's autobiography, the Caswells had given Wes three claims associated with the Mysterious Slide. Wes sold the claims for $15,000 to Martin Curran, who apparently later went into partnership with Ben on the same claims.

Things pick up on the 15th. *Borah came up from Weiser,* [E. H.] *Dewey also came on the 4 o'clock train. Borah and Dewey said we could do business now, that suits me fine.* The next day is a Saturday. *We got the papers and deeds all together and took them to the bank* [First National Bank of Idaho]. *Met Dewey and Borah there, turned over the deeds to Dewey through Moore and he gave us the check for $100,000.00. I put $15,000.00 on interest* [savings account] *and the rest on deposit to draw from* [checking account]. *We gave Johnson $100.00, all he asked for his trouble.* This is all of the comment on the windfall Lu makes in his diary. A large article in the Sunday issue of *The Idaho Daily Statesman* details the discovery and sale and shows a copy of the $100,000 check. The Statesman article and photograph probably do more to set off the gold rush to Thunder Mountain than anything else.

The check is made out to "Caswell Bros. and A. O. Huntley." However, it also is endorsed by Wesley Ritchey. Split five ways this would give each man $20,000. But it is not known if Ritchey received the same as the others, since the Mysterious Slide claims he had been given apparently were not a part of the sale. After the sale, Lu takes Miss Gillespy and Miss Burke to the show and the next day buys a mare from Duffy the stable man for $65, also . . . *a Sass Rope, a halter, a pair of boots and open shoes.* Prior to that, on the 14th, Lu also *Took Miss Gillespy to the show. Ben took his girl, Wes also got a girl to go* [along].

The sale of the mine alleviates the need to return to Thunder Mountain for the winter so Ben and Dan elect to remain in Boise; Lu says only that *Dan and Ben will stay out.* Just like that, he is left with the arduous task of taking care of the ranch full time, while his two older brothers get the luxury of the soft city life, the opportunity to court women, and a chance to travel.

Lu returns to Cabin Creek in the company of Wes. They leave with four horses (Bell a favorite saddle mare of Lu's, the stalwart Jim, Chub, and Kid) a day after receiving payment for the claims. They basically retrace the route Lu and Ben had taken coming in to Boise, except that Wes has to detour at Payette Lake to pick up his horses in Meadows. Also, Lu is pushing hard to get home before the weather turns bad in the mountains. They make overnight stops at

Dry Creek, Emmett sawmill, Foot Hill Ranch (20 miles past Emmett), Van Wyck (about 3 miles southwest of present day Cascade), Big Payette Lake, Burgdorf, Shiefer's, below mouth of Smith Creek, and Placer Bar.

On the first day, they get a late start and make only 10 miles. On the second day, they start at 8 AM but run into a series of problems. *Chub started back for Boise, run him about a mile before I could head him off. I lost my pocket book above Willow Creek and we went back about 1 ½ miles after that. Kid broke his halter and we lost some time there. So in all it spoilt our day's drive.* On the third day, they stop after only 6 hours of riding.

So far the best Lu and Wes have done is 20 miles a day compared to several days of 30 miles or better covered by Lu and Ben on the way to Boise. However, on the 21st they have an exceptionally good day and cover 42 miles in slightly over 10 hours. *Beat the stage by about 10 minutes. He started half hour a head of us.* The next day, they stop at the way station on Big Payette Lake and *Wes went on to Salmon Meadows after his horses. I took the shoes off of Bell and she traveled lots better.* On the 23rd, Lu has a leisurely start and Wes catches up with him about 4 miles above the Big Lake. They are now traveling with whatever horses Wes retrieved in addition to the original four. They continue on to the cabin at Upper Payette Lake and encounter an unexpected surprise that raises Lu's ire and causes them to go another 14 miles. *We was going to stop over night there as we supposed we had feed there, but the boss informed us that we had not feed there. I knew better* [on November 7, Lu had noted that Ben had given *Neighbours $10.00 to pay Rivis for hay and grain*] *but rather than to row with him, we drove on to Burgdorfs Hot Springs, got there at 9 PM. Horses pretty tired, hard traveling. 15 inches of snow on the summit, about 45 miles drive.*

The next day they stop in Warren before going another 14 miles on a steep mountain trail to Shiefer's, where they arrive after dark. While in Warren, Lu cashes a check for $100 to pay out, buys $9.10 worth of grub, and treats the crowd in the store to cigars. He also gets 288 lbs of oats from Tom Neighbours. The following day is November 25th and they begin to encounter snow reaching about two feet deep on Elk Summit. Fortunately the trail has been broken, so they push on till dark and camp just below the mouth of Smith Creek, in only 4 inches of snow. On the trail, they meet several men headed for Thunder Mountain. Some, like Sam Smith and Charley Meyers are hauling in grub and other supplies. Others are racing to get there to stake claims and/or set up shop before winter sets in and more people arrive. The following morning Lu and Wes head for Placer Bar but not without problems. *I had a hard chase after the horses, the boys let them go by camp and I got part of them headed again but Wes had to go to Smith Creek camp after them. Lost my china ring in the circus.* On the final day, they still have 5 hours of travel to reach Cabin Creek. *Put the shoes back on Bell and Jim, was getting pretty tender. Bell came in to camp and nickered all the time, when the horses pulled out yesterday. Met George Wood at the river crossing at the upper part of the Meadows, coming from Thunder Mt. with 13 head of horses,* [I am] *to winter 8 of his. No snow at the ranch, but snowed on us coming down.*

Cabin Creek (November 28 – December 31)

The day after Lu returns to the ranch, he has Bull take Bird and Bolley up to the Rush cabin to leave grub for the mail carrier Brewer. Lu goes down to the river with two other horses to help Wes, Jonas, and Wood across Big Creek on their way to the mines. Later he stows his pack outfit and sights in his new 30-30 rifle. On the 29th he *Went to work putting up wall cloth. I got white oil cloth to paper the house, got about half done. Looked after the new horses* [Wood's], *gave them sulpher and rosin, one of them is sick.* The next day he *Worked in the blacksmith shop most the day.*

December

December of 1901 is mostly snowy and cold, getting as low as 2 below, and, compared with other times, activities slow to a snail's pace. While Lu is away, Jake Galvino comes back to work but he stays only a short while longer and is replaced briefly by Tom Neighbors. Once Wes has taken care of business on Thunder Mountain, he leaves for Boise on December 8, before setting off by train for Gardiner, Montana. Jake spends much of his time cooking but works some on the cellar Lu is building. However, he quits abruptly on the 7th when Wes Ritchey and Bert Zeiber return and he learns they are headed for Warren the next day. Tom stops by on the 9th on his way to Thunder but stays around and helps with a number of tasks until the 16th.

Bull spends a lot of his time in the woods making rails for a fence Lu is planning to build in the spring, cutting logs, splitting sticks for roofing the cellar, and fixing the *Wagon Road* that goes up Cabin Creek from the ranch house to the woods. Some of the logs are intended for firewood and some for the cellar.

Lu botched the interior decorating job he had tried at the end of November, so on the 1st he tears it down and redoes it. Early in the month also, some stored root crops require attention. The turnips start to rot, destroying about a third of them. Bull and Jake sack up the rest and haul them up to the new cellar on the horse-drawn sled. Ten days later, the *root a bagas* present a similar problem. Another difficulty is that the *mountain rats are lugging off all our onions, set trap for them.* After Jake leaves, Lu is stuck doing the cooking again. One of Lu's other tasks is to check on the horses on Cave Creek. He also continues to treat Wood's old gray mare and brings her up to the haystack every day, waters her by hand, and regularly treats her with sulfur and rosin. Lu routinely bakes bread, drills and blasts rock out of the road to the woods, hauls logs down with a team, drives the cattle (eventually totaling 22) back up the river or up Cave Creek and gives them salt.

Lu hunts several times during the month. On the 12th he kills two deer with his new 30-30 Marlin and 2 days later *killed a fine deer with the Borchardt* rifle, *also a grouse* on Horse Mountain. Then on the 21st as he is coming over Vinegar Hill on the way from Cave Creek, he shoots another deer, *got a nice fat one, dragged it home with me, gutted it at the house so the dogs could have the entrals.* He also goes hunting Bighorn sheep a couple of times. On the 20th he writes, *Killed a ram sheep and the eagles got to working on it before I got back. Shot it twice, about 300 yards. Over 2 eagles were there when I came back, shot one of them, about 150 yards.* The ram's horns measure 14 3/4 inches around, so Lu skins out the head for mounting. After Bull brings in the carcass, they harvest the testicles and have *big oysters* for dinner. Lu works on the ram's head over the next week and gets it *all mounted with eyes and all.* The next day, he *saw an eagle up to where the sheep was. Went up to see if I could get a shot, got one, but it was a dim one. Missed at about 200 yards, shot to high. Saw some sheep and tried to get one, but to far off, wounded one, but don't know whether I killed any or not. I was shooting about 6 or 7 hundred yards. Took a trip across the hill to look with glasses after dinner, but could see nothing of them.*

Curley Brewer comes in the forenoon on Christmas eve with the mail and stays over night before heading to Warren. As usual, Lu spends the rest of the day reading mail and writing replies. He pays Curley $15 for the trip and sends five letters with him. On Christmas day, Lu has a bad cold and is not feeling well. He works a little on the wooden form for the sheep head he is mounting, takes in his washing, and generally spends the day tinkering around. On the 26th, he *Stayed in the house the rest of the day, felt to weak and sore to go out.* His cold continues to plague him through the rest of the month. On the 31st, he sees some sheep on the mountain. *Thought I would go up to see if I could get a picture . . . . I saw my pack outfit of horses but felt to bad to go any further, had not ought to of went that far.*

In November, Lu had noted simply that *Dan and Ben will stay out.* However, according to their grandniece, while Lu is focused on activities at the ranch, ". . . Ben and Dan spent the late fall and winter going to Pittsburgh, Michigan and Colorado where they were treated as celebrities." Prior to their trip, Dan had gotten engaged but his fiancé soon died. Later he proposed to another woman, then changed his mind, and she sued him for breach of contract. After all this, he decides to get away for a while and go back east with Ben to visit relatives and to advertise their gold discovery. Dave Burley, the passenger agent for the Oregon Short Line Railway thinks it will be good for business if they travel to Salt Lake City, Utah and set up an exhibit of gold from Thunder Mountain. In Pittsburgh, they meet with investors about their Sunnyside claims and are offered $100,000 for them. The investors are told that the Caswells intend to keep the property for at least another year and that it should be worth at least twice that of the Thunder Mountain claims. In Michigan, Ben and Dan visit relatives, including their uncle William and aunt Eliza Phillips and cousins.

Dan and Bertha Caswell shortly after their wedding (ISHS # P1987.28.51).

1902

Even as early as the start of 1902 a number of changes are evident in the lives and lifestyles of the Caswells and their partners. Ben and Dan are traveling in the East and, in the spring of 1902, Dan marries Bertha Phillips, his 32-year old first cousin, whom he meets there. Wes is in Montana courting his future wife Edith Spiker and A. O. is busy running his ranch and planning the construction of a magnificent house with which he hopes to win the heart of a woman he has his eye on. Only Lu continues on more-or-less as before and even his way of living soon undergoes significant change. No snowshoe trip is made to Warren this year because of increased mail service and an array of visitors providing contact with the outside. Also, he no longer needs to make extensive pack trips to the outside for supplies or to devote substantial amounts of time helping with the mining on Thunder Mountain. Lu's attention now focuses almost entirely on the Cabin Creek ranch and its operation and improvement. The garden is expanded and acres of produce are grown, especially root crops such as potatoes, carrots, beets, and rutabagas, in anticipation of selling them to the gold rushers. With the absence of his brothers and Wes, Lu becomes increasingly dependent on hired help and it changes in complexion. Although his long-time friend Bull initially stays on to work for Lu, he succumbs to the lure of Thunder Mountain in mid-May and is augmented and replaced by a cavalcade of mostly new people.

January – March

Cabin Creek (January 1 – March 22)

The winter seems colder and longer than usual. In mid-January it is cold enough that Lu goes over to the slough to try out his skates. By the 25th the river is *pretty well frozen over* and the following day the temperature is down to 12 below. However, 3 days later, Lu records *The coldest day* [16 below] *in the history of the thermometer*. On February 5, it is only 3 above at noon and has snowed 2 inches. Near the end of February, there is a glimmer of hope that an early spring is on its way with *Water running every where, snow about gone*, and deer feeding on some early shoots of grass. However, it turns cold again and remains so throughout most of March, including an all day storm on the 9th that drops about 4 inches of snow, interspersed with a few hopeful entries over the next few days such as: *Chickens gone to laying finally. Robin singing. Deer getting down for grass.* Lu's activities during the remainder of the winter are pretty much confined to the area around Cabin and Cave Creeks. He is raising over 20 head of cattle in addition to the Caswells' horses and Bull's horses and cows. Lu identifies his pack outfit as: Babe, Bird, Bolley, Browny, Daisy, Jim, Joley, Rily, Sandy, and Trixey. He also cares for several other groups of horses and some mules of George Wood, Jonas Fuller and Jack Roberts, Fred Holcomb, and C. E. Nickelson. Wood's bunch consists of 13 head, including the one in poor condition. Lu uses the flat across the river, as well as the Big Meadow at the mouth of Cabin Creek, Horse Mountain, and Cave Creek for pasture. However, he also feeds out an unusually large amount of hay in February and March, including a substantial portion that has been in the stack for 6 years. This goes mainly to animals that are kept around the barn and vicinity, such as the three milk cows, Lu's saddle horse Bell, the draft horses Deb and Poll, Browny—a utility horse of Lu's favored by Bull, and assorted sick and injured horses.

Lu gets through the winter mainly with the help of Bull, though they are aided by sporadic efforts from a newcomer Jim Nolan starting in February. Bull continues to spend a lot of his time during the winter working in the woods and hauling loads of bolts and rails (for future fencing) down to the ranch house with Browny but he also helps keep track of the cattle, helps with the chores (which, by February 5, include milking three cows), and performs a variety of other tasks like sawing firewood, cutting brush down by the barn and creek, partnering with Lu on the whipsaw to cut out wagon axles and bolsters, making a shed of slabs for the milk cows, and making fence posts, rails, and pickets. He is slowed and periodically "stove up" by rheumatism.

Jim Nolan has been making it on his own in Big Creek Country by hunting, trapping, and prospecting. However, he stops by Cabin Creek on February 6 and welcomes the opportunity for a break from the rigors of camping alone and subsisting on a largely meat diet and agrees to spend some time working at the ranch. First though, he spends a day *to gather up his things, he has scattered over the hills* and another day to get his pack at the upper forks of Cabin Creek. Jim is a good addition. He is versatile, requires little direction, puts out good effort, and can work on his own or together with Bull. He is around for 10 days before leaving for Monumental to do some prospecting. He returns briefly after four days and then goes back until March 5. He takes another day off on the 10th to go check his cache at Rush Creek. Among his various jobs he sorts potatoes and cabbages, cuts and splits fire wood, files the whip saw, helps Bull in the woods, makes pickets, digs rutabagas, and clears brush.

Cort comes down Big Creek from Thunder Mountain on January 5 for a short visit but leaves again by way of Rush Creek on the 9th. Lu reports that on the 7th *Cort went up and helped* [Bull] *cut a tree and run around over the hills then roared about sore feet.* Cort stops by the ranch again on February 18 with a man named Dan Colter [Cotter] and the next day goes up Cave Creek 2 miles to make what Lu thought was a *locations placer.* However, when Cort registers his action on the 26th, he files both a placer and a quartz claim and includes W. D. Bull as partner. On the 20th Cort and Cotter head up Big Creek and probably out of the backcountry.

When Ben and Dan left suddenly the previous autumn and did not return, Cort may have gotten a bit lonely and strapped for cash. He is not mentioned again in Lu's diaries but must have left the region soon after because on May 28 he marries Maude Lotus Griggs, one month shy of her 19th birthday, in Clarksville, Texas. Clarksville is only 35 miles by road southeast of Manchester, Texas where Cort had lived for several years with his parents and half sister before embarking for Idaho. After the wedding, Cort reportedly returns to Idaho with his wife. He puts Maud up in a Boise hotel and returns to Thunder Mountain for a while. This does not set well with her. They leave soon after and are residing near Cort's childhood home in Volinia, Michigan by the time their first child is born on September 7, 1903.

The arrival and departure of the mail to this remote outpost is always a major event but in 1902 becomes more frequent and less haphazard than in the past with the apparent institution of a "regular" paid carrier. The mail in the winter of 1902 arrives each month at the beginning of the third week and is carried in succession by Charley Meyers, Babendorf, and Claud Lockwood, who stay only one night on each visit before heading back to Warren. On the January delivery, Bull sends out two letters and Lu 14, including renewals for his two newspapers The Post Intelligence and Deseret News and a packet of Kodak film. In February, Lu sends out more letters, including a $15 check to Brewer for Ben, and packages of film and furs. In March, Lockwood brings in a special letter and returns with some signed papers so Lu pays him $50 for the trip! One other visitor is recorded during this period. On March 7, a man named P. (Pat) H. Rosche comes down from Thunder Mountain with some flour and returns the next day.

In addition to the routine tending of the livestock, Lu has to contend with an unusual number of ill or injured horses that require special, time-consuming care. George Wood's old gray mare with an injured leg requires the most attention. Lu often moves her to the haystack for better feed and waters her daily. At the end of January, Bell sprains an ankle and Lu puts balsam on it and wraps it, then checks on it periodically over the course of a week. However, she remains out of commission much of February. On February 10, Browny becomes sick and has to be treated with drenches but is back working within a week. In early March, Lu finds his horse Daisy on Cave Creek with a broken leg and has to shoot her. He later uses her carcass to bait a bear trap.

Often Lu's primary purpose is tending the livestock and the taking of animals, if it occurs, is secondary, as on a trip to Cave Creek on January 8th to check on the horses, when he kills an eagle from his horse with a pistol. However, there are a number of times when the taking of game or fur-bearers is the primary object and during the winter he records setting out or checking on poisoned bait for *lyons* (cougar); killing Bighorn sheep (one at 200 yards another at 190) using the entrails for bait and bringing home the rest to eat; and going after deer. Some of the places he traps and hunts seem to have no modern counterpart, such as *Brown Horse Range* and *Sheep Gulch.*

In most situations, if a dog of Lu's is caught chasing deer, he whips, shoots at, or kills it. For example, on February 1st Lu recounted that *Jack and Bell, the dogs, chased off some deer on the hill across the creek. I gave Bell a good sound thrashing, also old Jack a clout of the whip.* On the 4th, on a trip to salt the horses and cattle, he took the level of retribution up another notch: *Bell broke after deer, stopped her by shooting at her.* However, just a few days earlier, Lu described a hunt where he actually encouraged one his dogs to go after deer. *Saw some fine deer across the river, thought I would avail my opportunity by getting over the pup* [presumably the stag hound pup he purchased in August 1901], [the dog] *run it in to the river,* [the deer] *went under the ice and didn't come out for 200 yards, but got it just the same. Killed it with the Borchardt.*

Lu has acquired a new 32 caliber Marlin and tests it by shooting a squirrel offhand at 40 paces. He also shoots into a piece of knotty wood and finds that it penetrates 22 ½ inches. Finally in February, he has an opportunity to try it out on a large animal. The previous day he had found a deer carcass that coyotes had been feeding on. Then, on the 5th he *Went down to the carcas and shot a coyote, the first coyote for the new gun and the first shot at in daylight with it. Had quite a circus with the dogs, both got bit, Bell got mad and wanted to eat him. Brought it home. Skinned out the coyote and washed the blood off.* When Lu went back two days later to check the bait he *killed an other coyote, shot him between 2 & 3 hundred yards.* Lu gets another opportunity to test the rifle at the beginning of March when he: *Went up to the mouth of Cave Creek and killed a deer, shot in mistake for sheep, took* [the horse] *Bell and went up after it, after dinner.*

On March 3, Lu writes *Bull and the dog treed a cat on the river in the rocks. I went down to see if I could get him, but can not get to where he is, so will have to set a trap for him.* The next day, Lu sets two No. 4

traps for the cat. When he checks a week later, there is no sign of the cat having been around but within the next two days it comes back and is caught. Then, presumably because Bull saw the cat first, Lu makes him go up and bring it in.

As always, Lu has a couple of large new projects, as well as several smaller ones, to occupy his "spare" time. This winter the larger projects involve working on another hot bed, making a horse-drawn wagon for hauling logs, and refurbishing one flour chest and making another. Work on the wagon involves primarily the axles and a pair of logging bolsters and takes over a month, starting on January 19. After the wooden axles are dressed out, Lu fits them with iron skeins that fit into the wheels and hold them on. He breaks one of the skeins, tries repairing it, gets it too hot and ruins it, and has to send for another.

Once the axle and wheel combinations ("trucks") have been completed except for the broken skein, Lu begins working on the "logging bolster," a set of inter-digitating iron plates. Both plates are held in place by king bolts, which requires that holes be drilled in the plates—a time consuming task. The two plates are arranged in such a way that the top plate, which supports a crossbeam, rotates on the bottom plate and facilitates the hauling of long loads on winding roads. Apparently Lu made both front and hind bolsters and mounted them on the wheeled-axles he had made earlier, completing the job in only 15 days. During the same interval, he teams up with Jim and Bull and they put a log on the saw pit and use the whipsaw to cut out a brake stick, 2-inch plank, and some boards for the bolster cart and also several wagon and mower tongues.

Pat Rosche's arrival with flour on March 7th brought on the realization that mice had been gnawing on the existing flour box and that its capacity was inadequate for the additional flour. As a result, Lu overhauled the old flour box and built a new "flour chest"—a job that extended through the remainder of the month.

Lu continues to do most or all of the cooking. He also busies himself during the winter with completing a number of repairs and other minor tasks. He makes a singletree hook; fixes a split in the wagon tongue; makes a shelf for the clock; repairs the grindstone and sharpens several axes, a hand axe, a foot adz, a chisel, and the bit for his bench plane; remodels his new horse hide chaps; and rebuilds Bull's plow. In March, there is additional action at the saw pit and, between Lu, Bull, and Jim working in pairs, they get out twelve "sticks" to make a harrow bed and fourteen 12-foot long boards. Near the end of the month, Lu shows Jim a spot on the other side of Big Creek about 1 ½ miles from the cabin where he wants a hole dug. Lu uses the hole as the basis for establishing his "Cousin Nell" quartz claim.

Thunder Mountain (March 23 – 28)

When the mail comes in on 21 March, it includes an important letter, presumably from Ben, relating that agreement has been reached with the Belle of Thunder Mountain Mining Company from Pittsburgh to sell their Sunnyside mining claims for $125,000. The deal will be finalized on May 16, when the four original partners (Ritchey is not included) receive a check for $75,000 telegraphed to the Boise National Bank. The remaining $50,000 will be paid out July 1. The sale is brokered by Martin Curran, a close friend of Ben's. Both payments involve bank transfers and it is clear from Lu's diaries that he is not in Boise at the time; probably none of the other partners is either. The company also purchases an adjacent set of claims from their friend F. W. Holcomb of Salmon City and his partners for $65,000.

Dan and Ben are still in Boise, so it is left to Lu to go to Thunder Mountain to deal with some important business related to the sale of the claims. Gold rushers are all around and the Dewey Mill is in place. Lu apparently goes on foot up Big Creek and then up Monumental Creek on crusted snow and ice and so is able to make good time in spite of stormy conditions. He takes a 25 pound pack and sets off before 8 AM on the 23rd, reaches the *Wickey Up* by midday, stops for dinner, and gets to Taylor's cabin at 6:15 PM. He encounters several men on the way including one who is ill. Lu reaches the Dewey Mill at 1 PM the next day, has a look around, and speaks with T. D. Babbitt, who is now the chief engineer for

Dewey on Thunder Mountain. However, Lu hangs around the Caswell cabin all the following day because he is not feeling well.

The specific objective of Lu's trip is to: *Put up Water Notice on Sunny Side. Had them sealed, also Power of Attorney, recorded placer notice.* That done he *Looked over the mountain, 5 feet of snow on summit. 3 ½ feet below the mill.* On the 27th Lu *Cleared things up, took breakfast at the* [Dewey Mill] *boarding house. Put pack on my back and started for home, stopped at the Taylor cabin.* There are eight prospectors at the cabin that night, including Billey Dow, who accompanies Lu the next day as far as the Wickiup. Bill Garten, an eventual resident in the vicinity of Ritchey's Big Creek ranch, arrives while they are having lunch. When Lu leaves, he estimates that about a dozen men will spend the night there and he also sees *Lots of men on the trail.* One of these is Pat Rosche packing a deer on his back and accompanied by another man with a mule loaded with grub. In spite of poor traveling conditions, Lu makes it to the ranch in 6 hours and 25 minutes, compared to the 5 hours it took him going up, and he arrives just as Bull and Nolan are finishing supper.

Cabin Creek (March 29 – June 24)

After his return, Lu has a couple of leisurely days at the ranch in which he finishes up the flour chest (and later installs it in the storehouse), hauls the last of the hay out of the old stack, and writes a couple of letters. During the same interval, Jim Nolan cuts decking for the bridge, Bull hauls it to the construction site, and Jim finishes the bridge a few days later. On Easter Sunday (March 30), they "relax" and Lu *Fried up 4 eggs apiece. Saddled up Bell and went up to salt the horses.* He finds the bear trap sprung again and attributes it to a "2-legged bear." *Jim and Bull went up to cut and snake poles* [i.e., pull them out with the horses]. *Jim set a post below the house on ditch and repaired the fence.*

April-May

With the beginning of April and the arrival of two additional

Dewey mine and gold mill, at the base of the "Golden Reef," built after the Caswells and their two partners sold their first set of claims to a group of investors headed by W. H. Dewey. (ISHS # P1994.25.51 Hanmer Collection).

Rebecca Caswell on horseback in lower left, approaching the Caswells' Mysterious Slide cabin on Mule Creek. Dewey mine and mill and Golden Reef are evident in the background. (Photograph courtesy Stewart E. Taylor).

hired hands from Bear, Joe Warner and Wallace MacFerry, the pace of activities accelerates rapidly. One other person, John Graham, whom Lu describes variously as an *old fellow* and *slow as old Jobe*, comes down from Thunder on April 17 looking for work and stays on until May 10. John cleans ditch, sorts seed potatoes, picks rock off the fields, and helps some of the other hands in the short time he is there.

On April 5th, Nolan departs down Big Creek on foot to visit his home in Salmon and Bull goes along as far as Trail Creek to look for pasture for his cows. Before he leaves Nolan receives $74.40 in pay. Near the mouth of Trail Creek, Bull may have set eyes on the lush meadows on either side of Big Creek for the first time and liked what he saw because he overwinters his stock there.

The main focuses of work during the remainder of the spring are on an extensive fencing project, plowing and planting field and garden crops, and construction of a major new irrigation ditch. In addition to the crops, a variety of fruit trees are planted, mainly by Bull. These include well over two dozen plum trees and two dozen apple trees, a peach tree, and two pear trees.

Lu began anticipating the planting season in early March when he started making the hot bed. On April 4, he notices the grass is beginning to green up. Time is rapidly approaching for preparing the garden plots and fields but first he must complete the picket fence and repair the wagon, plow, and harrow. In early April, Lu puts in a new axle in the wagon and cuts down the wagon box (with the help of Wallace and Joe). On the 6th he writes *went up to the woods and got a load of poles on the new trucks. They run good.* Thus, he has begun using the "bolster wagon" he built earlier. And on the 9th, after hauling another load of poles for the meadow fence, he *Rigged up the wagon to haul pickets.*

Lu builds the harrow frame during the first two weeks of April. This includes making over two dozen metal bolts and nuts and threading them, to use for harrow teeth. Meanwhile, he fixes up the old plow by putting a new shoe and sand side on it. Then he tests it by plowing the onion patch. After finishing the harrow on the 15th, he hitches the horses up and harrows and plants the onion patch.

Also, in mid-April, Bull and Joe renovate the meadow on Big Creek Flat by "clearing rubbish" (probably by burning the meadow) and then draining the meadow. The first godowns appear on April 8th. Lu views them as a threat to his crops and irrigation ditches and shoots a large number of them periodically throughout April and May. On April the 17th he has a particularly good day and kills about 30 and does even better on the 25th, when he kills about 50 more.

The fencing project is a major effort and, at one time or another during April and the first 2 days in May, involves every one at the ranch and all but 4 days. For some reason, Lu chooses to continue to build a relatively labor-intensive and high-maintenance picket fence rather than, for example, a sawbuck-and-pole or split-rail type or barb wire, even though the fences are now a considerable distance from the ranch house.

Plowing and planting start on April 12, beginning with onions, but get into full swing on April 22, when the seed wheat is cleaned in preparation for planting it and plowing begins in earnest. Plowing finally ceases on May 7 but the main planting continues until about May 12, the same day Bull leaves with Tom Neighbors for Thunder Mountain. Some additional planting of garden crops occurs sporadically during the remainder of the month but attention mainly shifts to irrigating the crops already planted. Tilling brings plenty of rocks and roots to the surface, so an added task is to remove them from the fields. Wallace and John generally are the ones who "pick" or dig rock and "grub" roots, although on one occasion Lu *shot* [blasted] *2 that was to big to handle.* Lu, Bull, Joe, and Wallace drive the horses. Poll and Deb usually are the team employed for plowing and related jobs like harrowing, planking, and furrowing, but occasionally, when a second team is needed, Browny and Trailer or Jim and Bell also are used. Furrowing is done to direct the water to the plants during irrigation. On April 24, *Poll took the belley ake, got pretty sick. Gave her soda and linseed oil and acunite* and by the next day she was better.

The planting of onions and wheat is followed closely by alfalfa and oats, the latter three completed by May 4. Before planting, the wheat and oats are fanned to remove the chaff, soaked for several hours to enhance germination, and vitrioled to keep the seed from rotting in the cool, damp soil. Major planting of garden crops starts with cabbages on April 28, progresses through carrots, beets, peas, salsify, and parsnips (about 2 acres in all) on May 3 and 4 and concludes with more cabbages and onions, beans, rutabagas, sweet corn, and bush squash. Planting potatoes (about 2 ½ acres) begins May 8 and ends on the 12th. Lesser plantings include tomatoes and celery but all told the diversity is less than the previous year.

April and May see numerous visitors at the ranch, reflecting the increased traffic related to the pending gold rush. A couple of them are professional mail carriers and a few others volunteer the service but all stay at least overnight. Some, like Charley Campbell and Jonas Fuller, spend a day or two relaxing. Others, like Tom Neighbors help with the work. Dick Blackburn and Charley Curtis come down for vegetables and Lu sells them potatoes at 10 cents a pound. He also gives them some grub for a sick man, plus three letters and a roll of Kodak film to mail.

On May 10th, Tom Neighbors, George Wood, and a man named Wolf arrive from Thunder. A week earlier, Lu had taken Wood's horses up Cave Creek and found nothing amiss. But, when Wood goes to get them, he finds his bay horse dead. After paying Lu for pasturing his horses, he and Wolf head upriver with Wood's horses to go out. Tom has brought some fruit trees and he stays to help plant them, then leaves a day later for Thunder Mountain with Bull. Perhaps, he and Bull have decided to become partners. Bull leaves without apparent warning. This marks the end of his working at the ranch and considerable contribution to its success, although he continues to stop by occasionally to visit.

Near the end of May, Lu has another flood of visitors. Dan Cotter, Cort's friend, stops by with some mail on his way in from Boise before going on to Thunder. In the mean time, Tom Neighbors has come down from there, gets in on the visiting, and leaves "for home" the same day Cotter departs. Lu pays Tom $20 for a plow that currently is on the South Fork and will be brought in later. On the 29th a man named Sam Gundaken and his men come in from Thunder on their way north. Lu let Sam have an old saddle and Bull's horse Trotter to ride out and they leave the next day by way of Chamberlain Basin. After this, Lu seems to give up keeping track of individual people and simply writes *Lot's of outfits coming from Salmon with horses.* The rush for gold by newcomers is beginning to accelerate.

Lu decides on an ambitious project to build a hillside ditch on Cabin Creek, running along the east side of the valley from Cow Creek to Spring Creek, to provide additional irrigation water for fields east and south of the ranch house. As usual, the project is done amidst a myriad of other activities that keep Lu hopping. Fortunately, he is able to recruit an additional crew of men to do most of the work. In addition to Lu, who oversees the project and keeps the tools sharp, and Joe (who assists Lu, does the cooking for the whole ranch, and keeps up the house and chores), eventually a total of ten others are involved: seven work on the ditch and three on a professional survey crew.

Lu and Joe do the initial survey and lay out the line for the ditch, starting on May 12th. They encounter a bluff on the first try and have to drop down and rerun the line. Next they clear away the brush and Lu uses Browny and Trailer to plow the ground where the ditch will go, finishing on the 19th. The other men dig out the dirt and remove rocks. The work is pretty routine until the 20th, when they are slowed by rain, wet snow, and cold. On the 21st Lu and Joe survey the bottom of the ditch and conclude considerable work is still needed. Some places are solid rock and on the 22nd, Bob Skinner, one of the recruits is given the responsibility for blasting it.

The professional surveyors arrive on the 23rd and Lu keeps a close eye on their work. *Followed them all day to see that it was done right. They run 3 surveys before they got it right.* He also has them survey-in the location for a future tunnel. Lu pays them $30 the next day for their work and equipment and for recording the water right. Then he takes them over to Cave Creek to record the water right there at an additional cost.

Water is started through the ditch on the 24th and by the next day it has come half way, in spite of a big break due to ground squirrel burrows. Both Skinner and another recruit get sick to their stomachs on the 30th from what Lu attributes to drinking warm water out of the ditch. The job is completed at day's end on June 1. All of the recruits are paid off and leave on the 2nd, except for Skinner, who apparently takes an additional day to finish blasting.

June-August

The summer months are as busy as the spring but show a distinct shift in the kinds of events involved. With the receding of snow from the high elevations, there is a stream of new faces passing by the ranch between June 1 and July 21 on their way to or from Thunder Mountain. Lu refers to these gold stampeders as "campers" and they come from Dixie, across the main Salmon River to the north and down Cave Creek, from Salmon City to the east probably via Trail Creek, or from Thunder Mountain by descending Canyon Creek just opposite the ranch. They thread their ways onto and off of the mountain like ants at a picnic, hoping to lay claim to the remaining crumbs of prospects. The rush provides a market for vegetables, milk, and cattle raised at the ranch. Examples of the fare provided and the prices charged include 5 gallons of milk for $1.20, 10 pounds of potatoes or more at 10—15 cents per pound, radishes, turnips, strawberries, sugar, and meat. Occasionally, Lu will buy or trade for items from the visitors, e.g., potatoes plus cash for beans. Many other groups stop off at the ranch for equipment and supplies, to obtain help crossing the river, or to sharpen tools. Requests for packing loads across Big Creek become so voluminous that Lu begins charging 50 cents per load. Often Lu writes that he let an individual or group "have" milk or grub or some other item and it is not always clear whether the exchange is free or for cash but probably is usually the latter.

On June 9, two groups arrive but decide not to cross until the river level drops, then the next day they begin work on a bridge. They finish construction on the 11th but when Lu goes down to check it out he assesses it as *A pretty stringy thing.* The next day he *Went down and helped the campers put their horses across the river. Pinned the bridge so they could take their ropes off. River going down.* [Joe] *Went down and helped me some on the bridge. I had to get in the water up to my hips to pin brasers* [bracers] *on.* On the 23rd Lu notes that *The flat is covered with campers* and becomes concerned about losing horses. So on the 24th, he *Hunted up all of the horses: took* [wrote] *down some brands, brought in part of them and kept them in the corral till night.* During early July, Lu observes four to ten camps or tents and up to 25 horses on the river on any one day.

Several other main groups of ranch activities also stand out. These relate to irrigation of crops (for which Joe has primary responsibility) and maintenance of existing ditches, setting out additional plants, digging a ditch on Cave Creek, and haying. Breaks and filling up with sand, occur in both old and new ditches. Problems with the new irrigation ditch involve loss of water into the porous soil, muddy water, and bank cave ins. All require time and effort to address. In addition there is another, smaller fencing project. Interspersed among the major activities are others such as herding the cattle to keep them on the south side of Big Creek, checking on the horses, killing more godowns, and thinning and weeding plants. It is a real 3-ring circus because many events overlap and are further confounded by the comings and goings of many individuals and groups.

Besides visits from the "campers," Wood comes down on June 9 to retrieve some steers and Bull's horses, but the river is too high to get them across. Instead, Wallace MacFerry returns 2 weeks later to complete the job and stays another day to help thin carrots. Between Wood's and MacFerry's appearances, Jim Nolan reappears on June 13 when he comes down from Thunder Mountain with two companions. John Cameron and his son Angus are in need of work and Lu hires them for a little over a week to help with some of the less demanding chores, including thinning vegetables, pulling weeds, and digging ditch. John plays out after 5 days but Angus stays on another four. John receives $6.30 in wages and Angus $14.15. Meanwhile, Lu recruits Nolan to go out for the mail. He returns on the 22nd and is paid $50 for the trip. He also brings in "old Suse," a horse that had been missing since the previous fall, and Lu soon pickets her so she won't wander off with some of the "campers." Nolan, MacFerry, and the Camerons all depart about the same time at the end of June.

Cave Creek has become an essential area to the ranch for grazing horses and cattle, especially during the winter. For some time, Lu has been concerned about losing access to the valley to newcomers and has taken various steps to establish claims to mining and water rights. On June 15, he sends Joe and the Camerons over to dig three holes and thereby do *the representing work on the claims on Cave Creek.* In late June, he further asserts his claim to the valley by initiating construction of a quarter-mile (80 rods) long irrigation ditch and pays John McCoy and Mike Powers $2 per rod to dig it.

Thunder Mountain (June 25 – 28)

After getting the ditch started, Lu fits in a quick trip to the Dewey Mine to sell a large amount of root crops from the previous year's harvest. Joe accompanies him. They pack up 12 horses with 1743 pounds of potatoes and rutabagas and make it to the Rush Creek cabin in 6 ½ hours. Lu notes that there are several outfits already camped there. The next day, they arrive at the Dewey Mine around 4 PM and Lu has letters from Dan and Wes awaiting him at T. M. d'Atry's. One can imagine that the letters inform him of Dan and Wes' marriages. He may also learn that Dan is building a house and starting a new business in Boise and that Wes plans on visiting the ranch with his new bride in mid-August.

Sold all of the potatoes to Erwin [Frederic Irwin] *the superintendent for 15 cents a pound. Loaded up with provisions* [probably at Roosevelt] *and got back about ½ mile below Trap Creek at 7 o'clock. Feed very scarce. Bull was at the* [Burnt Flat?] *cabin and fellow took my picture. A town* [has sprung up] *at West Fork. Saw Bert Zeiber going out, tipsey as usual.* Lu *Packed up and started at 9:15* [on the 27th], *got to Rush Creek cabin at 2:30. A Salmon* [City] *outfit camped there, one woman with them. I bought 3 pair of* [horse]*shoes of a fellow,* [who] *came in loaded with shoes, nails and potatoes.* Lu and Joe arrive home the next day and find *An outfit was here, shoeing horses, that claimed to know me, but* [I] *didn't renew the acquaintance.*

Cabin Creek (June 29 – August 18)

The day after Lu returns to the ranch, he resumes his attention to the ditch project and rides Bell *up to see how the ditchers on Cave Creek was coming on. Had about a dozen rods of ditch dug.* He returns 2 days later and observes that the men still have a little blasting left to do. The ditchers finish the job on the 5th and the next day Lu settles up with them for $156.30 after deducting the amount for items they purchased.

One of Lu's diary entries on July 1 is *Billey Dow dead at Thunder Mt.* Lu had met Billey on Monumental Creek on his trip to Thunder Mountain in March and Billey had stopped by the ranch on June 11 with another man to get some potatoes. Billey was about 30 years old and had a camp on an upper branch of Rush Creek. About mid-June he was found lying delirious near the creek, where he evidently had crawled for water and was unable to get back to his camp. The two men who found him brought him about 12 miles on a horse-borne litter to the Dewey mill where he died about 2 days later and was buried near the mill.

On July 6, Lu notes that he *Built a grade up the hill across from the Brown's flat to haul timber for a new fence.* Interspersed over the next five weeks, he and Joe haul poles, posts, and picket bolts with one of the teams of horses and Wallace, Joe, and eventually Bert Scott (who comes down with MacFerry on August 2 and goes to work for Lu) dig and occasionally blast post holes and otherwise work on the fence until finished on August 13th.

About a week after Lu returns from the Dewey mine, the Brack outfit comes in with a pack-string load that includes a new mower. Apparently the ones Lu purchased the previous summer haven't worked out. He assembles the mower in a day then makes a tongue (then has to lengthen it by splicing) and adds a tool box. On July 15th he *Hitched up to the mower and went down to cut hay. Had a reck, got a bolt in rong. Joe came up and got an other. Worked fine.* A considerable amount of the grass can't be reached with the mower and must be cut by hand with a scythe.

After the downed grass is cured for a day or so, it is collected into rows with the horse-drawn rake, "cocked up" into piles and pitched by hand onto the wagon, then hand-loaded on to a stack, and covered with a canvas. Lu uses Browny to rake hay and Poll and Deb to haul it and probably to mow. The job requires the efforts of several men and takes over 2 weeks. Lu, Joe, and Wallace, do most of the work but on the 23rd Walter Davis is hired to help and Jim Nolan joins them later.

On the 24th Lu cuts the last of the hay he can reach with the mower and Wallace goes to work on the remaining patches with a scythe. Wallace gets some assistance from Davis but does most of the hand-cutting and then quits to start packing vegetables to Thunder for sale. Lu operates the horse-drawn rake and finishes gathering all he can by that means on the 28th. Joe and Davis put up and haul most of the hay with some help from Jim. Jim puts up some of the loose hay in the field and builds a fence around the hay stack. Joe and Davis finish hauling and stacking hay on the 30th. In his notes, Lu accounts for over 10 loads of hay.

In late July Wallace MacFerry begins purchasing vegetables from Lu and packing them to Thunder to sell. He makes several trips and also carries mail and other items. MacFerry apparently leaves during the second week in August, possibly to return to Bear. After he leaves, Tom Kirk takes over the delivery of vegetables. Tom first appears in late July when he has Lu examine his prospects (ledges) across Big Creek and help determine their value. During August and early September, Kirk packs up four loads of vegetables totaling about 2500 pounds to Thunder Mountain and in exchange brings three loads of supplies down (probably from Roosevelt) for Lu.

The last day of July, Jim Nolan and Walter Davis leave for Cottonwood Creek for a week. When they return, Lu swears Nolan in as a deputy game warden and also hires him to prospect the Caswells' placer on Monumental Creek with Davis' assistance. Davis returns with Nolan's horses 2 days later and, on August 12th, *Jim Nolan came down from Monumental, said there was no use sinking holes there. Pay was in the creek bed. He brought a prospect with him, nice gold all right.*

On August 13th, Ben, Wes, and Wes' wife arrive from Boise with a pack outfit. Wes married Edith Spiker in late April in Montana and she is already carrying his baby. This brief visit is the only record of Ben or Wes being in Big Creek country all year.

Wes and Edith Ritchey with Ben on the porch of Elkhorn Cabin during their honeymoon trip to Big Creek Country (Photograph courtesy of Stewart E. Taylor).

Over the next 2 days, Wes and Edith cook while the others work around the ranch. Lu and Joe shoe a total of nine horses to take as far as Bear, while Lu goes on to Boise. *We then rigged up the scales and weighed some of my horses. Babe weighed 1030 pounds, Jolley 1275, Bird 1170, Trix 1050, Barney 975, Bay Bolley 911. Bert burnt the straw from wheat . . . the other boys worked on the cellar. Ben went over and got some samples from the ledge across the river and pounded them.*

Before he leaves for Boise on August 16th, Lu has several last minute tasks to get done and he is held up by *the hardest rain of the season,* on the 17th, that leaves things *to wet to start* until the 19th. On the 18th, he cut most of the oats because Bert couldn't get the hang of using the grain cradle.

When Lu leaves, it is for the first time in over 10 months. He apparently expects to be gone for an extended period. He must feel a bit apprehensive because he is leaving the care of the ranch in the hands of Walter Davis and Bert Scott whom he has known only a short time—Davis since July 23 (except for a brief acquaintance in September 1901, when he was helping pack for Meyers) and Scott since August 2. However, neither side could be anticipating how long he actually will be away.

To Boise and West Coast via Warren (August 19, 1902 – January 30, 1903)

The remainder of the year is covered by a single entry in Lu's diary dated August 19 but apparently post-dated and actually written after Lu returns to the ranch in February 1903. *Started out with my outfit for Boise. Went through to Bear in 4 days. Joe Warren* [Warner] *went with me.* Lu takes the stage from Bear to Council and then catches the train to Boise. No mention is made of Ben, Wes, or Edith, who presumably stayed behind for a while longer and/or travel separately. Wes and Edith eventually go up to Wes' cabin on Thunder Mountain and stay until October. Davis and Scott remain at the ranch until October 8 and each receives $98 for his labor. By the time they leave, Joe's brother Amos Warner comes in to replace them.

In Boise, Lu stays with Dan and his new wife Bertha. He first attends to purchasing supplies and equipment for the ranch and arranges for Orr and Horn to haul it to Warren by wagon and then pack it the rest of the way. He later pays them $316.97 for their services. *Dan went over and got my pack outfit and over took the teams and took a load with them. I in the mean time got acquainted with a young lady by the name of Rebecca Hays.*

September – November

While in Boise, Lu looks for some real estate to invest in. On September 6 he visits the home of Mrs. Joseph H. (Helen) Hutchinson and family; a realtor, she hopes to interest him in a house she has

Luman and Rebecca Caswell (Photograph courtesy of Stewart E. Taylor).

for sale. While there, he happens to see a large picture of an attractive young woman who, Mrs. Hutchinson explains, is her younger sister Rebecca Hays, daughter of Judge Hays.

Lu immediately responds, half jokingly, that she is the one he wants to marry. She is in the hospital at the time but is about to be released. Her doctor Jack Taylor, stops in to visit the Hutchinsons while Lu is there and goes along with a plan for Lu to meet Rebecca. One thing leads to another and Lu quickly finds himself calling on Rebecca in the hospital that same day in Dr. Taylor's buggy. Rebecca is a good sport and agrees to go for a ride. The two hit it off and on the third ride, Lu proposes to her and she accepts.

In a curious twist of fate, though Lu can not have known it at the time and may never realize, Rebecca's father Judge Charles Marshall Hays had been a close associate of W. H. Dewey some 20 years earlier. Dewey had helped him get elected as sheriff and then prosecutor of Silver City. As prosecutor, Hays had watched as Dewey beat a prior conviction for murder. Hays also had been editor of the Owyhee Avalanche, which Dewey had owned.

Because the time before Lu has to return to the ranch is limited, he and Rebecca are married on September 20th, 2 weeks after he proposed. They leave immediately afterward for the West Coast for an extended honeymoon and travel in a style befitting a man of means. They visit relations on both the Hays and Caswell sides, ranging from Los Angeles to Seattle. While in the Seattle area, they call on Lu's uncle German Rouse and Rebecca's aunt Parker. Lu makes arrangements with her aunt's husband Captain John Parker to build a ship, to be named the "Caswell," for $3,000. They are gone about 2 months but cut short part of their trip due to a recurrence of Rebecca's health problems.

After returning to Boise, around November 20th, Lu and Rebecca alternate between staying with Dan and Bertha in Boise and Rebecca's parents in Nampa. They buy a two-story, furnished house to live in, just behind one Dan is having built for himself. The house has been owned by Ben but he decided to sell after concluding he did not want to get married. Lu also purchases some rental property, a bicycle, and several Shetland ponies and generally spends his time adjusting to and enjoying his new circumstances. However, while he dallies through December in the State's "banana belt" around Boise, weather conditions in the mountains are growing harsh.

1903

January

Boise to Cabin Creek (January 19 – January 30)

Lu has a rough trip during the dead of winter returning to the ranch from Boise. Lu's new brother-in-law Charles Hays accompanies him from Boise but has to turn back at Elk Creek and stay a while with the Shiefers to recuperate before going on. It is to Charles' credit that he makes it as far as he does and that he doesn't give up but eventually completes the trip to the ranch. It also is a measure of how single-minded and tough Lu is in continuing on to the ranch. Lu takes the train to Council where he is met by Ben Baird, whom he has hired to come with him and take the horses as far as possible. They go *as far as the old fishery with sleighs, about 42 miles from the railroad. Then by toboggen and pack to about half way up Elk Creek to the summit. We then put packs on our backs and came through, letting Enos Smith* [take] *the horses on Warren summit, to haul the men that was killed in a snow slide some time ago.*

Cabin Creek (January 30 – May 25)

Baird went on after Charley, starting on the first of February. I have done nothing much but rest up and give my sores a chance to heal. Cleaning around the house. Amos Warner whome I have on the ranch was very glad to see us.

Lu arrives to find that Amos seems to have been overwhelmed by his job as interim caretaker and let things seriously deteriorate. Cows are dying and the ranch house and surrounds are like a pig sty. However, Amos is versatile and generally indispensable so Lu keeps him on. Lu must realize how fortunate he was to have Amos assume responsibility for the ranch in his absence and without the opportunity to learn first hand what was expected. Lu also must have appreciated that Amos has been alone at the ranch for at least three months.

The trip seems to have taken a lot out of Lu and, though he keeps busy for the rest of the winter, he stays close to the ranch and limits his activities to ones that are not too strenuous. During February, he regularly bakes bread and does much of the cooking. In the longer term, Lu seems to adopt more of a supervisory role this year and his diary entries for the ranch are as much a record of what the others who work or visit there do as it is of his own activities.

During the previous year, Lu contracted with Jim Nolan for $500 to construct a 170-foot tunnel as part of the irrigation system Lu is developing. Nolan starts before Lu returns to the ranch at the end of January and continues to work on it until completion in April. It is not clear where the tunnel is located but it is far enough away that he does not stay at the ranch at night. Nolan is trusted to proceed on his own. He rarely visits the ranch during this period and Lu uncharacteristically checks on his work only once. Tunneling obviously involves a lot of blasting and, when Nolan does visit, it usually is to obtain materials such as powder and fuse. Nolan still has 15 feet to go when Charles stops by at the end of March but he eventually breaks through on April 9 and, on April 11, *Nolan got the tunnel done. Packed the tools down and we settled up. Paid him $467.25 dollars.* The remainder of the promised pay apparently went to cover the cost of items that Jim purchased from Lu.

In addition to Amos Warner, Jim Nolan, and Charles Hays, Lu employs a number of part-time workers, beginning in early February and extending to mid June, when Amos is on his own again while Lu is away for 7 weeks when Rebecca has an operation. They generally are paid at the rate of $1/day. The name "Barney" appears a number of times in the diary this year starting on April 6. However, this actually is a nickname for Amos, rather than some additional helper.

The first of the new part-time workers is Rob Duncan who works every day for Lu for a little over a month. Rob stays at the ranch during that time but lives nearby with his wife and father and continues to visit after his job ends. However, Lu is not impressed with the quality of Rob's effort (he refers to him as a *putterer around*) and *lets him go* at the end of the month.

After finishing the tunnel, Jim Nolan drifts in and out of the ranch, including stays of 5 days at the end of April and a month in May to early June when he works on irrigation ditches and digs post holes. For one of the weeks in May, he teams up with a man known only as Diamond to cut lumber for a new addition to the cabin. Diamond, apparently lives near Jim and the Duncans. He first visits the ranch on May 7 with Rob Duncan to get grub but returns the next day to saw wood with Nolan. Diamond mainly helps Jim saw for the next dozen days but he periodically reappears either to obtain provisions or, in August and September, to haul vegetables to Thunder to sell. Jonas Fuller, a familiar face around the ranch, comes down from Thunder Mountain with the mail in late March and stays several days to work in the woods making rails and posts for fencing. He returns for the month of May to clean ditch and help plant potatoes before going back to Thunder Mountain. Al Wood, whose horses Lu has looked after in the past, helps out for a little over three weeks starting May 22, including a couple of weeks as a replacement after Jonas returns to Thunder. Another familiar face is Jake Galvino, who stops by from Placer Bar in early February to get vegetables and again at the end of April.

February

Lu resumes his daily entries on February 3rd, though that one and the others for the remaining week are included with the 1902 diary. February 3—*I hired a Rob* [Duncan] *to work . . . For $30.00 a month. Amos found one dead cow, he fed her last eve. but she wouldn't get up so she was dead today. Had him run the best ones up the country and put 3 more in at the stack. He also got a lion that we set bait for yesterday. They are killing some deer around, but I will stop that pretty quick. We brought up the hams of one for the dog.*

February 4—*Cleaned up around the house, a terrible dirty house, burnt up a lot of papers. Two cows died, one black cow I got of Bruce and the other black spotted cow I got of Bull. Took up 3 cows to feed. Amos drove the cows up fast and robed one. He and Rob hauled wood forenoon.*

5—*Cooked. Stretched a lion hide. Shod Bird. She was very sore footed. Amos and Rob took Bert's* [horses] *up to feed the cows, was gone all day.*

The weather continues to be bitter cold with Lu reporting 28 below on the morning of the 6th. *Started up to the horses to give them some oats, saw they were on top of Horse Mountain and came back. I was afraid if I went up there I would get to chafing again. My old sores are hardly well yet. Got up Bell, saddled her up and went to the lion bait.*

Enos Smith (instead of Ben Baird) arrives with Charley Hays on February 9, probably bringing the horses Lu had left in his care on Warren Summit. Lu pays Enos $50 for bringing Charley in. Within a few more days, the routine tasks of the regular helpers are sorted out and continue through the remainder of the month and into March: Amos looks after and cuts browse for and feeds the cattle and horses, Rob Duncan cuts logs and peels the bark from them for an addition to the house and then cuts fence posts, and Charley Hays helps cook and wash the dishes and eventually also assists Amos. Charles is not much of a hunter but by April 5 he will have killed two deer. Lu or Amos periodically checks the baits for lions and occasionally gets one.

It seems like an inordinate amount of their time is spent getting the livestock to feed, tending the ill ones, and disposing of the dead. Apparently livestock feed is in short supply. In order to supplement it, Lu often has the men, particularly Amos, cut shrubs or cottonwood shoots for the animals, give them root crops, or drive the cattle into stands of cottonwood. One specific location Lu mentions is *cottonwood springs* which could be a grove at the head of Spring Creek. The horses come in to be fed more than in the past. The horses also are taken up on *Sheep Mountain* as well as to the traditional range on Horse Mountain.

The sickness and death Lu encounters when he first arrives continues through February and into the first of March.

February 10—*Old Browny died with indigestion or collic. Doped him all the forenoon to no avail. Amos got up the mares and drug him up the flat.* 14 – *The little spotted cow had a calfe, it chilled to death.* 18 – *Amos drove in 2 more weak cows . . . .* 20 – *Amos . . . Brought in an other cow.* 22 – *We have got 2 sick calves now, had to puncture one, it blotted* [bloated] *so. Gave it some soda.* 23 – *The black calf died, we did all we could to save it, but to no avail.* 24 – *Got up Bell and put the saddle on her. Snaked the dead calf off. Amos drove the cattle over on Sick Gulch. Charles helped him.* March 1- *Worked on the 2 year old heifer, Jill, trying to pull her calf from her, but gave it up and had to kill her after all.*

Soon after arriving back at the ranch, Lu begins making arrangements to add a bedroom on the cabin, in anticipation Rebecca eventually will come to live there. Thus, at least some of the work to be done is to find and cut trees in the woods and haul them down to the cabin site. Additional effort is expended to cut firewood and harvest poles for fencing.

Lu's old friend Bull is a regular visitor during February. Apparently, he, Rob Robinson, and Joe Surprise, are sharing a camp in the vicinity of the mouths of Trail and Rush Creeks and overwintering their livestock there. Bull comes up to return a harness soon after Lu gets back, then shuttles between the ranch and Ritchey's cabin for about a week before going back down to his camp. Surprisingly for this time of the year, Bull and his associates seem to be making regular trips to Thunder Mountain too. Bull's colleagues appear to treat the ranch as a convenience store, stopping by to purchase vegetables, tobacco, and other sundries whenever they are in the area. However, there is no record of Bull ever visiting the ranch again. He must have gone back to Thunder Mountain or out to Warren, probably in the early spring, because he is not at his camp on Trail Creek when Lu visits in April. Also, Lu writes on May 13 that *Robinson came up and said Bull had got back.* Otherwise, nothing can be discerned about his whereabouts or fate from the diaries. Popular lore has it that the "Bull brothers" lived for a while at Trail Creek and may have later built a cabin there but this is not confirmed and is somewhat questionable because there is no mention in the diaries of a Bull brother ever being in the area.

Mail delivery during the month is somewhat haphazard with only one delivery by an official carrier. However, it also is fairly frequent due to the comings and goings of Bull's associate Robinson. Periodically, Lu records paying the mail carrier as on the 9th: *I paid the mail carrier 6 dollars for my mail, Amos paid $2.00. The rest are to pay two dollars each.*

Roosevelt, Idaho after the original tent city (erected in 1902)had been replaced by more substantial structures (Photograph from the Hanmer Collection ISHS # P1994.25.5).

On February 12, Lu notes that *a man by the name of Lewis Vogan came down from Roosevelt with the mail, got two letters from my wife and some papers.* The next day he adds *Wrote letters most of the day. Vogan went below.* There are two things of significance here outside of the nature of Lu's mail. One is that this is Lu's first specific mention of the new town. Between the summer of 1902 and mid 1903, the Thunder Mountain boom-town of Roosevelt expands from 1400 to over 7,000 people, from 7 to 14 saloons, and from one to two or three hotels, plus additional eating places and stores, and includes assayers, carpenters, doctors, dentists, lawyers, and undertakers. With the establishment of a post office at Roosevelt, it appears that most of Lu's mail now comes through there, rather than through Warren, transported by whichever visitor is coming from or bound for Thunder Mountain. The other significant point is that this is the first record of the mail carrier going down Big Creek further than Cabin Creek. In this case Vogan probably went down another 6 miles to Bull's winter camp. Between 1915 and 1918, this location will become the home of Cougar Dave Lewis, Lu and Ben's former neighbor on Big Bar on the Snake River, and much later the site of the University of Idaho's Wilderness Research Station.

Six days after the mail delivery by Vogan, *Joe Surprise brought down the mail. Got 2 letters from my wife, one from Dan, one from a stranger in Boise, one from the Deseret News.* One or more of the letters reveal that *Ben Caswell got married on the 12th of Feb.* With this announcement, four of the five partners have entered into life-changing agreements within 18 months of having sold their first set of claims. Over the following week, Lu pens a number of letters including several to his wife and others to his father, sister Melvina, cousin Helen Lake, and a couple of his wife's relatives—Elma and Irene. These are all given to Robinson, who is headed to Thunder the next day.

Lu does manage a modicum of repair and maintenance work during February. He sets up his combination and blacksmith's vices and works a lot in the shop sharpening all his blacksmith tools and over 10 picks and a crow bar and fitting up dozens of horseshoes. He also mends a halter rope, brazes a catch on the cupboard door, fixes up the peavey hook, and makes some pick handles.

March

The arrival of mail is always a big deal for Lu and when it comes he often drops everything else to attend to it, as on March 2nd: *The mail came in . . . just after noon. Read letters and papers the rest of the day, got several letters from my wife, 4 or 5 from Dan, one from my father-in-law, one from my cousin. Davis's wife had a girl baby. I paid Robinson 10.00 for mail,* [including for] *Charles and Amos.* As a consequence of these distractions, Lu accomplishes little else for the day except to cook.

Another interesting diversion for Lu and one that provides opportunity both for socializing and information transfer is afforded by visits from passers-by. These occasions occur for a variety of reasons but increasingly result from local awareness of supplies that can be purchased from Lu. For example, during March there are 8 days when such visits occur involving Robinson, Surprise, Nolan, or the Duncans, each two or more times, to obtain items ranging from butter, flour, potatoes, and bacon to catolene (similar to kerosene), coal, and tobacco. The Duncans also begin coming by to collect Lu's dirty clothes to wash in exchange for vegetables and butter and they obtain three spools of thread and some shears for mending clothes.

During March, harvesting trees and tending the livestock continue to be the two activities requiring the greatest amount of effort. Also, as in the previous month, the trees being cut and hauled to the cabin are mainly for house logs and fence rails. Amos is assisted by Rob Duncan initially and later by Charles. Poll, Deb, and Bell are used to snake the logs out of the woods and haul them in. The cows that are about to calve and others needing close attention are kept in or near the barn below the house but the main bunch is kept further away and fed almost daily on a nearby hill with a supplement of root crops. On the 8th, Lu observes that the cattle seem to be doing pretty well. The next day, the *bald face cow had a heifer calf* and toward the end of the month the rhone cow has a steer calf.

Only occasionally does Lu go hunting during the month and then mainly for meat. In one case he kills a buck at about 300 yards. However, throughout the month, Lu continues to bake bread and to chip away at the endless task of "repair and maintenance." Lu's versatility and creativity continue to find expression through his work in and around the shop. During the first half of the month he repairs a broken plow handle, the wheelbarrow, and a brace for the wagon box and marks a lot of his tools. In addition, he rebuilds the rack for the wagon, puts in a new stake, and makes a nut for the queen bolt. He makes a spear and two grab hooks and two links for log chains, replaces an axe handle, half-soles his gum boots, and sets up the hillside plow he had purchased from Tom Neighbours. He also makes a complete harness, including the back band and pairs of reins, traces, and tugs, and has it assembled and oiled within 5 days. During the second half of March, Lu rebuilds an old harness, makes a log toboggan, repairs a chair, mends his spurs and Deb's halter, and makes several more items with the forge, including another grab hook and a clevis and pin for the plow.

Early signs of spring are evident in Lu's urges to clean some of the outbuildings and the *door yard* around the cabin. During the second week of March, he straightens up the shed and has Amos clean out the chicken coop. The chickens also begin to lay during this spell. Then during the last week of the month, several days are spent cleaning up the yard area, including removing wood from around the house and re-stacking it in preparation for building the new addition.

In mid-March, Lu notices that some of the stored vegetables are in need of attention. He has Charles sort over the onions and help Amos sort potatoes to remove the spoiled ones. However, the cabbage is in the worst shape and requires more-drastic action. They trim up the cabbage heads to remove the rotten portions and cut up all the rest to make kraut. Lu washes and scalds two 5-gallon kegs and a barrel to hold the salty brew and estimates that the 20 gallons together hold 200 pounds of cabbage.

Jonas Fuller comes down from Thunder Mountain with the mail in late March. Among other things, Lu receives several letters from his wife and his garden seeds. Jonas spends the next day going down to check on his horses but then stays several days to help get the hotbed ready and to work in the woods with Lu and then Amos making rails and posts for fencing.

April

As in previous years, a large amount of time during the growing season is devoted to raising grain and garden crops, and to building and maintaining fences and, increasingly, the irrigation ditches. Relatively little time in April is devoted to fencing and is restricted to the first 2 weeks. Jonas splits out another 32 posts and 30 rails, Amos hauls in those and others already stockpiled, and Lu chars 103 posts to help preserve them. These materials are set aside for use in May.

The planting season starts this year on April 2nd when Lu *Cleaned the poles and brush and sun flowers off of the upper potato ground and Grubbed some stumps.* Next, Amos plows that area and Charles and Jonas dig up the onions so Amos can plow the patch. On the 7th, they plant the hot bed, finish plowing the oat ground, and plank the onions. Two days later, Amos finishes harrowing the oats, Lu cleans up the garden in the house yard, and Charles sets out two rows of onions. Amos continues to do the bulk of the plowing and also most of the harrowing, planking, rolling, and marking.

Lu has conceived the notion of making a "roller" to use for packing the fields before they are seeded. At the beginning of April, he has Amos and Jonas cut a log to serve as the actual roller. The first is too small but Lu finds a big pine that will do. They cut it, then have a tough time hauling it in. Next, Lu squares off the ends of the log with Jonas' help and builds a frame for it. He finishes on the 9th and immediately uses the new machine on the oats. He also has acquired a new combined seeder/cultivator and, after setting it up and testing it on some onions, uses it to sow the oats prior to harrowing them in. About this same time, the garden patch (presumably in the house door yard) is plowed and harrowed and Lu uses the seeder to drill in beet, lettuce, onion, parsnip, radish, and turnip seeds. However, on the 13th he specifically mentions Amos planting *the rest of upper garden in corn, melons & beans.* This "upper" garden presumably was located on the irrigated flat uphill from the 1895 cabin. In mid-April, they *set up the old marker and put the wagon tongue in it for 2 horses.* Lu adds a couple of plum trees to the orchard. Near the end of the month, the little hillside plow breaks and Amos has to use the big plow to finish plowing. They ultimately plant acres of oats and wheat and large areas of carrots, beets, onions, and rutabagas in fields separate from the two garden patches.

Work on the ditches begins April 2 and continues for about two months. Jim Nolan completes the tunnel on April 11, a few days later Lu hires Rob Robinson and Joe Surprise to dig a ditch extending from the tunnel, variously estimated as being 230 to 462 feet long. At the same time, Lu and Amos survey another ditch to go onto the oats. Lu repairs picks and sharpens picks and drills to facilitate the new work. Charles does most of the ditch cleaning, with occasional help from Jim Nolan, including an extended period at the end of April (for which Jim receives $15) and a day in May. Altogether, Charles spends most of 20 or more days during April doing ditch-work. Collectively he digs out over 200 feet of ditch in sections that have become choked with sand and rock or where the banks have caved in, often in stretches of 15 to 50 feet a day but sometimes, in bad sections, progressing only a few feet a day. Next, on eleven days during the first half of May, Jonas Fuller (who had returned at the end of April) "chars" out long stretches of ditch (including 580 feet on May 1) to clear out plant debris. Finally, during the first 3 days of June, Lu digs and otherwise cleans out the recently constructed "upper" ditch and gets water running through.

There is a surprising amount of traffic between Cabin Creek and Thunder Mountain during April, compared with previous years. Except for a man named Johnson, all of the visitors to the ranch are past acquaintances, notably Joe Surprise from further down Big Creek and Jim Nolan, but also Rob Duncan, Jonas Fuller, and Joe's frequent companion Rob Robinson. All play a role in transferring mail between the two points and, as a result deliveries and incentives for writing letters come fairly often. On one occasion Lu writes ten letters (compared to one each for Charles and Amos), on another five, and on the 29th he *Wrote letters most of the day.* There is only one record of payment for mail delivery this month—$5 to Surprise on April 3. An especially important letter from Rebecca arrives on April 11; indicating that she had undergone an apparently successful operation on March 24 in Portland, Oregon for a blocked uterus. Besides numerous letters to and from his wife, he receives one from his father and orders a book on the Rough Riders.

Joe Surprise occasionally buys goods from Lu, like a can of catolene or 100 pounds of flour and some fruit for $14. Jim Nolan purchases potatoes on one occasion and tobacco, coffee, and sugar on another. On April 9, Jim purchases quinine for his friend Robinson, who is sick. Rob Duncan stops by three times during the month to deliver Lu's washing and take back more for his wife to do, in exchange for vegetables. On the 22nd he also picks up mail to take to Thunder Mountain.

The burden of caring for the cattle eases as the snow recedes and grass appears. However, calving continues and, when Lu goes to check on them on the 19th, he finds that a black heifer has a day-old black spotted calf with her. Two days later when Amos goes back up to the cattle, he *found 2 dead, one the black cow and rhone. Black swamped and rhone rolled, couldn't find the black calf.* The next day, they *Went up to look for the calf, found it, the* [cow] *had it cached.* On the 23rd, Lu rides up to *4 mile*, gathers up the steers, and puts them on better feed across the river.

When the godowns emerge from their burrows in numbers in April, Lu finally provides a comparative basis for evaluating his marksmanship. On one occasion, when they all went hunting together, Lu got 20 compared to 9 for Amos and 2 for Charles. A few days later, Lu kills 16 with 18 shots and two days later he is 11 for 11 shots. In between these two times, he killed another 30 godowns and a hawk. They also find time for another, more profitable, pastime: fishing (or, as Lu more accurately terms it, salmon *hunting*). On one particularly memorable time, Lu and Amos *got 11 salmon, over one hundred pounds of fish.* They put them all in the smokehouse for curing over the next several days. Of course it doesn't all go smoothly. On the first try, the salmon fall down and have to be washed and a rack built for them. One notable catch occurs when Amos lands a *speckled trout about 14 inches long.*

In mid-month, Lu saddles up Bell and goes down Big Creek looking for a missing brown horse. He makes it all the way to Trail Creek without finding the horse. However, he is surprised to find instead that *Bull had my tent, mantas, and lots other stuff.*

The last week of April, Nolan comes up and has a long talk with Lu. The next day, Lu shoes Jim and Bolley, puts together a camping outfit, and goes back down Big Creek to check out Nolan's claim on Trail Creek. The claim is located about 2 miles up from Big Creek. Lu gets back to Bull's camp, near the mouth of Trail Creek, about 5 PM and finds Surprise and Robinson there. He stays overnight and returns to the ranch before noon. On the way down, he killed a mountain lion and left it but on the way back he loads it up and later skins it and stretches the hide.

Work on the new cabin addition progresses slowly during the month. Getting the long logs and twelve joists hauled down are important accomplishments. In mid-April, Lu notches the logs and cuts the mortises for the joists. With the frost finally out of the ground, Lu is able to put down the stone foundation and joists and begin laying up the log walls. With knowledge of Rebecca's successful surgery indicating they will be able to have children, he modifies his original plan and adds a second, smaller bedroom to serve as a nursery.

May

With the logs already staged and the foundation in place, Lu is able to make sporadic progress on the addition during May. He has four more rounds of house logs up by the 7th, then notches the logs on the 12th. During a ten-day period starting on the 9th, Nolan and Diamond team up to whipsaw lumber for flooring. They produce a total of 770 feet of boards from six logs in 4 full and 3 partial days of work. Lu works only a few more days on the house during this time but by the 25th, with the help of Jonas and Wood, the house is *covered* and the shakes on.

From April 28 to May 9, Amos prepares the *upper field* for planting potatoes and he, Jonas, and Lu plant both red and white varieties. Before planting, the white potatoes are cut into pieces but the reds are planted *whole seed*. After planting about an acre, they cut an additional eight sacks worth before continuing. Two weeks later, Amos prepares some more ground and they plant more potatoes. Also during May, Lu also sets out 13 plum trees and some cabbage and cauliflower plants, plants a lot of peas and radishes in the yard garden, has Nolan and Diamond sow onions, and, with Amos' help, plants sweet corn, cucumbers, melon, and squashes in the upper garden. Ever the optimist and longing for tomatoes, Lu sets out 58 tomato plants in the upper garden on May 15th. Not surprisingly for this growing zone, they all are killed by frost that night.

In May, Lu also undertakes the largest renovation and expansion of the meadow on Cabin Creek flat to date. It starts on the 4th when he *Commenced to fire the meadows, it burnt pretty well.* The work extends over 6 additional days to the 23rd when at various times Lu, Amos, Jonas, and Charles clean, clear, or otherwise remove brush.

Rob Duncan continues to visit the ranch at intervals of every 1 to 5 days. Lu writes that *Duncan came over . . . They are camped on the General Bar.* At other times he indicates that *Rob Duncan came down from Thunder.* He variously buys flour, potatoes, and other provisions and picks up or delivers the wash. On one occasion Duncan, his wife, and Diamond come over together. On another, *Surprise and Diamond was over and got some provision*, indicating that they all were camped in the same general area. However, on yet another time, Lu says *Surprise and Robinson came down and got 54 pounds of potatoes. They all went back up the river* which suggests some trading-around among locations.

Lu periodically engages in salmon hunting during the month. He spears three *fine ones* on the 4th; gets two more, weighing 23 pounds on the 5th; and three others on the 9th. He harvests another six fine ones the next day and finishes off the month with four more salmon on the 19th.

The fencing project for which Lu has been preparing begins to materialize during the month. Amos hauls the posts and rails, Charles digs holes and sets posts, and Amos and Jonas and Nolan and Charles pair up to attach the rails.

On the 19th, Lu notes that "the boys" *killed a deer in the onion patch, saved a ham and the loins.* The availability of fresh meat and the lack of a way to keep relatively large quantities away from flies, mice, and other pests, appear to motivate Lu to build a *meat cage*. The cage takes the equivalent of several full days to make. It probably is a large, rectangular container, with doors and shelves, and with the framework of the container, doors, and shelves covered with screening for circulation of air and to keep away flies and other animals. It is put to use as soon as it is finished.

The month ends with a flurry of last minute preparations to transport food items to Thunder Mountain and Roosevelt to sell. All available hands participate. Lu *Set light bread, put the outfit together and got ready to pack. Nolan patched up the riggin. Amos helped fix up and put lumber under cover. Jonas & Wood put the shakes on* the roof to the new addition and *finished cleaning the meadow. Nolan and Charles finished the fence. Amos, Jonas and Wood finished planting the potatoes.* The crew also gathers up potatoes and other remaining root crops from the previous growing season. The potatoes have been stored over winter in one or more pits, probably covered with straw. In mid-April, Amos and Charles remove most of the potatoes, sort and sack them, and place them in the cellar in anticipation of selling them to the miners. The goal had been to leave on the 25th but they do not quite make it and leave the next day instead.

Thunder Mountain (May 26 – 30)

The morning of May 26th, they pack up 13 horses with potatoes, parsnips, onions, the camp outfit, and their personal gear, and head for ready markets on Thunder. Jonas Fuller, Amos Warner, Jim Nolan, and Al Wood all go along to help with the pack string and drive seven steers. Charles stays behind to look after the ranch. They intend to take Amos' mule but she throws a fit and they pack Al Wood's mule instead. Still, they are on their way by 9:30 AM and make it to the Rush Creek cabin. They do better the next morning and are on the trail by 7:30 AM. They go over the summit above Milk Lake, through 3 feet of snow, pass down Milk Creek to Monumental Creek, and stop at noon just below where it is joined by Holy Terror Creek. There they set up camp. *We butchered the 2 big steers, Willie & Nuban, they dressed 694 & 699 respectively. Got done at dark.*

The following day, Lu gets Jake Galvino to tend camp for them and they *Packed up at 8 o'clock, 6 head with potatoes and 6 head with beef, went up to Roosevelt and the Dewey, sold all but had to hussel around to get rid of the stuff, got back at dark.* The next morning, they *Loaded up with the rest of the potatoes and took them up to Roosevelt & sold them, I went up to Thunder to get my pay for the beef, got back to camp just behind the boys* [i.e., Amos and others] *with the* [pack] *train.*

Most of the crew returns to the ranch on the 30th except Jonas Fuller. This is the last mention of Jonas by Lu. A short time later, having sold his H-Y Mine in 1902, he moves to Grangeville and dies there of heart failure, alone in a hotel, just before Christmas 1906. His obituary noted his "frank, openhearted manner" and his generosity toward other miners in distress.

Elk Horn Ranch (May 31 – June 14)

Upon returning, Lu cleans out a section of ditch, and with Al's help sets out cabbages and cauliflower. Amos and Jim have decided to build a boat to facilitate crossing Big Creek. They start sawing lumber for it as soon as they return. Al helps saw lumber but mainly gets busy making a riata or lariat rope from Willie's hide. He cuts out thin strips, stretches, then braids them. While Al is making a second rope, Lu makes three hondas out of sheep horns Rob Duncan has given him, to form and hold open the small loop or "eye" at one end of each rope.

June

Amos and Jim finish sawing lumber for the boat on June 1 and Jim immediately starts to build it. He finishes construction two days later and gathers up some pitch for caulking. An additional 2 days are spent making the oars. Jim oils and paints the boat on the 6th, loads it on the wagon, and uses the team to haul it to the bridge. The next day, Jim and Lu try out the boat. The river is very swift but they make it across and Lu discovers the tracks of the red cow he has been searching for. On the 8th, Jim starts for Thunder Mountain. Lu goes down to put him across in the boat but one or both of them think better of it and he crosses on the bridge instead.

A major push to complete the new addition to the house is implemented at the beginning of June and the bedrooms are ready for occupancy by mid-month. Lu lays the floor in the big bedroom on June 1 and in the little bedroom the next day and cuts the doorway between them. He continues working the next 3 full days followed by 3 half days. On the 9th, Al and Charles chink the walls and the next day everyone works on the house. On the 11th, Lu gets two doors hung and both windows in. The final touch, a writing table, is added the next day. Sadly, Rebecca proves to be more frail and attached to city life than Lu has anticipated and never comes to reside at or even visit the ranch.

Work on the garden continues during the first 2 weeks of the month. Undaunted by past catastrophes, Lu sets out another 100 or so tomato plants on June 1 and some more a week later and this time is successful. He also sets out the rest of the cabbage plants, cultivates the onions and other plants using the combined seeder/cultivator, thins the plants, and has the boys spend over a day sprouting potatoes. During this same interval, Amos and Al clean ditches and irrigate.

Nolan takes two letters and some film with him to Thunder for Lu. When he returns 2 days later on the 10th, he has a new man John Night with him, looking for horses. They visit the ranch again on the 12th before leaving. Diamond comes down with an associate on the 9th and gets a load of vegetables, including radishes and lettuce. Lu puts them back across the river in the boat. Lu spends most of the 14th getting ready to move. He also pays Al Wood for services to date and Al presumably leaves soon after.

To Boise and Portland (June 15 – August 4)

Lu and his wife have made plans to return to Portland for additional major surgery in early July. Lu leaves Amos Warner in charge of the ranch and on June 15th heads out to Boise and nearby Nampa with Charles Hays and Jim Nolan. They encounter a bad section of trail and make a major detour but eventually make it out of the backcountry and go on to Salmon Meadows. There they split up. Jim and Charles catch the stagecoach headed south, while Lu takes the pack string on to Bear and leaves it in care of the Warners. Then he goes on to Council and catches the train to Weiser, where he meets his wife, who is there with her mother. In the morning, they go to the Hays home in Nampa and in the evening "Becca," her sister Elma, and Lu continue on to Boise and spend the night. The next day, Lu introduces his wife to his folks, who have recently moved to town. *Started for Portland on the eve of the 28th to have Rebecca operated on for kidney and appendix trouble. Met Dr. Smith and had him examine her again. We set Friday the 3rd of July for the day.*

July

The surgery is successful, in spite of encountering some unexpected adhesions. Rebecca is hospitalized for about 3 weeks. On July 8, Ben arrives with two more of Rebecca's relatives and curiously continues on to southern Oregon the same day. On the 12th, Lu takes the train to Olympia, Washington to watch the launching of the "Caswell," a 70-foot wooden sternwheel passenger and freight steamer he commissioned to have built the previous year. He is accompanied on the trip by Rebecca's sisters Elma and Rowena and another relative named Bessie. After returning to Portland, Lu heads back to Idaho. *I left for Big Creek on the 15th, bringing the girls back to Nampa & Boise with me. Stayed in Boise till the 23rd, when I started on the home stretch.*

After reaching Bear and paying Charles Warner $20 for taking care of his horses, Lu has problems contacting Jim Nolan by telephone so goes on alone to Salmon Meadows, where they finally link up. Around Payette Lake, they encounter difficulty finding feed for their horses because *The sheep has the country all run down.* Lu and Jim return to the ranch on August 4, first stopping off at Roosevelt to contract for vegetables. The contract apparently is with Diamond, who shows up for the first load on August 8.

August

Cabin Creek (August 4 – 21)

After Lu returns to the ranch, he and Amos do all of the work until joined by Joe Pettigrew on September 17. Jim Nolan also is around for a few days. Lu buys Jim's mule Molly for $75 and Nolan leaves on the 7th to locate some claims on Cottonwood Creek. Lu busies himself with weeding, thinning onions, and irrigating. When Diamond arrives for a load of vegetables, Lu provides him lettuce, beets, cauliflowers, and onions at 7 cents per pound and potatoes at 2 cents per pound. The whole load comes to $46.52 and probably weighs about a ton.

After Nolan and Diamond leave, Lu and Amos concentrate on harvesting the hay and grain but also continue irrigating. Most of the wheat is for animal feed rather than for flour and two loads are placed in the barn on the 10th. On the 13th, Lu weeds the carrots and cuts *the water off upper potatoes.* The next day, he switches the water over to the orchard. Two days later he brings some string beans and squash down from the upper place and notes *The garden growing fast.*

The oats are cut by hand, using a cradle scythe, which keeps the oat stalks and heads together and allows the stalks to be bunched and tied into shocks. Harvesting of the oats begins on the 11th, is completed on the bench field on the 13th, and on the remaining portions the 17th. They start to bring in the oats on the 16th but get greedy and pay the price. *Amos got some poles from the meadow and we put on a pretty heavy load of oats. Struck a ditch at the foot of the bench and broke down, broke the reach and a hame to the wagon, had to unload.* Lu works on repairing the wagon for the next 2 days; they resume hauling oats on the 19th and complete most of the job the following day. Around gathering the grain, the grass hay is cut, raked, and hauled, mostly on the 12th to 14th. They bring in the last of the wild hay on the 21st.

Jim Nolan returns from Thunder on the 20th with several letters for Lu. The next day, Lu shoes two horses and he and Jim get ready to go to the Middle Fork of the Salmon.

To Middle Fork Salmon River (August 22 – 28)

Jim Nolan and I packed up and started for Middle Fork of Salmon River to look at his big ledge. We got to the Johnson cabin the first night, trail pretty rough. Found some rich quartz float but no ledge. Their likely route was down Big Creek to Trail Creek. At the time, direct access to the Middle Fork via Big Creek was blocked by a narrow gorge, forcing them to go up Trail Creek then down some manageable tributary, such as Bernard Creek to the Middle Fork. Nolan is known to have worked a 17-mile stretch of the Middle Fork between Nolan and Survey Creeks. There is evidence of an old mine at the head of Survey Creek. Perhaps they went there the next day by riding north along the west bank of the Middle Fork. *Packed up and went up and went to* [his] *old camp and sampled the ledge, a big wave, but it didn't pan out to suit me. We came back and camped across the river.* There is a ford across the river at Survey Creek.

Lu writes that the next day they *Came up the river to Brush Creek and up Brush Creek about 8 miles to camp.* So, at some point they must have re-crossed the Middle Fork and gone up the South Fork of Brush Creek to near the base of Shellrock Peak. Lu adds . . . *Met Rengle on the road, who has the ranch at the mouth of Brush Creek* [now known as the "Flying B"]. *Commenced to rain and rained all night, but we camped in an old cabin.* On the 25th they apparently head south along Norton Ridge *and came to the head of Little Indian Creek to camp, we eat the last of our grub for breakfast.* The next day they *Came to* Bruce's *Camp on Monumental, stopped at Roosevelt and got some grub.* George Bruce apparently is an acquaintance of both men and owes Nolan $10. Lu and Jim spend the night at Bruce's camp at the West Fork and in the morning Lu leaves for home on his own, arriving at 4 PM.

Cabin Creek (August 29 – September 8)

The day after Lu returns, they cut some more wheat and spend the remainder of the day in a classic confrontation. *Got up Bell and Suse and went after a bull to run with the milch cows. Had a duce of time getting him down. Broke our ropes and wore him out, had to leave him in the river bottom, he broke one hoof off.* The event continues the next day. *Got up mares and went after the bull, had a big hunt for him, went most to the top of the mountain, but found him in the brush on the river. He was awfull stubborn. Put him in the barn yard. We shod Bell and Suse behind, they were awfull tender* [from the encounter].

Rabbits are eating the bark off the apple trees so Lu makes screen collars and puts them around the bases of the 26 trees. He also put horn hondas on the rawhide lariats that Al Wood made for him. On the last day of August, Lu and Amos cut the oats and wheat in the upper field and bind it.

September

On September 1 they haul in the wheat and oats and Amos builds a fence around the oat stack. A small amount of the wheat is "goose wheat," which is thrashed for grain and yields them about a sack full. Also on September 1, Lu starts getting another load of vegetables ready to haul to Thunder Mountain. He thins out the onions and harvests two wheelbarrow loads. He also pulls up and tops two sacks full of rutabagas, several sacks of turnips, some young onions, and some beets and plows up 6 rows of potatoes and sacks them up. He waits until the last minute to cut some cabbage but has everything ready to go on the 6th. While Lu is working on the garden, Jim Nolan and George Bruce arrive on the 3rd with the mail and leave the next day for the Middle Fork.

Lu plans to take the mule he bought from Jim Nolan on this next trip. He makes a special set of shoes, to fit her small feet, and puts them and the packsaddle on her on the 6th to let her get use to them. The next day, they *Put in the day packing up, lashing and baling loads and weighing. Load made up of potatoes* [2200 lbs.], *onions, rutabagas, turnips, cabbages & beets.*

Thunder Mountain (September 9 – 12)

Lu and Amos rise before dawn on the 9th, but with 13 horses and mules to pack, don't get away until noon. On the way up Canyon Creek, they meet Dan, who has come to do the annual assessment work that is required for him to hold on to his claims. Dan eventually abandons them even though they ultimately prove to be quite lucrative. Dan goes on to the ranch. Lu and Amos stay the night at the Rush Creek camp and arrive at *Bruce's old camp at West Fork at 6 o'clock.* However, they must have gone further up Monumental Creek to camp, possibly to the Burnt Flat cabin. In the morning, Lu *Got up the horses but found Suse, the bay mare had rolled and broke a front leg and ruptured herself, had to shoot her.* Lu expresses no emotion over the loss but his grief must have been considerable because she had become one of his favorite horses to use. *We packed up and went to the Dewey with my loads, got there at 2:30. Got back to camp at 6:30, put on camp* [packed up] *and came down to Bruce's with Bell.* The trip home the next day is a tough 6-hour ride. *Stormy, snowed all day awfull. Bad traveling, got wet through.* When they finally pull in to the ranch at 4, Nolan and Bruce are there along with Dan. When Nolan and Bruce leave for Monumental Creek the next day, Lu estimates there is *About 6 inches of snow on Rush Creek summit.*

Dan stays in the area until Lu goes out to Boise for the winter in early October but he doesn't do much around the ranch. He leaves the day after Lu's return and goes back to Thunder, where he spends the next week doing assessment work. Dan also goes on a number of hunting trips by himself for grouse, bear, and deer, including overnight trips up Cabin Creek and to Trail Creek, and a 5-day excursion up to Rush Creek.

Cabin Creek (September 13 – October 4)

Their first day back, Lu dries out his gear and goes with Wood to drive the cattle back across the river. He also meets with *Some fellows . . . that* [had] *come to look after the timber reserve business.* Their visit may have been in response to a letter Lu wrote on the 6th involving *certificates and application for survey.*

There is a heavy frost the morning after their return and they spend the day salvaging as many of the tomatoes as they can. Amos puts tomatoes in the store house and Lu spends most of the next 6 days cooking tomato *preserves.* He also spends another day cooking preserves from melons Amos harvested, along with beans, from the upper garden. Apart from the tomatoes, Lu mostly focuses on last minute preparations before leaving for the winter and waits for Diamond to finish hauling out the last of this year's produce.

Once Amos put the tomatoes into the store house, he hitched up the mower and cut the alfalfa in the irrigated field along Cabin Creek south of the ranch house. It is allowed to cure for a week before he rakes it up. Joe Pettigrew comes to work at the ranch on the 16th, the same day Nolan and a man named Cameron come down from Roosevelt. They get 117 pounds of potatoes and 20 pounds of onions from Lu before heading for the Middle Fork with Robinson the next day. Apparently at this time Lu finishes paying off Nolan the balance of the $35 he owed for his mule.

As soon as Joe arrives, Lu and Amos go to work harvesting rutabagas and turnips and thrashing oats. The thrashing continues for a week, except for time out to haul alfalfa and dig potatoes, with Amos helping Joe most of the time. They get three loads of alfalfa and nine sacks of potatoes. *On the 24th The boys got through thrashing. We took the fanning mill down and cleaned oats all the afternoon, but did not get through.* The next day, *We finished cleaning oats. I made an other grain box, had enough oats to fill both boxes. Got about 30 hundred weight of oats.* After finishing the oats, Amos and Joe go after firewood and fencing for a few days. They also finish shocking up the straw, clean out the grade below the house, and enlarge the stock yard.

On the 19th, Lu and Amos saddle up Bell and Jim and round up all the cattle. They castrate five of the male calves but leave old Lizzie's as a future bull. The next day they drive the cattle up on the range. On the 21st, Lu goes up to Cave Creek for a day to fix a wash out and a cave-in on the ditch. He doesn't get done and is delayed for five days before he can finish the repairs and get water running in it.

Diamond still has two more round trips left. While Lu is waiting for him, he has time to kill. He fixes his boots, goes grouse hunting and looking for bear and deer, cleans up and fixes up *around*, puts up the saddle blankets, repairs the garden scythe, makes some horseshoes, and otherwise just "tinkers around." Tom Kirk comes in on the 23rd to do his assessment work. He stops by the next day to get a shovel and pick and to sharpen tools.

Diamond's pack train gets in on the 26th and leaves the next day with over 2400 pounds of vegetables. After it goes, Amos and Joe gather up more potatoes, onions, carrots, and turnips, sack them up, and have them ready for Diamond's return on the 30th. They complete the harvest of potatoes and turnips while Lu helps Diamond and finishes getting ready to depart for Boise.

October

October 1 – *Helped Diamond off with a load, took 2025* [pounds]. *Packed my grip, cooked and put away some things.* 2 – *Got up my pack outfit and shoed them, had to go on top of Horse Mountain after Trixy. Shod 6 head. Dan got in from Rush Creek, brought 2 deer with him.*

3 – *Packed up and got ready to go out, brought the horses off of Horse Mountain. Dan went up and fixed the trail across the river.* When Lu and Dan leave the next day to go back to Boise, Amos Warner and Joe Petigrew are left in charge of its operation. At this point Lu's journals cease.

PART III

Epilogue

When Lu rode out of Big Creek Country in October 1903, his life was fast becoming more complex. He had a new and ailing wife of barely a year, whom he was just getting to know. They were about to conceive a daughter (b. August 1904); lose his stepmother (d. May 1905), a set of twins through miscarriage (1905), a son at birth (1906), and his father (1907); and produce another daughter (1908), all in the short span of 5 years. He probably returned to Big Creek by the next spring to check on the livestock, harvest and market the crops, and see if

Ben Caswell's sawmill on Mule Creek circa 1906 with Mysterious Slide cabin in the background (Photograph courtesy of Stewart E. Taylor).

Dan (on right), Ben (center), and possibly Lu Caswell at sawmill on Mule Creek around 1906 (Photograph courtesy of Stewart E. Taylor).

Amos and Joe would stay on for another year. He held on to the ranch a little longer but soon sold it. By 1906, it had become clear to Lu that, with a growing family and business interests in Boise, it was impractical to try to keep the ranch on Cabin Creek going. He had not been able to live there for an extended time since he left in the autumn of 1903. So, in 1906 he sold his squatters claim to Elkhorn Ranch to John Conyers, a saloon keeper in Roosevelt. For the most part, Luman's adventuresome life in the wilds of Big Creek Country, had come to an end. Later, near the end of his life, he would lament "I left my paradise on earth when I left Thunder Mountain. All I did after that was get older."

By March 1904 only the Dewey Mine was in operation. While Colonel Dewey had managed to have the parts for a 10-stamp mill packed in on the backs of 60 mules by mid-August 1901 and operational in 1902, the other mines were still waiting for a wagon road into the area to be completed before hauling in the heavy equipment for their stamp mills because of the prohibitive expense of packing by mules. It wasn't until September 30, 1904 that the first wagon load of freight over the new road arrived in Roosevelt and the road was still in need of improvement before it could accommodate heavy machinery. From 1902 to 1907, the Dewey Mine produced about $265,000 in gold; the Sunnyside and other mines took out considerably less. In fact, by 1905, it was evident that the Belle of Thunder Mountain Company had seriously overestimated the ore values of its mine. The high grade ore rapidly played out and costs of operating in this remote area were excessive. The Dewey mine closed during the fall of 1907; the Sunnyside was already idle by then but closed officially in 1908. The other mines also shut down around this time and only the smaller operations continued, leaving just a few miners in Roosevelt and the surrounding area.

As the mines closed, the population of Roosevelt declined and by 1907 was well below the peak of 1903 and 1904. A few diehards believed things could only get better and even the Caswells built a new sawmill on Mule Creek in 1906. But they were all wrong.

On May 31, 1909, a gigantic mudslide began on Thunder Mountain, proceeding down Mule Creek, and burying everything in its way, including the saw mill. The Caswell and Curran placer property [Wes Ritchey's old Mysterious Slide claim] was destroyed and hydraulic piping and giant (the large nozzle-like structure used in hydraulic mining) were buried. The slide was reported to have been 2 to 3 miles long, 200 feet wide, and 20 to 100 feet deep. It blocked Monumental Creek below town, backing up the water, flooding the town, and creating what is now Roosevelt Lake.

The slide took 3 days to reach Monumental Creek, a distance of about 2 miles, and the dozen or so people still living in Roosevelt had plenty of time to safely vacate the area. However, Monumental Creek was swollen by melting snow and, once dammed by the slide, began to rise rapidly causing the residents and men from nearby camps (including Busby, Holcomb, Johnson, and Morgan) to work through the night moving the contents of stores and cabins to higher ground. By the next morning the town was submerged under 30 feet of water. Even faster than it was born Roosevelt had died, interred in a watery grave crafted by the Caswells' quest for gold.

Lu was at home in Boise when reached by the news correspondent for *The Idaho Daily Statesman*. He was quoted as saying, "It is a very unsafe place for a town to be built. While I regret very much that the people there were overwhelmed, at the same time I am not surprised. It was something that might have occurred at any time. The wonder is that it had not occurred before." He said that his brother Ben had been at Roosevelt for some time working the placer claims owned by Ben and by Martin Curran of Boise. The claims were located near the head of Mule Creek and were being worked by hydraulic mining. Lu believed the slide was started by hydraulic operations. That the slide started 3 miles above town, indicated to him that it started at or above the Caswell and Curran placer claims, on the side of Thunder Mountain. He believed that the Dewey buildings probably were safe as did E. H. Dewey when the newspaper contacted him. The news correspondent was Mrs. Neal Wayland, wife of the Roosevelt postmaster (the post office continued to operate until 1915). It is noteworthy that she did not mention Ben as being one of the people present in the area at the time and had not contacted him. By the time of the 1910 census, there were only 11 people living in the vicinity of Roosevelt. Ben, who was the last of the five partners to reside there, was not among those listed.

The Big Creek area became part of the Federal Forest Reserve System in 1919, though filings for homesteads and mining claims were still allowed. In 1927, a group of people including Idaho Governor H. C. Baldridge and S. C. Scribner, Supervisor for the Payette Forest, went into Big Creek to examine it as a possible primitive area, a designation that would protect it from further development and road building. In 1930, Baldridge and Scribner proposed a large area south of the Salmon River, that included Big Creek, as a primitive area and the following year it was established as the 1.1-million acre Idaho Primitive Area by the Forest Service Chief R. Y. Stuart. In July 1980, Big Creek country, except for mining exclusions at

Thunder Mountain mudslide that destroyed Roosevelt, Idaho (Photographs from the Earl Willson Collection ISHS # 66-74.167, 66-74.157, and 66-74.160, respectively). Top left: Site of the origin of the mud slide, 500 feet wide by 90 feet deep.

Left: Path of the mud slide (mainly left of center) and Caswell sawmill destroyed by slide.

Below: Roosevelt, Idaho being flooded by back waters from the mud slide.

the head of Big and Monumental Creeks, became protected from development as part of an officially designated federal wilderness, the 2.3 million acre "River of No Return Wilderness." It was later re-named the Frank Church—River of No Return Wilderness in honor of the Senator who guided passage of the enabling legislation through Congress. In anticipation of wilderness designation, the private in-holdings on Cabin Creek, which encompassed the original Caswell Ranch, were purchased by the U.S. Forest Service. In 2005 the Trust for Public Land, a national environmental conservation group, purchased an additional 645 acres of land and 272 mining claims in the historic Thunder Mountain Mining District from the Thunder Mountain Gold and Dewey Mining Company. The purchase ended the potential that a new mine could be built in the drainages of Monumental and Marble Creeks and returned the area to public ownership, thus completing the cycle begun by the Caswells over a century earlier. The Trust eventually transferred the land to the Payette National Forest to protect a total of 6,000 acres.

The Golden Years

1901 – 1919

The era beginning with the sale of the two main sets of Caswell claims in the early 1900s and extending to about 1919 would be considered by many to be the best of times for the three Caswells and their two partners. During that period, the actual extent depending on their individual personalities, choices, and fates, they married and raised up families, lived comfortably or even a bit extravagantly, and invested some or much of their windfall in what seemed to be wise choices. The economy was booming during this period both nationally and throughout much of Idaho, especially in the Boise area where Ben, Dan, and Luman initially settled along with their parents, sister Melvina, her husband Clarence Higgins, and their children. As the state capitol, in a potentially productive river valley, and with nearby forests, Boise possessed special advantages over other areas of the state. However, its growth and development generally reflected that of much of the region. Large-scale expansion of Boise's regional farming and forest resources fueled economic development and an influx of people. Real estate sales and building construction boomed. Even the outbreak of wartime hostilities in 1914 aided the economy as the dislocations in Europe affected local farm markets favorably.

Marriage and acquisition of new homes seemed to be the first major order of business in the pursuit of the new-found good life for each of the five former partners. This was followed by involvement in various business ventures and the begetting and raising of children. Dan Caswell began the marriage procession in the spring of 1902, followed closely by his friend Wes Ritchey. Lu married 6 months after Dan, and Ben capitulated about 4 ½ months later in early 1903. A. O. Huntley held out another year after Ben but spent the additional time carefully plotting his move.

Lu Caswell

Luman followed his brother Dan into both marriage and business. Dan saw opportunities in serving the home construction industry and established a paint and roofing store, whereas Lu sought to deal in the properties on which the homes were built. Luman had a history of being careful with his money: banking most of it, keeping a smaller portion in a checking account for expenses, and keeping careful records. After the sale of their claims, he invested heavily in real estate and, throughout the golden years of 1901 to about 1918, generally did well.

Lu and Rebecca remained in the house they had purchased from Ben at 221 Washington in Boise until about 1920. In addition to the two-story house, there was a triangular shaped piece across the street, containing a barn and corrals, where they kept horses. Lu and Rebecca's first child, Helen was born August 28, 1904. She was named after her aunt, Helen Hays Hutchinson, who had been instrumental in Lu and Rebecca first becoming acquainted. Their final child Louisa was born July 23, 1908 with pulmonary problems that plagued her continuously for the first 2 years. She required the constant care of a live-in nurse during that time.

In relating those times later to Louisa as part of his autobiography, Lu recalled "We lived the life of Reilly. Rebecca was a good hostess [and they probably entertained often]. I spent most of my time taking care of my real estate business. Set up a home office equipped with a roller [roll-top] desk and typewriter." "Becky liked to travel and when business didn't prevent it, so did I." "In the beginning Becky and I took several trips, mostly to Portland, Oregon. Her sister Helen Hutchinson now lived there." They also toured the World's Fair in Portland in 1905.

Lu continued to maintain his interest in gold. He was listed as "an owner of gold mines" in the 1910 Census and, from 1905-1911, the Boise Directory alternately listed Lu's profession as real estate or mining. These references to mining and several photographs from his albums suggest that he periodically returned to Thunder Mountain during this time. However, the assessment work on his remaining claims generally took all summer (about 30 days per claim) and so, at least during the early part of the period, he hired Ward Roberts to do the work for him and afterward the claims probably were sold or abandoned. Also, after the sale of the ranch to John Conyers in 1906, he had little incentive to visit Cabin Creek.

In addition to his own home, at one time among other properties, Lu owned 500 lots in Boise's Eastside Addition and a large ranch in Pleasant Valley 12 miles south of the Boise River and east of Kuna. He bought the lots for $6,000 down and $18,000 balance and sold them off gradually over the years. In 1914, business was still doing well enough that he bought a brand new 4-door Cadillac. It was a 5-seater with shiny black leather upholstery. But, in keeping with Luman's practical ways, it was a "Touring" model, which was the low end of the Cadillac line and sold for about $1975. Perhaps not so coincidentally, in February 1914 Lu and Becky sold the triangular piece of their residential property across the street from their home, which contained the barn and corrals, indicating that they no longer had a need for horses, at least in town, but did need a car.

The Pleasant Valley Ranch was established on 640 acres acquired in 1915 from the Bureau of Land Management in conjunction with the development of a new irrigation canal by the Pleasant Valley Land & Irrigation Canal Co. According to Lu, "It consisted of a large ranch house and a bunk house that could accommodate twelve men. Barns, corrals and a small lake." He had intended to make it a stock ranch but instead it became a "hay and wheat ranch."

Over the years, they were able to afford a number of accouterments that gave other evidence of their financial well-being. For example, at various times they employed a housekeeper and a variety of other domestic helpers. At the time of the World's Fair, Lu purchased a twelve-place set of "Roosevelt" dishes, that he believed was the only one of its kind, and twelve settings of crystal with a silver mounted center piece to go with them. In 1917, Lu and Rebecca still were able to afford the best education available in Boise for their two daughters. They began sending them to St. Teresa's Academy, a Catholic school for young ladies that was only a block away from their home. It was the same school that Rebecca and her sisters had attended and she and Lu knew their daughters were getting an excellent education and being taught very good manners. The girls started as day scholars and later became boarders.

However, even during the good years, Rebecca's health was an ever-present concern. She was hospitalized at the time Lu met her and underwent two operations soon after they married. She had an uneventful pregnancy and birth with their first child in 1904 but the next year she miscarried twins, and the following year lost a son in a tragic accident at birth. Her health progressively deteriorated, the doctors lumping it into the catchall category of the day of "female trouble." She spent considerable time bed ridden or in the hospital. By 1917, her condition had gotten notably worse, so much so that Lu began looking for other ways for reducing her work load. "Before I had always hired [domestic] help but now Rebecca was in need of lots of help and care herself." Also, the main reason for enrolling their daughters as boarders at school probably was due to Rebecca's deteriorating health. Rebecca's second home became Saint Alphonsus hospital—a never ending expense (along with domestic workers and boarding school for their two children). They visited old Dr. George Collister so often that he also became a family friend.

Dan Caswell

In December 1901, Dan invested $3500 in 9 lots in the North Locust Grove Addition on Harrison Boulevard in Boise, an upscale area next to some property purchased by Ben. When Dan and Ben traveled east during the winter of 1901-1902 and visited relatives in Michigan, he struck up a close friendship with their first cousin Bertha Rouse Phillips. Bertha was petite (4' 11" and 80 pounds), vivacious, and attractive. She also was very feminine and liked dressing up in fancy clothes and wearing jewelry, all of which were especially appealing to Dan. Bertha came back with them from Michigan and shortly after, on April 9, 1902, the two were married in San Francisco. Soon after returning to Boise, Dan purchased property at 210 State Street for $6,500 and built a house on it that was just a few houses away from the one Ben had purchased at 221 Washington. The two-story, stone-faced house had an oak staircase, hardwood floors, and piped-in hot water for heating. Dan and Bertha later sold one and a half of the associated vacant lots in 1906 for $6,000. Their daughter Donnabel was conceived soon after they were married and was born in the new house on 4 February 1903. Just two days earlier Dan had been a witness at Ben's marriage. Also in 1903, he began operating the D. G. Caswell Paint Store in the upscale Union Block, located on the 700 block of West Idaho Street, and remained in business

Dan and Bertha Caswell's home at 210 State Street in Boise on land they purchased in 1902 (ISHS # 76-5.53).

there for several years. According to his ad in the Polk Directory, he sold wholesale & retail paints, oils & glass, and P&B roofing.

Dan and his family remained in Idaho until 1908 or early 1909. In April 1907, he and Bertha sold 80 acres of property in Boise to Lu for $2500 and in September, they sold their palatial home for $8500 to their neighbors the Laidlaws. Dan also sold his paint and glass store in about 1907. By the time of the 1910 census he, Bertha, and Donnabel were living in Los Angeles along with Bertha's mother.

This major translocation from Idaho to California apparently was due to Bertha's health. They may have hoped that the warmer and sunnier climate would be beneficial for her. In Los Angeles Dan bought a nice house, reinvested in real estate, and had another paint and glass store. He also built a summer bungalow in what is now Beverly Hills, that supposedly was the first summer house built there. Periodically, Dan would go to Mexico to prospect for gold and on the 1910 census his occupation was given as "Mining" of the general nature of "Mine and Stock."

While in Los Angeles, Dan and Bertha lost a set of twins at birth and then a son, who may have been stillborn, a set of unfortunate circumstances very similar to that experienced by Lu and Rebecca. The babies' deaths weighed particularly heavily on Bertha, who may have been predisposed to depression. Dan had done charity work with a nearby orphanage. Soon after their son died, the orphanage called Dan about a newborn boy [b. June 14, 1910] that he and Bertha decided to adopt and name Phillip.

Several years later Bertha reportedly suffered food poisoning while eating out, went into a coma, and nearly died. Whether from this event, the onset of dementia, or both, Bertha's health rapidly deteriorated. She wouldn't trust anyone to give her food, lost her appetite, became very thin and weak, and required a great deal of care. When Lu learned of their problems, he wrote and suggested to Dan that he come back to Idaho and help run the ranch Lu had recently acquired south of Boise. It wasn't long after that Dan sold their home and the family left Los Angeles.

Dan returned to Idaho with his family around 1915. They lived with Lu and his family for a while in Boise and Lu's wife Rebecca helped care for Bertha. But soon Bertha had to be placed in the state sanitarium in Blackfoot, on the opposite side of the state from where Dan and the children were living and where visits from them were impractical. Lu characterized her behavior as "nervous hysteria" but she eventually was diagnosed as having *melancholia dementia*, the most common form of which is now known as Alzheimer's Disease. She was only 44 when she died at the sanitarium in June 1917. Donnabel was 14 and Phillip just 7. Bertha's body was taken by train back to Boise. In keeping with the times, when mental illness was treated with embarrassment and lack of understanding, she was buried unceremoniously in an unmarked grave in the Caswell plot in Morris Hill Cemetery.

After Bertha was hospitalized, Dan (who had become Lu's working partner on the ranch) built a small house east of Lu's ranch house and moved there with his two children. Donnabel looked after her stepbrother while Dan ran the ranch. Dan and his daughter (she preferred the name Donna) became very close after Bertha died, as he tried to make up for the loss. He remembered his unpleasant childhood after his own mother died. In fact, he may have chosen not to remarry because of the bad experience he had being raised by a stepmother and a desire to spare Donna that pain. Their closeness also may explain why he later shared his home near Idaho City with her and her husband and eventually moved to Boise and to Bremerton, Washington to live with them in his old age.

Ben Caswell

Of the three Caswell brothers, Ben was the instigator and the dreamer. He was the true prospector and above all the others had the skill for finding gold and the perseverance to keep after it until successful. However, Ben also seems to have been more of a loner than the others, to have made a number of questionable decisions without consulting with them, and to have been carefree with money. Lu believed that some of Ben's problems stemmed from his overanxious and impulsive nature and that difficulties they had encountered in the sale of the two main sets of claims had come from that. But Lu felt that "Ben's worst fault was his damn stubbornness and he was forever getting us in jackpots because he wouldn't give in and because of his cocksure attitude." Ben savored being in the limelight and he basked in the notoriety and adulation that came from striking it rich. He also enjoyed the accompaniments of the good life, such as fine Havana cigars and a well-stocked sideboard in his hotel suite. Both of these traits converged to rapidly deplete Ben's earnings from the sale of the claims.

Less than a month after the first set of gold claims sold, Ben purchased 10 lots (= half a city block) in the Locust Grove Addition for $1500. The front half of the lots were on the west side of the prestigious Harrison Boulevard and the other half were just behind them. Later that winter was when he and Dan traveled to Michigan to visit relatives. After returning from their travels, Ben bought the house at 221 Washington Street that he later sold to Lu. Although Ben made sound investments in real estate, he generally was loose with his money and did not keep track of expenses. To some extent, he relied on Lu to watch after his savings and settle accounts for him.

Ben first met Anna Marie Larsen in the vicinity of Warren on his travels to and from Thunder Mountain. She had immigrated from Denmark in 1892 and worked with her two brothers, Hans and Andrew, on their placer claims on the Secesh River outside of Warren. She immigrated and was married under her middle name but later in life used her first name on legal documents and in directory listings. Ben had known her several years prior to the sale of the gold claims. Their relationship was a rocky one almost from the start. Ben proposed to her in the spring of 1902. However, by autumn, he had decided not to get married and sold the house and associated buildings to Lu. Therefore, it was a bit of a surprise for his relatives and friends when they learned that he and Marie were getting married on February 1, 1903. He was 42 and she was 30 and their differences in age and ethnic backgrounds probably caused problems from the outset. Ben and Marie eventually built a house on the property Ben had purchased on Harrison Boulevard. On November 3, 1905 Marie gave birth to their only child, a son they named Arthur Benjamin (Bennie).

In 1906, one or more of the Caswells completed a new sawmill on Monumental Creek, just below the Dewey mill site. Although all three brothers may have had a hand in its construction and operation, the primary owner probably was Ben. The sawmill was in operation until it was destroyed by the mudslide that inundated Roosevelt in 1909, which probably also was about the time that the "good life" ended for Ben. According to Lu, Ben had been at Roosevelt for some time working on the placer claims owned by Ben and Martin Curran. All of their equipment was buried by the slide and may never have been recovered. However, for the moment, all may not have been lost because on July 7, 1909 *The Idaho Daily Statesman* noted that, "In spite of the destruction wrought to buildings and workings, miners are rejoicing because of the new ground which has been opened up by the huge slide back in the mountain, which would have meant the expenditure of thousands of dollars to uncover by manual labor." At about this time, Ben dropped out of sight and did not reappear until the 1920 census, when he was working in California as a farmhand.

A. O. Huntley

A. O. Huntley labored to carve out his ranch along Indian Creek and develop it into a productive cattle operation. Since having first known the Caswells, he worked persistently to improve his ranch and living quarters. He put in long hours and, it is said, commonly did the work of two men. He also engaged in lumbering, speculated in mining, and worked some on his Swan Lode about a half mile west of the ranch. A. O. was the last of the five partners to marry. He bided his time, apparently to increase his eligibility as a suitor. He and his future wife actually lived relatively close to each other as the crow flies but the way was obstructed by Hells Canyon and some formidable mountains. According to Huntley, "Several years before [the sale of the Thunder Mountain gold claims] a neighbor and myself had driven a bunch of beef cattle to La Grande [Oregon] . . . it was on this trip I first met the young woman who afterward became my wife." Pearl Payne had moved with her family from Wisconsin to Cove, Oregon, near La Grande, around 1873 when she was about 5. At the time of their meeting she was a school teacher in Cove and lived there with her widowed mother and a sister.

A. O. and Pearl Huntley on their wedding day. (Photograph published in the Idaho Statesman January 21, 1934).

A. O. used his earnings from the sale of the Caswells' Thunder Mountain claims to further build up his ranch and improve his livestock herd. By July 1902 he was making plans for "building a palatial residence on his ranch near Cuprum" with which he hoped to woo the "girl of his dreams." The 14-room Victorian style mansion, located in a sparsely-inhabited rural area, had three stories plus a basement and was equipped with running water, electric lights, and central heating. A few years later, reportedly between 1905 and 1910, Huntley added a magnificent barn and began raising and selling registered Hereford cattle. The barn also was three stories tall. The north-south axis measured 40' wide by 100' long and a east-west leg of comparable size extended off the west side of the barn. The interior was illuminated by incandescent lighting. Hay

A. O. Huntley's mansion on Indian Creek near Cuprum, Idaho (ISHS # 62-220.7).

chutes with tip boards sped up the feeding process, water troughs filled automatically, and four-wheeled carts mounted on rails on the bottom floor facilitated manure removal.

A. O. and Pearl were married April 18, 1904 in Ft. Atkinson, Wisconsin, near where she had been born. He was 40 and Pearl was two years younger. On their wedding trip, they purchased the furnishings for the new house at Marshall Fields in Chicago.

A. O. did well on the cattle ranch for another dozen years or so. He was able to increase his land holding to over 1000 acres, employ a number of domestic and ranch helpers, and invest in local mining and real estate opportunities. In 1908, their only child, Marion Eloise, was born. A. O. and Pearl saw to it that she was well educated. Later the Huntleys arranged for Marion to attend the Intermountain Institute in Weiser for her high school education. The Institute's students pursued a college preparatory curriculum but also were required to take manual training or domestic science courses.

Thus, through hard work, the good fortune of having backed the Caswells, and astute investment, by the end of World War I A. O. Huntley and his family were benefitting from and enjoying the full fruits of his efforts. Their futures looked bright and it seemed that the formula that had worked so well for Huntley in the past would continue to do so in the future.

Wes Ritchey

Wes closely followed his good friend Dan Caswell into marriage when he (age 28) exchanged vows with Edith Spiker (age 18) in April 1902, only 20 days after Dan and Bertha had tied the knot. Unfortunately Dan could not be present because Wes had returned to their old stomping grounds in Gardiner, Montana to be married at the ranch of Edith's parents John and Louisa Spiker. Wes had first become acquainted with Edith around 1897 when he and Dan were working in the area.

Apparently, Wes had initially planned that he and Edith would settle down in Boise. But Edith didn't take to city life and, before the year was out, they left Boise, went back to western Colorado where they both had come from years earlier, and began homesteading outside of Hotchkiss. In December 1902 Wes paid Charles H. Gray $3,000 for half interest in a fully equipped 160-acre ranch. The property was within 5 or 6 miles of where the Caswell homesteads had been when he and Dan left Colorado in 1894. Wes later, in 1909, augmented this with an additional 120 acres adjacent to the original property. They built a solid but unpretentious single-story stone house nestled at the base of a conical hill. Although only about 12 miles from Hotchkiss, Ritchey's ranch was located in rugged, juniper-covered terrain that was difficult to access and remains so even today. Because of this and Edith's introverted nature, the Ritcheys apparently never developed strong social ties within the community and were largely self-reliant.

Their son Raymond Daniel was born at the ranch 2 ½ months after they arrived. In autumn 1905, Edith was seriously injured in a fall from a horse. After she left the hospital, they rented out the ranch and moved to Gardiner, where they built a cement-block house and Wes operated a general mercantile store for the next 7 years. After Edith's mother and stepfather moved to Filer, Idaho to operate a chicken ranch, Wes and Edith returned to Hotchkiss in 1912. Their second son Maurice Amsden was born in October 1913 while Edith and their son Ray were staying with her mother and stepfather. After that, Wes and Edith remained on the ranch with their sons until the 1920s where they lived busy but (for ranchers) relatively routine lives.

Wes and Edith Ritchey farm house north of Hotchkiss, Colorado (photograph by author January 2009).

Return of the Hard Times

1920 – 1940s

It seemed as if they had it all and that it would never end. Yet in a few brief years and in virtually the blink of an eye their fortunes were gone. Luman, Dan, and A. O. seemed to rise the highest and in the end fall the furthest of the five partners. Ben's good fortunes ran out the fastest, while those of Wes Ritchey persisted the longest largely because Ben was the most prodigal and Wes the most frugal in their spending and life styles. Ben's good fortune ended by about 1910 and he essentially became a drifter, ever in search of another El Dorado. The others maintained their fairy tale lives for a half-dozen or so more years but then were caught up in the economic downturn that would plague much of the nation for the next twenty years.

With primarily an agriculture-based economy, Idaho and Boise did not do well after about 1919 contrary to national and regional trends. Postwar economic dislocation on an international scale was particularly hard on Idaho farmers and ranchers due to wartime inflation followed by a severe postwar price collapse. Between 1919 and 1922, prices for Idaho's crops and livestock plummeted and a relatively large number of Idaho banks failed, including some from Boise. For example, in Idaho the price farmers received for a bushel of potatoes fell from $1.51 in 1919 to 31 cents in 1922, while that for corn went from $1.65 in 1919 to 50 cents in 1921. Farmers and ranchers who invested in land and equipment when prices were high were unable to make payments when prices for their products dropped.

As demand for farm and ranch products fell, agricultural income was reduced by half or more, loan payments and taxes could not be paid, and mortgages were foreclosed by the banks, many of which themselves were overextended and failed, further restricting credit. To compensate for low agricultural prices, farmers and ranchers generally raised more, creating a surplus which drove prices even lower. This resulted in a deadly cycle in which the high surplus and lower prices necessitated borrowing money to stay in business and in turn created debt leading to increased production to pay the debt. This cycle continued to impact rural Americans throughout the 1920s and 1930s and eventually did in the majority of them including Lu, Dan, and even A. O. Huntley. Wes Ritchey, being in Colorado, may have been better insulated from the economic maelstrom that struck Idaho plus he apparently was not caught with a large mortgage or heavy real estate or stock market investments when the downturn occurred.

Lu and Huntley were hit the hardest of the former partners by the economic downturn of the late 1910s and early 1920's and essentially lost everything during that time. Banks failed, businesses went bankrupt, and they were overextended at both. In addition, in such an economic climate no one was buying land, building houses, or purchasing pure bred cattle. It is especially ironic that Lu, who once could do the work of several men and oversee a large crew of men working concurrently on multiple tasks, would soon be reduced to being a construction crew member himself. He also eventually would go from having helped determine the fate of a city to that of doing maintenance work for another city and from having been an owner and operator of two large ranches to being a simple roustabout ranch hand under the direction of a foreman. Ultimately he would build and occupy a cabin very similar in size to first one he and Ben had built on Big Creek and end up doing farm chores and "piece work" utilizing his carpentry skills in order to cover expenses and remain at least marginally independent. Huntley's fall was equally abrupt, though he eventually was able to acquire a small farm and maintain his dignity and financial independence longer than Lu. Dan also acquired a small farm and several "prospects" and remained financially viable until the 1929 stock market crash, when he too struggled to make ends meet.

Lu Caswell

In 1904, Lu got caught up in a real estate deal that, in retrospect, seems like a scam. Lu was approached by the sheriff Mosley about 500 lots in the East Side Addition of Boise that he wanted to get a commission on. When Lu went to the owner Mr. Off, who was president of the Boise City National Bank, he was told that Off would only deal directly with him and not through Mosley. Lu in his naivete lacked two critical pieces of information about the property that might have alerted him to the inadvisability of the deal. One was that Lu would be liable for taxes and any improvements provided by the city, such as sewers and sidewalks, that cost three to five thousand dollars per transaction. The other was that an investment company from New York was about to initiate a large development on the West Side of Boise. The unexpected expenses and competing development didn't seem so serious at first but, as Idaho's economy began to go down and other financial commitments of the family mounted, the financial drain they created became insurmountable. "Up to that time I had been doing very well with my business deals, but this became the straw that broke my back."

In addition, by about 1917 the adverse financial conditions on the ranch were becoming increasingly apparent and the specter of Becky's hospitalization always loomed on the horizon. Although the ranch provided plenty of meat, eggs, and vegetables for the family and relatives, it was becoming exceedingly difficult to make it pay. Lu stated "The percentage of profit was never what it should be per acre because of lack of water and destruction of the hay and wheat crops by hordes of jack rabbits." With the losses already sustained by the East Side fiasco, the ranch showing a deficit, and little prospect of a buyer, Lu and Rebecca decided to stop the financial hemorrhaging and let the ranch go for taxes. Dan had seen the end coming for Lu and in 1921 bought a little ranch in Pleasant Valley on Ten-mile Creek and acquired some of Lu's stock and ranch furnishings for his place.

Lu and Rebecca's remaining asset was their home on Washington Street. After much anguish, they sold their home and moved into a much smaller house across from the Academy to be near their daughters. About the autumn of 1921, Lu found a small 80-acre farm near Caldwell, with a partly-finished house on it. At this point, Louisa was still at the Academy but Helen was in nurses training at St. Alphonsus Hospital. The inter-urban transit station was only a block from the house and made for convenient transportation to either Boise or Caldwell. Thus, it was easy for the girls to come home on holidays and the station was close to where Rebecca's mother had been living since Judge Hay's death in March 1917. Things were looking up.

After arriving at the farm, Lu managed to get the first year's crop harvested and was finishing the interior of the house in his spare time. As Lu recalled "Just when we got settled here Rebecca was again suffering illness that confined her to her bed . . . Winter had rolled around again [probably 1921-1922] and as usual I banked the fire in the small kitchen range for the night. The range had come with the house. What I didn't know until later, a broken tooth in the grill fell off and when something woke me up, the whole house was on fire. Only had time to roll Rebecca in blankets and carry her outside. Laid her on the snow and dashed back to try to rescue something, but by then it was a raging inferno. The house burned to its foundation . . . Some evil genii was dogging my footsteps. My luck had really run out." Lu carried Rebecca to the neighbors where they stayed until Lu could rent a furnished house in Caldwell. Louisa came home from boarding school for the Christmas holidays and, because her mother needed her, she didn't go back. Down to the last little bit of money they had in the bank, Lu decided to drive to Boise and ask Roy Struve, a former employer there who owned the Boise Implement Company, for a job. Struve agreed to hire Lu again and in a position that paid relatively well and was "Sorta head mechanic, did everything, carpentry and rebuilding car bodies."

Struve also had dealings in California and on a hurried trip back to Boise asked Lu to come down and take charge of a theater renovation project in Oceanside. He was desperate for Lu's experience and capabilities. "In four days I had to decide what possessions we could take in the car and what we had to leave behind. Struve told me not to worry, that I could store things in his storeroom at the Implement Co. We could send for them when we got settled."

Lu left Idaho in December 1925 with Rebecca and Louisa and arrived in Oceanside the week before Christmas. (About this same time, A. O. Huntley and his family also left Idaho, driven out by economic conditions.) Helen remained in Boise to work at St. Alphonsus Hospital. She later came to visit her parents and met a man whom she married in 1928. Lu immediately went to work as head carpenter for Struve on the renovation of the Palomar Theatre. The next year (1927) he helped build the San Onofre bridge and, after that, worked on the reconstruction of the Bonsall bridge. The only housing Lu could find when they first arrived was a beach house. As soon as he could, Lu bought property and, after work and on week ends, built a "garage house" so they had a place to live. He had intended to eventually build a house on the same property but conditions became such that he sold the garage house and moved into a rental.

Luman had found a short respite from the financial depression in Idaho by retreating to California. But in 1929 he was slammed again, this time by The Great Depression. He never really recovered after that, at least financially. He had recently turned 60 and could find little or no work. So he sought salvation in the one means that had been his resurrection in the past—gold. Lu left Rebecca and Louisa in Oceanside and went to work as a miner in Quartzite, Arizona, about 190 miles east of Oceanside. Rebecca and Louisa stayed in a rental house, next door to Helen and her husband. Rebecca's health continued to deteriorate. In addition to her "female problems," she had diabetes and was partially blind. In one of her letters to Lu in Arizona, she wrote that she hoped that he found gold so that they could have money again. From Quartzite, Lu moved to Nevada and, in August 1930, filed on the Midas claim in Bull Frog Mining District in Nye County. Next it was on to Hornsilver, Nevada in October and then back to Oceanside for the Christmas holidays and to congratulate Louisa on her December marriage to Clement Hensler. He indicated that he had made one good strike in Nevada but that it turned out to be on government ground and disallowed. Unfortunately Lu's luck had run out and he was seldom able to make expenses let alone find another big strike. Eventually, he and Rebecca moved to Escondido, where he got a job with the city. However, he was thrown from a work truck, seriously injuring his wrist, and wasn't able to work as a result.

In 1934, Rebecca's body had taken all that it could and she passed away December 4 in Escondido at age 56. After she died, Lu moved further south to Poway, to work on a ranch, though he continued to prospect when he could find time. In order to stretch his slim pay, he moved into a nearby abandoned cabin at "Big Rock" that he refurbished to make livable. While he was living at the Big Rock cabin, Lu's car, the Cadillac he had driven from Idaho, stopped running. Because it was hot in that part of the State and the cabin was poorly ventilated and its bed uncomfortable, he used the cushioned back seat of the once elegant auto for a bed.

After working for several years at Poway, Lu sold his 1914 Cadillac for $25 and moved onto a farm owned by his daughter Helen and son-in-law. He was given a quarter-acre plot back by the barn and built a small house. Initially, he had only an outhouse but that eventually was replaced by an addition to his house that had a cold water shower and toilet. According to his grandson Stewart Taylor, "He had a wood-burning stove and there was a water bin if he needed hot water. I supposed he shaved with hot water. He washed his own clothes. I don't recall him using mother's Easy washing machine. He was pretty independent. So was mother."

Lu probably did odd carpentry jobs to support himself. Stewart indicated that, "Grandpa had lots of carpentry tools. I know after he moved to my folks property in Oceanside and during the time he was building his 'cabin' he did some carpentry work for my dad & mother." "Grandpa kept track of the hours he worked for Mother & Dad doing fencing, working with the animals, hauling water to them etc. And they paid him." In 1948, Lu contracted colon cancer and died October 22 in the county hospital in San Diego. He was 81 and had outlasted both of his brothers and the other two partners. He is buried in Oceanside, where he had first settled when arriving in California 28 years earlier.

Ben Caswell

It might have helped if Ben had remained married, tempered his ways, and given some thought to the future. But, after the birth of his son in 1905, Ben began spending increasing amounts of time on

Thunder Mountain and in 1907 he and Anna Marie divorced. According to Lu, "... she was always accusing him of being too friendly with other women and this was a major reason for Ben leaving." Lu also stated that after the divorce "Their only child, Bennie. . . was taught to hate his father and Ben wasn't permitted to see much of his son. She was always vitriolic whenever he tried to see Bennie so he quit trying." In June 1909, Ben sold his Harrison Boulevard properties and closed out his investments in Boise.

After the divorce, Ben returned to Thunder Mountain and apparently soon went broke. In 1908, his place of residence was listed as Roosevelt, Idaho on his deceased father's probate, and Lu's ledgers indicate that he sent money to Ben there. Most likely Ben was on Thunder Mountain on May 31, 1909 when the mud slide inundated Roosevelt and destroyed the Caswell sawmill and mining operations. In 1910, Lu's ledger records show that "Ben had his brown filly bred to Lockhair," indicating that Ben was still in the area. But no 1910 census record was found for him in Warren or Roosevelt Precincts and, with the closing of the Dewey mine and the flooding of Roosevelt, there was no compelling reason for him to remain in the area. On March 16, 1916 the *Idaho County Free Press* noted that "[J]. P. [Pringle] Smith is advertising in the [Idaho County] *Free Press* for A. B. Caswell to pay his portion of the assessment of several claims in the Thunder Mountain mining district or forfeit his portion of the claims", also indicating that Ben was no longer around. As far as is known, Ben lost contact with his son and his former wife after leaving Boise.

After leaving Thunder Mountain, Ben essentially became a drifter. He surfaced again, but only briefly, at the time of the 1920 Census when he was recorded as living in northern California, 25 miles southwest of Yreka—a single, 59-year old, farm hand, working for Morris Lewis (age 86), his son (age 55), and two daughters (ages 59 and 48, respectively). Ben lacked the permanency of place and the family ties that would have helped preserve a record of his life on Thunder Mountain and afterward. He may have kept journals of his own and had a camera, but no personal records are known to remain.

As was the case for many others in these financially troubled times, no census record was found for Ben in 1930, when he would have been 69 years old. However, he reportedly was living in Colorado in the early 1930s when he made one last trip to Thunder Mountain. Ben is said to have traveled by train to Nampa, Idaho in the spring of 1931 and stayed at the Dewey Palace Hotel while getting his prospecting outfit together. The outfit consisted of a horse, pack mule, and supplies. He apparently followed an established route from Nampa to Emmett and then up the North Fork of the Payette River and over to Knox to reach his goal. On the way to Emmett, he went through the small community of Frankland where he was spotted as he passed by a farm run by his sister Melvina Higgins and her family. Otherwise, his presence in Idaho might never have been recorded. He may well have gone to Colorado after leaving Oregon, to try to weather out the Great Depression. However, after leaving Idaho in 1931 he is believed to have gone to Arizona and in March 1934 he wrote to his sister from Congress Junction, Arizona, where he was prospecting and working in a mine.

They exchanged a number of other letters over the next few years, including six short ones that he wrote to her. In January 1935 he was still doing some prospecting "chasing through the hills when it doesn't rain." In his February reply, he indicated that he currently was out of work and in debt. In this letter and a later one he complained of his rheumatism bothering him.

In October 1935, Ben's letter to Melvina indicated that she and Clarence may "Be out of a home [because of a fire]" and offered to send them money he had saved to buy another horse, if they needed it. He also wrote about people losing weight as they got older and stated that he had gone from 180 down to 160 and was now about 150 and feeling the better for it. This substantial weight loss suggests that he had been sick and/or not eating well but had not wanted to admit it. In the next letter, posted August 3, 1936 he noted that the mine was shut down again.

In February 1937, he wrote Melva that Lu had stopped by and had taken some pictures of Ben and his team. Ben included a couple of the photos in his letter and wrote "When you see how old I look I don't know if you will want me to come back to Idaho or not. I was scared my self, I hadn't looked in [the] glass in so long." In evident reply to a query that Melva had made earlier, Ben offered some observations about pensions. He stated that he was not receiving one but that Lu was getting $35 from "Californey."

Ben also said he had a visit from Wes and Edith Ritchey. He noted that "Ritchey is the same as he was when in Thunder Mountain. He only stayed a few days and I heard from him since they left." Wes later wrote of the visit, that virtually everything Ben owned was in his wagon and that the only thing of value he saw was an automatic pistol.

The final letter from Ben to Melva was written May 20, 1937 only 10 days before he died. It had not rained for 3 months and everything was drying up. He indicated that he was back at his old job and was now getting $50 a month. He expected to hold down the job at least through the summer "unless the mine is sold." He also had $15 on hand. Earlier he had received a copy of Zane Gray's recently published book "Thunder Mountain" a fictionalized version of the discovery of gold by the Caswell brothers. He thought that it was "Pretty well riten for hot are [air]. . . Yes dear girl, it thunders under ground in that mountain, some day they will find it is hollow. In the spring when the snow goes off it, it sometimes makes lots of a racket." In closing, he reminded Melva that he was getting paid now and had indicated earlier that he would be able to send her a little any time if she needed it.

A few days later Ben was driving his wagon and team in front of the Arrowhead Service Station in Congress Junction, when his new horse shied and lunged forward. Ben tried to hold the team back and calm them but he was jerked to the ground, further startling the now unrestrained horses, and the wagon rolled over him. In a telegram to family members, Dan wrote "He landed on the back of his head and the wagon ran over him breaking his back. He . . . lost consciousness almost immediately after the accident and died within the hour after reaching the hospital."

Dan Caswell

World War I was underway when Dan and his family arrived back in Idaho in about 1915, though America did not officially enter the war until April 1917. The war initially increased demand for American agricultural products by the Allied countries and increased income to U. S. farmers and ranchers as they responded to fill the need. This increased financial opportunity may have been one reason for Dan's returning when he did. After Bertha died, Dan and the two children moved to his 160-acre homestead on what is now the Kuna-Mora Road and began the process of "proving up." The place was next to Lu and Rebecca's recently acquired, 640-acre Pleasant Valley Ranch and the nearest post office was only a few miles away in Kuna. Dan obtained the patent on his homestead in June 1920 and in August 1921 purchased an additional 160 acres for $750 located only 3/4 mile northeast of the combined ranches. Of the total 960 acres, only the latter apparently was irrigated; most of the remainder seems to have been sagebrush—grass rangeland.

Dan and his young son Phil (age 9) stayed on in the Ten Mile area for several years after Lu but by the time of the 1920 census Dan (age 55) was reduced to renting a place for them to stay and apparently was working as a farm laborer. However, he had been looking for an alternative place to live, possibly one where he could prospect for gold and pursue more of a subsistence type life style, and in that same year paid $4000 for a 120-acre farm on Bear Run just north of the old gold mining town of Idaho City. The new place had a big bungalow, barn, chicken house, and garden and was partly forested. He paid $500 down and completed the purchase in September 1923. It probably was around this time that he left the Pleasant Valley ranch and went to Bear Run. In April 1924 in Idaho City, Dan filed a placer mining claim of 80 acres on the South Fork of the Payette River. Then in May he filed three placer claims of 20 acres each, that he had located a week or so earlier, along Mores Creek about 2 miles northeast of Idaho City. The Mores Creek claims were very near his place on Bear Run. The next year Dan sold all three of the latter claims for $1500 to the Boston & Idaho Gold Dredging Company.

An even more significant event in 1924 was that Dan, now listed as living in Idaho City, transferred the entire 120-acre Bear Run property and "half of all money and Personal property in Bank or otherwise" to his daughter Donnabel [age 21] for $1 on May 21. He may have done this as protection against creditors and as a step to provide her with some security should he die. Philip may not have been included in the transfer because he was only 14 and under age but he probably was still living at Bear Run with Dan and Donna at the time.

Donna left to begin attending the University of Idaho in Moscow in the fall of 1927 and continued at the University, except for summers, until late October 1929 when Dan sent her a telegram stating that she needed to return home for financial reasons. The stock market had just crashed and Dan apparently had lost most of what he had been able to hold on to after the initial economic downturn in 1919.

Dan and Phil were not listed in the census the year following the crash, suggesting that they were in a remote area, probably in the vicinity of Idaho City, trying to eke out a living, and had simply been missed by the census taker. Dan and Phil probably went to work for the gold-dredge mining company about this time but this would not have been considered suitable work for Donna and she worked in Boise as a waitress for several years (~1930-1933). Dan also worked for the Forest Service part of the time he lived at Bear Run, probably around 1930-1935, when he was in his mid to late 60's. He may have been a fire lookout in the summers or at least packed supplies to them.

Donna probably met Kenneth Johnston when she was working in Boise and they were married in November 1933. After the wedding they moved in with Dan at Bear Run. In the summers, Dan, Ken, and Phil worked on the dredge to make enough to carry them through to the next year. The family would "live from one summer to the next." These were difficult times but they managed to get by. Besides a big garden and chickens, they had goats for meat, milk, and butter and they hunted deer in the nearby forest.

Dan wrote his brother Ben in 1935 that he had made a gold strike and was going back to do some work on it and locate more ground. Two years later, Dan (age 72) was still living on Bear Run, near Idaho City, when he received news of Ben's death. Ben's few remaining belongings were disbursed among his siblings and, in a letter to Melvina, Dan noted that Ben's tent "will be useful at our prospect." However, his free-ranging life as a prospector would soon come to a close.

Dan, Donna, and Ken moved from Idaho City to Boise around 1938, probably because of the greater availability of work there. After they left the place at Bear Run, Dan rented it out in order to be able to pay the taxes but within a short time the renters had a chimney fire and the bungalow burned down. While in Boise, Dan did custodial and home-repair jobs and Ken did carpentry, mechanic, and machine work. They lived for a time in a boarding house near St. Alphonsus hospital (on 5th and State streets) and they were living there when Donna and Ken's only child Linda was born in 1942. Later they may have rented a place on Harrison Street or lived with "Aunt Marie" (Ben's former wife) for a time.

After the United States entered World War II in December 1941 and the birth of their daughter, Donna and Ken decided to move to the West Coast, where the economy was booming and better-paying work was available, and they convinced Dan to go with them. They packed up everything and stored most of it at Walter and Vanja Higgins' farm on Orchard Avenue and Midway Road. Walter had inherited the farm from his parents Clarence and Melvina when they both passed away in 1941.

In March of 1943, Donna and Kenneth bought a home in Bremerton, Washington and Dan moved in with them. When they arrived in Bremerton, the 77-year old Dan went to the draft board and volunteered to go into the Armed Forces in place of some other younger man "who might still have his life ahead of him." Eventually Dan was given a job working on the dry docks doing maintenance—picking up scrap and related work. Dan continued to work there until shortly before his death from a stroke on March 7, 1945, just 20 days shy of his 80th birthday and about five months before the war ended. He was buried in Bremerton because his daughter and son-in-law did not have the means to take his remains back to Boise.

A. O. Huntley

A. O.'s run of good fortune rapidly dissipated after the close of World War I. In August 1917, he and Pearl had mortgaged all of their real property for $50,000 at 8% interest. This loan possibly was related to some speculative scheme of the Huntleys to capitalize on the increase in agricultural commodity prices associated with America's entry into World War I the previous April. But this huge loan also could have been related to increased feed and operating costs and a depressed market for purebred cattle. This mortgage was continued over the next several years, indicating an inability to pay it off. The end officially came for Arthur and Pearl, on November 26, 1923 when they signed over all of their real property amounting to the 960 acre ranch on Indian Creek, six lots in Cuprum, 60 acres and three lots around the Blue Jacket Mine, and 154 acres and two lots near Bear. The entire package was purchased by E. M. Hoover, a banker in Boise, for $550 in cash, all outstanding property taxes, and, presumably, some portion of the remainder of their mortgage. At the time of foreclosure, Huntley also had over 600 show quality Herford cattle.

By April 25 of the following year, the Huntleys had left the ranch and moved to a 20-acre farm in Cove, Oregon to be among Pearl's relatives. They apparently were able to hang on to their personal items; however, most of the house furnishings, including brass beds, a massive roll-top desk, and a book collection had to be left behind.

After only a year and a half in Cove, they moved diagonally to the opposite end of the State to a 125-acre farm outside of Myrtle Creek, because of its milder climate, less necessity for a super-strenuous life, and cheap land prices. They soon found a place and tried to resume their lives by growing fruit and vegetables on a small truck farm. They were well received in the community and he became a member of the Grange (National Grange of the Patrons of Husbandry), a social/political self-help association of farmers for their mutual welfare and advancement. Their daughter Marian moved to Portland in 1927 and went to work as a cosmetician. In early 1929,

Arthur purchased an additional 40 acres of public land adjacent to his farm on South Myrtle Road. In the 1930s, economic conditions worsened further. In defense, Arthur, then in his mid to late 60s, became an active supporter of the Townsend Plan, which was designed to alleviate suffering among the elderly, many of whom had seen their savings and retirement incomes wiped out by the Depression. The plan challenged national old-age policy for more than a decade and contributed to passage of the Social Security Act in 1935.

In mid-1932, Pearl became ill and died on Thanksgiving day at age 65. Her passing left a great void in A. O.'s life. He made it mostly on his own after that but went to Portland for a while, to work as a carpenter, in order to augment his farm income and to be near his daughter. But, near the onset of WW II, Marian moved to Hawaii and A. O. returned to Myrtle Creek until a short time before his death at age 81. He was hospitalized for 27 days at the Good Samaritan Hospital in Portland for an enlarged prostate (Benign Prostatic Hypertrophy or BPH). A. O. died alone and in pain from complications of BPH on March 8, 1946. His funeral expenses were paid by his nephew Herbert Huntley Maschmedt in Seattle, suggesting that A. O. was living in virtual poverty at the end. He had sold a few parcels of his farm for small sums of cash beginning in 1943. After his death, the remaining 135 acres and his home were sold for $4,000. After settlement of out standing debts, his net worth was judged to be closer to $3,500.

Wes Ritchey

Colorado may have been less vulnerable to economic upheaval of the 1920s than Idaho. In addition, the Ritcheys' rural location and more frugal lifestyle made them more self-sufficient and allowed them to stretch their funds further. However, the downturn in the economy and in Edith's father, John Spiker's health conspired to take the Ritcheys to Oregon temporarily by the end of the decade. Though probably not realizing it, they were within 100 miles of where the Huntleys had moved in 1925. In 1930, Wes and Edith were living with her now elderly father in Watkins, Oregon, where both Wes and John engaged in gold mining, probably in an effort to weather the Great Depression. John died the next year in October and, after his burial in the Log Town Cemetery, near Jacksonville, Wes and Edith returned to their ranch in Colorado.

In March 1938, their son Maurice Amsden Ritchey married Leah Collins McKee in Jacksonville, Oregon, near where his grandfather John Spiker had lived. Later that same month his namesake (Edith's stepfather), Beam Amsden, passed away in Gardiner, Montana. In 1945 Edith and Wes left the ranch in Hotchkiss for the last time, though they did not sell it, and returned to Gardiner to be near her widowed mother who was then 84. However, Wes was not feeling well and in early September went to Los Angeles to seek medical treatment, possibly at the urging of his stepbrother who lived there. A short five months later, on February 12, 1946, Wes (a heavy smoker for most of his life) died of lung cancer (age ~71) "at home" in Sherman Oaks, Los Angeles County, California. He was buried in Greenwood Cemetery, San Diego probably because his oldest son Raymond D. Ritchey was still living in San Diego.

Profile Summit as seen from the upper end of Big Creek Flat near Edwardsburg (photograph by author August 2009).

Reflections

And so it ended. The dream that had become a reality now is only a faded memory. Like prospectors in general, the Caswells and their partners were optimists to the last. Even after losing virtually all of their possessions they never gave up and to a man, to one degree or another, returned to prospecting in the hope that another redeeming gold strike was just over the hill or around the bend. However, neither wealth nor fame returned. In their old age and poor estate when they died, little note was made of their passing. All of the partners died far from the mountains they loved, four of them on the West Coast. Perhaps only Ben, ultimately the poorest of them all in worldly possessions, died doing what he loved best—driving a team of horses and living the relatively care-free life of a miner/prospector.

Their real legacy lies not in fame and wealth but in the satisfaction of hard work and a job well done, in the adventures they lived, and in the challenges they met and overcame. It resides in the diaries and other accounts they wrote and in the other remembrances they left behind. Though they were just trying to do their best, many now recognize they were making history.

Much of the tangible evidence of their former presence in Big Creek Country has disappeared, some of it through natural processes of erosion, plant death, decay, and regrowth. Other evidence was lost at the hand of subsequent owners who moved, tore down and reused, or destroyed the materials and structures for their own purposes. This includes certain members of the US Forest Service who have chosen to erase most of the traces of even historic buildings through "scheduled removals," including incineration, to fit their vision of wilderness. But, over a century later, vestiges of the Caswells still remain. Some are obvious but others more subtle. There are the obvious markers like the remains of the mud slide at the mouth of Mule Creek, the lake where the town of Roosevelt once stood, and the "reef" at the Dewey mine site. There are also the remains of decaying cabins on Thunder Mountain and the miraculously-preserved, though somewhat re-arranged and displaced, 1898 cabin on Cabin Creek. Much of the existing trail system and remnants of no-longer maintained routes, like the "Caswell Cutoff" between Cave and Crooked Creeks, still stand as tributes to their vision and hard work. Less obvious but still discernable are outlines of the foundations of the 1894 and 1895 residences and of terraced fields on Cabin Creek and traces of partially filled-in irrigation ditches along both sides of Cabin Creek and on Cave Creek. All of these signs, whether self-evident or largely hidden, still provide reminders of a more difficult, tenuous, and exciting time.

A short distance from the Caswell and Larson family burial plots in the Morris Hill Cemetery, Boise, sits a large granite boulder with the following quote, in tribute to the role Frank Church played in helping craft the Wilderness Act of 1964 and Wild and Scenic Rivers Act of 1968 and in securing four Idaho wildernesses, including the River of No Return Wilderness, for posterity:

> I never knew a man who felt self-important in the morning after spending the night in the open on an Idaho mountainside under a star-studded sky. Save some time in your lives for the outdoors, where you can be a witness to the wonders of God.
>
> *Frank Church*—May 1961

Few who read this inscription will appreciate the significance of the juxtaposition in space of the Church and Caswell memorials and the overlapping of elements of their lives. Frank was born in 1924 and took an early interest in political science. While in the eighth grade in Boise, he wrote the editor of the *Capitol News* defending the policies of then Senator William Borah. The letter was so well written it was published on the front page. Church was impressed with Borah's abilities and patterned his speaking style and career after him. Interestingly, when Church announced his candidacy for the presidency in 1976, he did so from Idaho City where his grandfather had been a banker and where Senator Borah

Rugged terrain of the Frank Church Wilderness in the vicinity of Thunder Mountain (photograph by author May 2009).

had announced his candidacy 40 years earlier. This is the same William Borah who had been Dewey's attorney during negotiations with the Caswells and their two partners for their Thunder Mountain gold claims. Merl and Jean Wallace, who acquired and made their home in the Caswell 1898 ranch house on Cabin Creek, named their son after Borah. In addition, Senator Borah was instrumental in setting aside the Idaho Primitive Area, of which Big Creek Country was a part and which later served as the nucleus of the River of No Return Wilderness. When Frank was told, during the final stages of his losing battle with cancer, that this wilderness had been renamed in his honor, he was elated that he was able to share with his boyhood hero, Senator Borah, the distinction of having a natural landmark named after him. It seemed for him, the best of all memorials, and so too is "his" Wilderness for the Caswells, their partners, and friends.

On my journeys into the wilderness and at home, I continue to ponder the obstacles faced and surmounted by the Caswells and the others who were part of their story. Now, at the end of most of my research and writing on this book, as I reflect back over their lives, I am in awe at the challenges they faced, the amount of work they did, and the variety of different tasks they completed. I am amazed by the wide array of animals they hunted and trapped, the diversity of crops they grew, the number of cabins and other structures they built, the hardships they endured so matter-of-factly, and their perseverance and lack of complaint. I also am inspired by the high degree of independence, stamina, skill, and physical prowess that they exhibited. I am deeply impressed with their horsemanship as riders, packers, and teamsters and of their ability to train and to care for their animals. I know firsthand, though on a much more limited scale, the skill required to have worked with so many different horses in such diverse settings and kinds of activities and yet to rarely have experienced the loss of an animal or the upset of a pack load or packstring.

One day in the summer of 2002, I camped on Marble Creek, on the flanks of Thunder Mountain, with two of my graduate students. We had already had a challenging trip, during which a friend had been seriously injured in a fall from a horse and the horse itself had become exhausted and unable to carry a load. We arrived near sunset and were just unloading the remaining horses when we were deluged by a rain storm that lashed at us for over an hour. Every few minutes we were startled by bolts of lightning and the cracking of thunder that then rumbled down the mountainside and rolled over us as we huddled beneath a hastily deployed blue-plastic tarp. It was pitch dark when we emerged from our clammy shelter and finished unpacking our gear. It was a bit of a struggle locating everything, pitching our tents, and preparing supper in the light of our headlamps, but around midnight we were finally able to a call it a day. Fortunately, our tents and sleeping bags had been protected by the canvas covering of the manty loads and we were able to get a good night's rest. The next day was even more demanding, as major sections of the trail along our route had been washed out in the cloudburst of the previous night. However, we eventually made our way through the morass and several days later successfully completed our research trip.

As I think back on the storm, I am reminded of a similar occurrence (actually one of many) experienced by Lu and Ben in the summer of 1894, that gave rise to the name of the mountain where they soon discovered the gold that bonded them to the country for another decade. In the memory of the storm and of the entire trip, I find an additional kinship with them and with the land they came to know so well. Meeting and successfully dealing with unexpected and extraordinary events that draw on our own resourcefulness and push us to new limits of physical endurance and accomplishment are perhaps the greatest gift wilderness has to offer in this modern world. In addition, it is in shared kinships across time, such as with the Caswell brothers, Wes Ritchey, A. O. Huntley, and their frontier acquaintances, that we gain a fuller appreciation of our own roots, of obstacles met and overcome, and of the perseverance and fortitude exhibited by the early explorers and settlers in this demanding land.

I've returned to Big Creek Country several times since beginning this book and camped in peaceful glades along the trail and on the verdant meadows at Cabin Creek. I find joy in the snow-capped mountains, lofty trees, and secluded places of this formidable land and I delight in the cold, sparkling waters of its spring-brooks and the gushing rapids, deep pools, and placid glides of Big Creek itself. I continue to be impressed by the vastness of the area, the difficult terrain, the extremes of the weather, and the remoteness, solitude, and tempestuous beauty of the land. Though still challenging by today's standards, my journeys into the area and relatively brief stays pale in comparison to the accomplishments of the Caswells and their partners. Yet I am grateful to them for putting my efforts in perspective and enriching the breadth of my experience, and I am thankful to William Borah, Frank Church, and other such visionaries for providing the opportunity for me and future generations to experience the wonders and solitude of this glorious and historic country. Buoyed up by their self-confidence and spirit of adventure, I can't wait to return to seek new paths and to follow once again in their tracks.

Bibliography

My primary sources for this work are the unpublished 1895-1903 diaries and autobiography of Luman G. Caswell. A typed transcript of the full set and originals of the 1895-September 1900 portion of the diaries are in the Idaho State Historical Society Library and Archives (ISHSLA, Boise, ID (MS2/437). Luman's grandson Stewart Taylor of Chula Vista, California has a typescript of the autobiography and originals of the December 1900-October 3, 1903 portion of the diaries; he provided me a copy of the typescript and images of selected pages of the diaries. A one-page outline of major events covered by the autobiography up to the brothers' arrival in Mineral also is on file at the ISHSLA. The diaries, of course, were written soon after Luman experienced the events and are considered factual, within the limits of his powers of observation. The autobiography, however, was recorded from oral recounts, probably done entirely from memory, and taken and transcribed by his daughter Louisa Caswell Hensler near the end of his life. These remembrances were clouded by the passage of time but, outside of the period covered by the diaries, are the best information available on the personal aspects of his life. An abbreviated account, based mainly on these two sources, has been published by the Caswell brothers' grandniece Freda Babbitt in her chapter "Gold is Discovered on the Mountain that Thunders" (Valley County Idaho: Prehistory to 1920, Donnelly, ID 2002). I have relied on her work for some information not contained in the two primary accounts.

Parts I and III are strongly influenced by the autobiography and Part II by the diaries. However, all three sections are extensively augmented by information obtained through my own research or provided by individuals listed under Acknowledgments. In particular, Parts I and III and the sections in Part II concerning Wes Ritchey and individuals other than the Caswell brothers rely heavily on genealogical information obtained from US Census, state and county birth, marriage, death, claim, deed, and probate records and, where available, family trees.

Substantial amounts of additional information on the five partners are from the following sources: Details about Luman and Rebecca also come from telephone interviews and email correspondence with his grandson Stewart Taylor and from Lu's ledgers. Details about Dan and Bertha were obtained through telephone interviews and written correspondence with their granddaughter Linda Kiesel and from Lu's autobiography, the Boise City Directory, county records, and Morris Hill Cemetery records. Details about Ben Caswell were gleaned from the April 13, 1902 issue of *The Idaho Daily Statesman* and letters from Ben to his sister Melvina Higgins on file at the ISHSLA The report of the final sighting of Ben in Idaho comes from Elsa Higgins Phelps in a letter to Stewart Taylor of March 25, 2009. The principal source of information about A. O. and Pearl Huntley is the article he wrote for the January 21, 1934 edition of *The Idaho Daily Statesman*. Additional information was culled from issues of the *Council Journal* (July 3, 1902), *Adams County Leader* (June 29, 1934), and *Weiser Signal* (April 20, 1916). Heidi B. Cole's book *A Wild Cowboy* (Cambridge, ID 1992) contains valuable information on A. O. Huntley and his property holdings. Key information about Wes Ritchey is given by his daughter-in-law Leah Ritchey in her contribution "Family of Wes and Edith (Spiker) Ritchey and John and Louisa Spiker/The Spiker Family in Gardiner" in *History of Park County, Montana* (Dallas, TX 1984).

Information on Colorado geology and the Grand River is summarized in Halka Chronic's *Roadside Geology of Colorado* (Missoula, MT 1992). Meredith O. Wilson provides an excellent account of the history of the Denver & Rio Grande RR in *The Denver and Rio Grande Project, 1870-1901* (Salt Lake City, UT 1982). The history of homesteading and fate of the Ute Indians in the Delta area is reviewed by David Bradford, Floyd Reed, and Robbie B. LeValley in *When the grass stood stirrup-high: facts, photographs, and myths of west-central Colorado* (Lawrence, KS 2004). The history of Delta County and Hotchkiss is given by the Hotchkiss Bicentennial—Centennial Brochure Committee in *Hotchkiss and Crawford 1881-1910* (Delta, CO 1976).

I have relied extensively on historical maps and accounts (as well as modern ones) especially in retracing Lu and Ben's trek from Colorado to Idaho. In addition, I have visited all but a few short segments of their journey, as well as that of Dan and Wes. The Old Spanish Trail portion of the Salt Lake Wagon Road, that ran from Delta to Salt Lake City, is covered by Leroy R. and A. W. Hafen in *Old Spanish Trail, Santa Fe to Los Angeles* (Lincoln, NE 1954). Well-researched accounts of the Pony Express/Overland Stage route across Utah and Nevada are given by Leroy R. Hafen in *The Overland Mail 1849-1869* (New York, NY 1994) and David M. and Susan C. Jabusch in *Pathway to Glory: The Pony Express and Stage Stations in Utah* (Salt Lake City, UT 1994). The Nevada towns and history are described in Shawn Hall's *Romancing Nevada's Past* (Reno, NV 1994), Judith K. Winzeler and Nancy Peppin's *Eureka Nevada: a history of the town in its boom years 1870-85* (Ely, NV 1982), and Edna B. Patterson, Louise A. Ulph, and Victor Goodwin's *Nevada's Northeast Frontier* (Reno, NV 1991). The route north from Blackfoot, Idaho into Montana is detailed in H. Leigh Gittins' *Idaho's Gold Road* (Moscow, ID 1976). Julia Randolph has brought together material from various sources to compile *Gibbonsville, Idaho: The Golden Years* (Gibbonsville, ID 1982). Brief accounts of Pierce and Elk City and the discovery of gold in Idaho are given by Cort Conley in *Idaho for the curious—a guide* (Cambridge, ID 1982) and Margaret Fuller in *Trails of the Frank Church River of No Return Wilderness* (Weiser, ID 2002). Norman B. Willey described the route from Mount Idaho to Warm Springs in the July 25, 1890 issue of *The Idaho County Free Press* and I made further adjustment to account for crossing the "Wire Bridge." Information about mining and mining towns in the vicinity of the Seven Devils and elsewhere in Idaho is presented by Merle W. Wells in "Gold camps & silver cities: nineteenth century mining in Central and Southern Idaho" in the *Bureau of Mines and Geology Bulletin 22* (Moscow, ID 1983). Muriel Dudgeon's recounting of *John Flynn's Stories of Mineral* (Fruitland, ID 1966) includes a description of the town of Mineral. Heidi B. Cole's book *A Wild Cowboy* is invaluable for information on the Warners and Smiths of Bear, ID.

Access to newspaper accounts of people and events in the Warren, South Fork, and Big Creek areas was facilitated by Cheryl Helmers' creative compilation of the *Warren Times: a collection of news about Warren, Idaho* (Wolfe City, TX 1988). Two other valuable resources for this information are the reports for the Payette National Forest's Heritage Program: "Wilderness of the Heart" by Sheila Reddy (1995) and "An outline of the cultural history of the Frank Church—River of No Return Wilderness" by Peter Preston (McCall, ID 2001.)

Details of gold mining techniques are addressed by Rodman W. Paul in *California Gold: the beginning of mining in the far west* (Lincoln, NE 1965)and Bradford Angier in his *Looking for Gold: the Modern Prospector's Handbook* (Mechanicsburg, PA 1980). Details of the sale of the first set of claims are reported in the July 9 and August 1900 issues of *The Idaho Daily Statesman.* Annie L. Bird also gives a reliable summary in her article in the February 23, 1970 issue of the *Idaho Free Press.*

The development and early history of Roosevelt, Idaho is covered in the April 13, 1902 issue of *The Idaho Daily Statesman*, in articles by Paul Swayne "From an old hunter and guide" in *Scenic Idaho* (Volume 4, No. 2 1949) and Annie L. Bird "Town of Roosevelt grew up at Thunder Mountain site" in the March 7, issue of the *Idaho Free Press*, and in the unpublished manuscript of C. W. Neff "The road to Roosevelt: an account of Idaho's last gold rush and life in the town of Roosevelt in 1902" (Payette National Forest, McCall, ID 1941). Neff also provides details about Jonas Fuller, and the death of Billey Dow. The death of Jonas Fuller is chronicled in the December 27, 1906 and January 2, 1907 issues of the *Idaho County Free Press.*

The demise of the mines on Thunder Mountain is described by Annie L. Bird in her article "Thunder Mountain activity slowed after early boom" in the 14 March 1970 issue of the *Idaho Free Press* and by Merle Wells in his 1983 book. The destruction of Roosevelt is recorded in the June 3 & 6 and July 3, 1909 issues of *The Idaho Daily Statesman* and by Swayne in his article in *Scenic Idaho.*

Merle W. Wells describes the history of Boise and the political and economic forces at work, including details of the economic fortunes preceding and during the Great Depression, in his perceptive *Boise: an illustrated history* (Woodland Hills, CA 1982). Most of the details about Frank Church and the wilderness named after him, including the quote by him and the one by his wife Bethine about his regard for the distinction of having a natural landmark named after him, are from Fuller (1987).

Order Form

Streamside Scribe Press
G. Wayne Minshall, author & co-owner
1783 S. Old Highway 91
Inkom, ID 83245-1700
email: streamsidescribe@gmail.com
website: www.streamsidescribepress.com

We accept orders from individuals and supply booksellers. We offer quantity discounts on orders of three or more copies. Prices will be provided on request. Send check or money order to the above address. Include the number of copies ordered and your complete address with telephone number or email address.

Made in the USA
Coppell, TX
04 December 2020